This book is due for return on or before the last date shown below.

2 6 APR 1998

Don Gresswell Ltd., London, N.21 Cat. No. 1208   DG 02242/71

THE LIBRARY
NATIONAL ... ...ION FOR
EDUC... ...RCH
IN ... ...ES
THE ... ...RK
SLO... ...2DQ

DATE
22.4.91

CLASS
Jm, Nm   NEI

AUTHOR
Neill, S.

Classroom Nonverbal Communication

Nonverbal signals are less easily controlled than words and thus, potentially, offer reliable information to both teachers and children on each other's true intentions. But such signals are also more ambiguous than words, and this makes them valuable when teachers or children wish to send a message they do not want challenged. Even so, misunderstandings can occur, for example, between different ethnic groups. Sean Neill explores how children's skill in using and understanding nonverbal signals increases with age.

The appropriate nonverbal signals for teachers differ from those used in informal conversation because of the teacher's controlling, instructing and encouraging role, and this creates problems for new teachers, who also find it difficult to interpret the limited feedback from the class. A detailed coverage of teachers' and children's signals leads on to a survey of how teachers acquire nonverbal skills and research on effective training. *Classroom Nonverbal Communication* provides the only comprehensive survey of these areas for staff involved in the initial and in-service training of teachers, and in staff development.

Classroom social arrangements are permanently reflected in seating layout and room design, which can allow teachers and administrators to influence classroom interaction through advance planning. For these groups, this richly illustrated volume assesses how effective such planning really is.

Sean Neill has researched room layout and nonverbal communication in education since 1975 and has published many papers dealing with these issues. He provides a uniquely comprehensive survey of the research evidence on classroom nonverbal communication.

International Library of Psychology

Editorial adviser,
Developmental psychology:

Peter Smith
University of Sheffield

Classroom Nonverbal Communication

Sean Neill

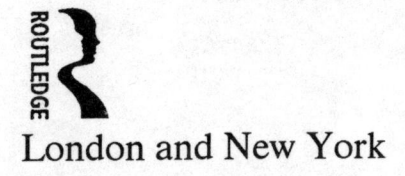

London and New York

First published 1991
by Routledge
11 New Fetter Lane, London EC4P 4EE

Simultaneously published in the USA and Canada
by Routledge
a division of Routledge, Chapman and Hall, Inc.
29 West 35th Street, New York, NY 10001

© 1991 Sean Neill

Typeset from the author's wordprocessing disks by
NWL Editorial Services, Langport, Somerset

Printed and bound in Great Britain by Mackays of Chatham PLC, Kent

All rights reserved. No part of this book may be reprinted or reproduced or utilized in any form or by any electronic, mechanical, or other means, now known or hereafter invented, including photocopying and recording, or in any information storage or retrieval system, without permission in writing from the publishers.

British Library Cataloguing in Publication Data
Neill, Sean (Sean Rupert St John) *1945–*
   Classroom nonverbal communication. – (International library of psychology).   1. Schools. Classrooms. Communication
I. Title   II. Series
371.1022

Library of Congress Cataloging in Publication Data
Neill, Sean (Sean Rupert St John) *1945–*
   Classroom nonverbal communication / Sean Neill.
   p. cm. – (International library of psychology)
   Includes bibliographical references (p.) and index.
   1. Nonverbal communication in education.   2. Nonverbal communication in children.   3. Interaction analysis in education.
   4. Teachers – Training of.   I. Title.   II. Series.
LB1033.5.N45   1991
371.1′022 – dc20
                                    90–39816
                                        CIP

ISBN 0–415–02663–6

To my mother and the memory of my father

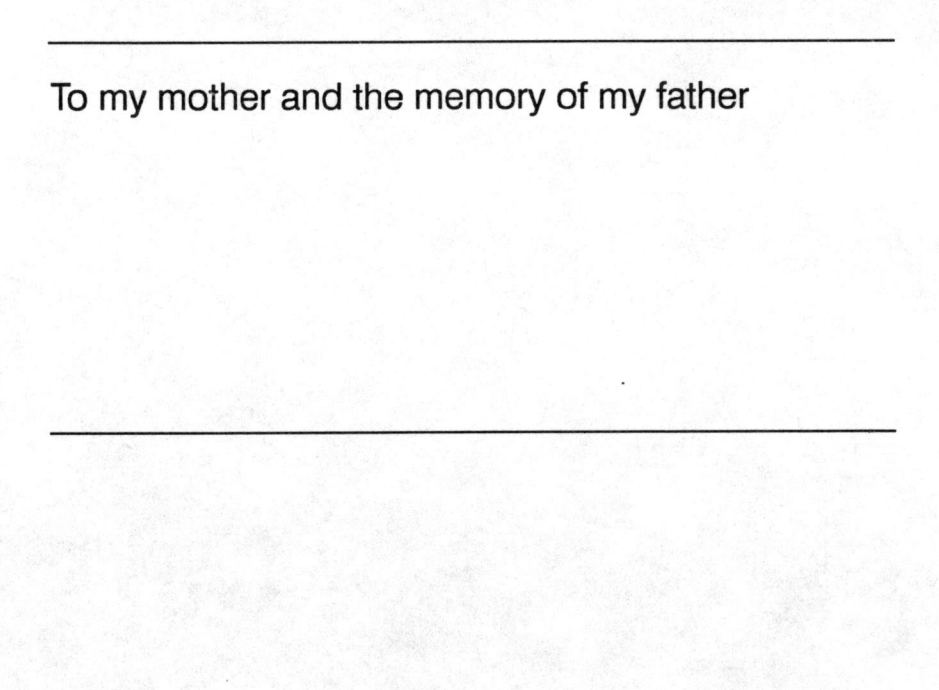

Contents

Acknowledgements	viii
Notes	ix
1 The classroom context	1
2 Children's nonverbal abilities and their development	13
3 Signals of dominance and uncertainty	26
4 Attention – positive and negative	47
5 Conveying enthusiasm	64
6 Showing interest and friendliness	80
7 Interpersonal distance and classroom layout	93
8 The use of space	119
9 Differences between groups	133
10 Implications for teacher training	147
References	166
Name index	183
Subject index	189

Acknowledgements

Many of the ideas in this book derive from research supported by the Nuffield Foundation. Many children, teachers and student referees participated willingly in this research. I thank them for their cooperation, despite no prospect of personal benefit, especially the teachers who allowed me to videotape their classrooms. These videotapes have already been extremely valuable directly to many student and probationer teachers who have been able to watch them, and I hope they will help others indirectly through the illustrations in this book, which are based on them.

I have also found comments from colleagues invaluable, especially John Robertson and Chris Caswell from whom I have gained many ideas, and Peter Smith, the editor of this series. The views expressed, and their errors, remain my own.

Notes

For clarity the pronoun 'she' is used to refer to teachers, and 'he' to pupils, throughout, except where the text refers to specific individuals or to behaviour shown by one sex only. With these exceptions, the behaviour described applies to both sexes. In the illustrations, outline drawings without shading have been used for clarity, including illustrations of non-white individuals. In illustrations based on videotapes or photographs (taken by C. Caswell) appearance and sex have been changed as necessary to maintain anonymity.

Chapter 1

The classroom context

Why should nonverbal behaviour in schools be of interest? The development of human culture is very largely due to our ability to pass on information verbally, so that new knowledge can build on to old (e.g. Humphrey 1976). The school is an institution designed to achieve this strategy, and we might expect the verbal to be paramount over the nonverbal there. However, there are two major reasons for the importance of nonverbal signals. The first is the complexity of classroom life, especially for the teacher, who has to deal with 25 or 30 other people at once. Both when assessing the situation, as it changes from moment to moment, and when she wishes to influence the children's behaviour – often several of them at once – she gains from extra communication channels besides her voice. As we shall see when we look at how the teacher conveys her enthusiasm for her subject (chapter 5) or the children's response to it (chapter 6), the extra communication channels can modify or support what she says. The importance of the teacher's 'manner' has long been recognised (Perry 1908, Waller 1932); the lack of change since Perry's descriptions 80 years ago is striking!

Nonverbal channels are more ambiguous than speech, and this is a second reason for their importance. As outside the classroom, it is often desirable to maintain flexibility and not to take too entrenched positions, especially if there is some degree of conflict (chapters 3 and 5). The ambiguity of nonverbal communication makes it ideal for delivering in a non-attributable way a message which might otherwise have caused offence – for example older children may find overt, direct praise condescending. If their contribution is received with real enthusiasm in facial expression and voice – a smile of surprise and delight, with vocal stress on the appropriate words 'That's it, *exactly*!' – older children, or adults, will feel it has been welcomed genuinely and without condescension.

The implicit nature of much classroom communication is the cause of many of the problems encountered by new teachers (chapter 10) and where teacher and children have different backgrounds (chapter 9). In the third section of this chapter, therefore, we look at the nature of the classroom social system. The classroom differs from other social settings, but not always in the

Figure 1.1 Finger point (left); palm point (right). These two points would probably be interpreted as communicatively equivalent, the differences being related to the medium (paper or blackboard) the teacher is working with. In Grant and Hennings' (1971) terms the teacher would be 'directly wielding' the book in the finger point, and 'instrumentally wielding' it in the palm point (in which the book has no communicative significance). His orientation counts as 'indirect wielding'. Thus in the palm point his orientation half-way from the class is explained by the need to see the blackboard and does not have the communicative significance of avoidance it would have if he were reading from the book

way which would be expected from explicit definitions of what education is about. Classrooms are supposedly about learning, whether this involves teachers transmitting a specified body of knowledge or children learning on their own initiative. Children do not, though, conform to adults' definitions of their role, but exert strong influence over classroom processes. In this chapter we look at some of the influences on their behaviour; in chapter 2 the development of their nonverbal behaviour is considered in more detail. First however, we need to consider what should be included in the definition of nonverbal behaviour as it applies to the classroom.

WHAT IS NONVERBAL COMMUNICATION?

'Nonverbal communication' in education has been taken to cover a wide range (Smith 1979), but in this book attention is concentrated on communicative behaviour, over the school age-range from about 4 to 18. Studies of babies and toddlers before they enter preschool have been excluded, except where they illustrate important points for the school age-range. Much research has been done on adults, especially university students (usually psychologists). Much adult behaviour in non-educational contexts is relevant to the behaviour of teachers; for example the behaviour of other public speakers. Studies of informal social behaviour have also been used to clarify the distinctive features of teachers' nonverbal repertoire. In many of these studies the 'adults' are students. Studies of university students, as students, have been used mainly where they illustrate points about teacher–student interaction which have not been investigated with school-age children. The emphasis on the learner's responsibility in university education, together with the adult level of sophistication which students have reached in their nonverbal behaviour, makes university students a poor model for many of the features of behaviour in statutory-age education.

A number of aspects which have been included as nonverbal communication by other authors are excluded here. Much of teachers' behaviour is 'wielding' (Grant and Hennings 1971) – either 'direct wielding' (handling books, chalk, apparatus, etc.), 'indirect wielding' (looking at the objects she is using) or 'instrumental wielding' (moving into position to use objects) (Figure 1.1). Though these movements have communication significance they vary according to circumstances in a way which makes it impossible to draw generalisations. Thus, after asking a question, one teacher may pick up the chalk (direct wielding) and walk away from the class towards the board (instrumental wielding) while another walks towards the class and the overhead projector and picks up the projector pen. These actions have communicative meaning, but mainly because they are accompanied by more specific communicative actions – waiting for the class's response and gazing at the class, which are described in chapter 6. These communicative actions have to be more invariant to serve their purpose, in the same way as words have to be relatively invariant. Some of the problems which arise when different groups use or understand the same communicative actions in different ways are discussed in chapter 9. The ways in which communicative actions develop are dealt with in chapter 2.

Included are personal space and individual distance (chapter 8), as some authors have felt that these are part of 'human nature'. The use and arrangement of space in buildings, which represents a fixed formalisation of individual distances and relationships, is included (chapter 8), but architectural features such as the presence or absence of windows or the colour of walls, which have been felt to influence mood (Smith 1979, Weinstein 1979), have been excluded.

There has been considerable debate over whether nonverbal communication implies the conscious sending and receiving of messages (e.g. review by Smith 1979). For this book, communication may either be under conscious control or not. As discussed in chapter 2, it appears that in many cases nonverbal signals originate as evolutionarily based actions, which come under conscious control with increasing age. Some signals, such as the leakage of uncertainty discussed in chapters 2 and 3, never come under as complete control as their makers would consciously wish. We might also include fixed signals such as room arrangement, since there is no direct conscious link between their originators and their recipients.

THE VALUE OF NONVERBAL SIGNALS TO THE TEACHER

The ORACLE study (Galton, Simon and Croll 1980) showed a contrast between the activity and amount of speech produced by the children and the teacher. Primary teachers spent 78 per cent of their time interacting verbally, while pupils spent 84 per cent of their time not interacting. The picture is similar for nonverbal communication. As we shall discuss in chapters 4 to 6, teachers use a wide range of signals to communicate with and control their class. Children's roles in the classroom, and therefore the range of nonverbal signals they use, tend to be more limited. In the later primary and secondary years especially, much of their time is taken up in essentially solitary work (even if a class is working together on the same topic, they may be working in parallel) or listening to the teacher. In these situations their opportunities for active communication are restricted relative to hers. This may suggest that the teacher does not need to know about children's nonverbal abilities.

However, the teacher's problem is in knowing what is going on in the classroom. She can of course check that the class is learning effectively through their written work. However, this involves a delay in feedback; in addition, incorrect answers often do not give enough information on how the child came to make the error. If it is apparent that a substantial proportion of the class is having problems, the teacher may have to repeat her explanation of the topic which caused difficulty. As well as wasting time, this may cause confusion if the class has by then gone onto other work and the repeated work is out of sequence. What the teacher needs is immediate feedback so she can correct any errors or fill in any gaps in understanding as they arise. In normal conversation listeners have ways of signalling to speakers whether they understand the message (Wardhaugh 1985). We explore this topic in more detail in chapter 6, but at this stage we can note two aspects of the problem.

Children may go for long periods in the primary classroom without their serious misunderstandings of topics being corrected when they are doing individualised work, even when they do go to speak to the teacher on a one-to-one basis (Bennett, Desforges, Cockburn and Wilkinson 1984). Bennett et al. attributed this to the teachers' apparent determination to teach the children rather than to find out what their problem was. There was a failure of communication between the teachers and these young (6–7-year-old) children. This was probably at least partly due to the children's inability to recognise and convey to the teacher that her efforts were not getting through.

Talking to the whole class is the most effective way for the teacher to communicate complex ideas (Galton and Simon 1980). This approach does have the disadvantage that the opportunity for individual children to verbally check potential misunderstandings is very limited. Constant interruptions are likely to disrupt the clear organisation of the explanation which is necessary for understanding (Brown and Armstrong 1984). Once children are habituated to the conventions of whole-class teaching they may not interrupt when they do not understand. The teacher may therefore be heavily dependent on assessing whether she is carrying her class with her from their facial expressions. Less successful explainers seemed not to monitor children's expressions and were unaware that they were repeatedly using terms which the class did not know (Brown and Armstrong op. cit.). However, assessing children's response from their facial expressions itself has problems, as discussed in chapter 6. There are severe limitations to their ability to communicate nonverbally, especially in the early years of schooling.

When children first enter education, at 5 or under, their level of communicatory skill, and the social relationships they communicate, differ considerably from those of adults, for two reasons. Firstly, both their transmission and reception of signals are less sophisticated than those of adults, and they may use signals in different ways or not at all. Secondly, since their social relationships with peers and adults differ from those of older children, the selection of signals they use tends to vary correspondingly. For example, young children are more dependent on adults than older children, and more likely to turn to them when distressed. The decrease in touching behaviour with age (chapter 7), in school settings at least, is likely to be primarily due to their changing relationship with the teacher. Older children are seldom in a state of distress where they need a shoulder to cry on.

THE AMBIGUITY OF NONVERBAL SIGNALS

One major implication which can be drawn from ethological study of nonverbal communication in animals is the ambiguous nature of many nonverbal signals. In the human case, firstly, nonverbal signals differ from words in that several can be emitted spontaneously with the same signal having different meanings according to which other signals are combined with it, and, secondly, in many cases people are not consciously aware of the nonverbal signals they produce in detail and cannot describe them accurately or name them (e.g. Bull 1987). The combination of these two points means that nonverbal signals are less 'attributable' than words and can be used to get a message or attitude across which would not be acceptable if conveyed in speech. There are ways of 'hedging' statements and views in informal social speech such as 'I'm afraid I don't agree' (Wardhaugh 1985) but because of

Figure 1.2 Non-communicative intention movement, from a videotape. The teacher leant forward in order to rise from the desk he was sitting on and move away, when the girl touched him. Her touch constituted a challengingly flirtatious invasion of his personal space, as discussed in chapter 7

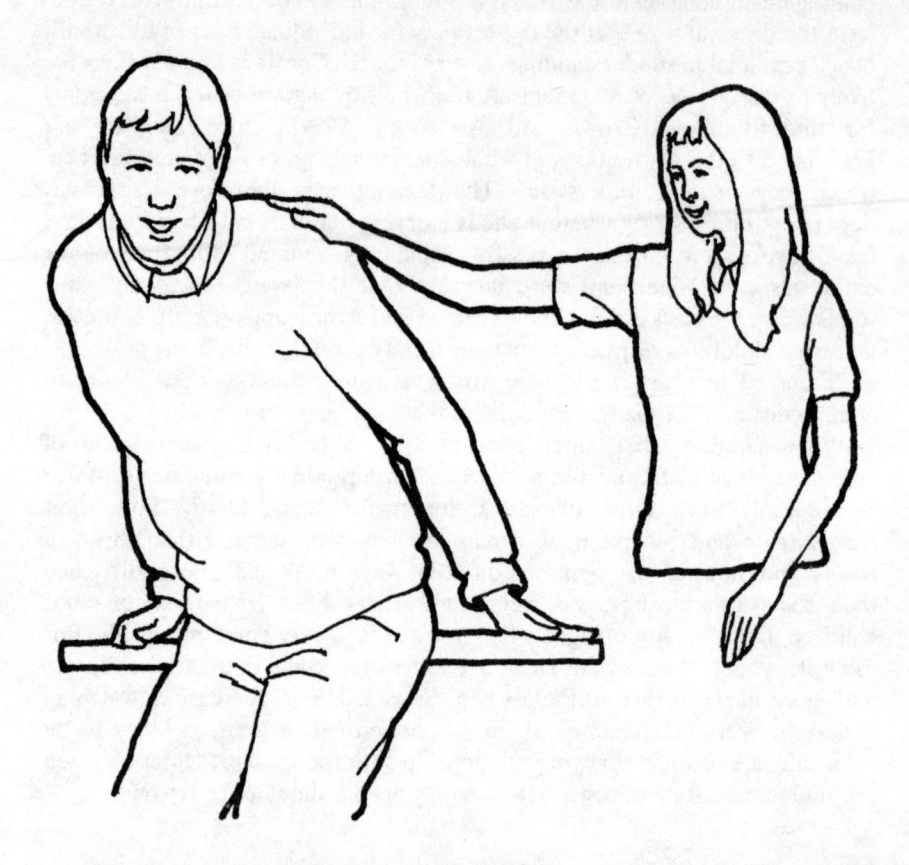

Source: Reproduced with permission from Neill 1986a

their greater explicitness they are often less appropriate to the more formal and unequal position of the classroom, though they can be valuable in the right circumstances. The general argument of this book is that nonverbal signals are often substituted for verbal ones in the classroom – by moving nearer to a child the teacher can control his behaviour without any overt reprimand, for instance (chapter 7). We will deal with these points in order.

The potential ambiguity of nonverbal signals is well illustrated by increased gaze and forward lean (chapters 4, 6). Like many nonverbal signals, they have their origin in *intention movements*, which represent preparation for action (Hinde 1974) (Figures 1.2, 1.3). Sustained gaze allows closer monitoring of what someone else is doing, and therefore increased information and greater

Figure 1.3 Forward lean as an intention movement of involvement. These two pictures were used in a study of the relative effects of posture and facial expression (Neill 1989a). Though the posture was seen positively, as cheerful, friendly and interesting, its effects were weak; children based their judgments primarily on the facial expression

accuracy in reacting to them, taking action against them or risking a closer approach. Forward lean places one in position, if seated, to get up, and, if standing, to launch oneself towards the other person (chapter 7). Increased closeness places one in a better position for a variety of actions – affectionate, supportive or hostile but, because it exposes one to a similar variety of actions from the other party, it increases the emotional temperature of the interaction. Increased gaze has a similar function; both intensify the effect of accompanying signals rather than conveying a specific emotion. Signals with a range of meanings which depend on the context are widespread among animals as well. A great variety of messages can therefore be obtained from combinations of a relatively small number of signals.

As an example, the level of interest listeners feel in a speaker can be conveyed by posture (Bull 1987; see also chapter 4). Normal speakers respond to these signals, for instance by handing the conversational initiative over to someone else if it is obvious that their listeners are beginning to become bored, without either party explicitly drawing attention to the signals – to do so would be a social gaffe. For a teacher to draw attention to and correct children's listening posture requires a reorientation of attitude (chapter 4). Equally, because of this lack of conscious awareness, emotions which a speaker would prefer to remain hidden may be revealed by *nonverbal leakage* (Ekman and Friesen 1969a). Ekman and Friesen found that mental hospital patients who were anxious, but not yet ready, to be released, expressed confidence verbally, but leaked their uncertainty, especially through hand and foot movements. The development of children's ability to avoid nonverbal leakage is discussed further in chapter 2.

It has been suggested by Trivers (1985) that the development of conscious awareness has led to self-deception precisely to minimise the leakage which would happen if conscious deception was occurring. The argument is that if a person genuinely believes something to be true, for instance in their own lack of responsibility for a harmful event, through a process of discounting evidence of their responsibility, their more genuine denials will be more readily accepted. A similar argument applies to the characteristic tendency of preschool children to overestimate their status position in their group. While accurate judges of other children's position, they rate themselves higher than reality, as assessed from observation and the views of the other children (Freedman 1980; Sluckin 1980). This unjustified self-confidence would reduce the signals of uncertainty which they leak (see chapter 2). Though there are disadvantages to excessive over-confidence, (chapter 3), a moderate degree of over-confidence may be especially valuable in early childhood. As discussed in chapter 2, children develop a 'style' in relation to dominance signals during childhood. By accenting the positive at the start of this process, they may increase their chances of developing an effective style.

ARE CLASSROOMS UNIQUE?

The classroom is a highly distinctive social system; neither children nor most adults spend much time otherwise in large highly organised groups of this nature, whether instructional or not. It is not therefore surprising that infant teachers have to spend a considerable amount of time getting across to their charges what the task of being a pupil involves (Willes 1983) and that secondary teachers feel it necessary to spend a considerable time distinguishing the work they plan to do and its organisation from what children have been used to in the primary school (Delamont 1983, Edwards and Furlong 1978). However, both teacher and children have to use words and nonverbal signals which originate in their experience outside the classroom. In general children interpret the same signals from teachers and non-teachers in the same way (Neill 1989b).

Though each classroom is likely to develop its own distinctive subculture (Walker and Adelman 1976, Grant and Hennings 1971), there has to be a degree of communality between different classrooms and between classrooms and other situations. If behaviour in each situation bore no relation to behaviour in any other, the participants, like the proverbial Martian, would be unable to cope on the basis of their previous experience. In some cases the similarities between classrooms and other situations may be because the other situations draw on skills which have been developed in the classroom. As Wardhaugh (1985) points out, teachers and lawyers in court are among the few people who ask questions to which they already know the answer and where the actual answer is likely to be evaluated in front of third parties. Here, in terms of individual experience, the ability to cope with lawyers may depend on experience from the classroom. Though mothers do use such questioning with young children, it is much more characteristic of teachers, and causes children problems when they first encounter it (Tizard and Hughes 1984).

Many of the features of classroom life derive from constraints imposed by the ratio of children to adults (chapters 5 and 6). Simple mathematics show that the amount of contact an individual child can expect to receive from a teacher is very limited, and observational research confirms that, though the primary teacher, for example, spends the great majority of her time talking to individual children, each child spends only a very small minority of his time being talked to by her, and most of this when he is in a class group rather than individually (Galton et al. 1980). The great majority of children's learning time occurs without direct interactions with the teacher, though her influence acts through the materials she has supplied. This situation places a heavy responsibility on the child to develop effective strategies for attracting the teacher's attention if he wishes to do so (chapter 4), but equally offers many opportunities for him to avoid her attention if he wishes to do so, since the pressure on her time prevents her from having such a complete view of what is happening in her classroom as her pupils (Hook and Rosenshine 1979). Different types of classroom organisational strategies have different unintended side-effects resulting from the main behavioural tactics the teacher adopts (Neill 1986b). Thus individualised primary teaching styles, where the teacher tends to be absorbed in a queue of children at her desk, encourage intermittent work by children, in which they spend alternate periods in intense work and social talk (Galton et al. 1980), while the greater degree of surveillance in the secondary classroom encourages the same children to adopt an 'easy rider' style where the demands of work are mitigated unobtrusively (a 'closed challenge' – chapter 4) by taking a long time to carry out the administrative aspects of the tasks set.

Much of what goes on in the classroom derives from social skills and relationships which are not strictly educational. The distinctive feature of Western education systems is the teaching of a rational, heuristic approach to the world (Gladwin 1970), in line with the success of the rational scientific approach in understanding the physical world and enabling technological advance (Olson 1976). The current development of a national curriculum in the United Kingdom (National Curriculum Council 1989a) is an example of the concern that children should receive an adequate grounding of factual knowledge and analytical techniques. However, informal social skills play a large part in a wide variety of types of work under modern conditions, and official training schemes for young school leavers include explicit training in such skills (e.g. Berry 1985). Informal social processes are also of major importance in children's social lives both outside the school and in the playground (e.g. Foot, Chapman and Smith 1980, Sluckin 1981) and in the classroom in their relationships with each other and with the teacher (e.g. Macpherson 1983, Turner 1983). Recently ethologists have come to stress the primacy of social over non-social knowledge in the evolution of intelligence (Whiten and Byrne 1988; but see comments on Byrne and Whiten 1988). Since the pioneering work of Hargreaves (1967) it has been apparent that classroom behaviour could be understood in relation to social pressures, especially between pupils. These social pressures differ radically in different contexts. However explicit the formal rules or legal framework which surround teaching, in the great majority of cases they are enforced through informal procedures; the teacher can hardly call the police in if her 7-year-olds refuse to take their nationally standardised tests. She has to rely on her relationship with the class.

Such relationships and the social groups and sociocultural structure to which they contribute do not have an independently measurable existence; they are realised in the individual interactions between participants. Hinde (1987) discusses the relationships between these different levels of complexity at which social behaviour can be analysed. Links have been drawn between classroom behaviour and the sociocultural structure (e.g. Bellaby 1979); but such discussions tend to involve questions of political philosophy which it is inappropriate to deal with here. At the other end of the range of levels, Hinde (op. cit.) links interactions to the physiological characteristics of the participants; these, though affected by individual experiences, also have an evolutionary basis. In the case of nonverbal behaviour, a number of signals, such as smiling, are universal in humans, though modified by cultural differences, and have close parallels in primates (Hinde 1987). In some cases it may be useful to draw formal comparisons between human use of nonverbal signals and their use in the simpler social systems of animals (e.g. below, on the ambiguity of signals; for dominance, chapter 3).

Parallels can be drawn between classroom social processes which nonverbal signals subserve and processes occurring in traditional societies. By traditional societies are meant those in which technological change is slow, and social mobility is low, so that children can reliably expect to spend their whole lives in the group into which they were born. Social control was found to be extremely strong (Shorter 1976, Gillis 1975). Such groups persisted in traditional industrial areas until the 1950s (Young and Willmott 1957). Seabrook (1982) claims that the increased economic welfare of working-class people has been accompanied by a disintegration of their previous networks of social support, and Hargreaves (1982) has suggested that schools need to provide children with groups to which they can affiliate to compensate for their loss of suitable groups outside the school. Otherwise, in Hargreaves's opinion, children will satisfy their need for affiliation by affiliating to unsuitable groups. I have suggested elsewhere that children's decisions are largely taken in terms of the social value of whatever behaviour they adopt. The classroom implication of this is that children will take classroom decisions in terms of immediate social rewards rather than taking into account the long-term financial benefits of education (Neill 1983b; see also Heath 1981). This again places emphasis on the social interaction skills subserved by the nonverbal behaviour described here.

Most attention has been given to difficult classes (Hammersley and Turner 1980) and the tactics which pupils use in opposition to teacher authority. These tactics, and the teacher's counter-tactics, are dealt with especially in chapters 3 and 4. In the top stream of Hargreaves's (1967) school, by contrast, the peer group reinforced the school's values. However, this is no less behaviour in response to social pressures; here tactics of cooperation and reward, described in chapters 5 and 6, come to the fore. Both cooperative and disruptive behaviour are usually carried out to conform to social pressures, often the pressures exerted by the peer reference group (see also Neill 1983b). This applies as much to the public-school pupil doing Greek as the disruptive pupil. The former will have peers, as well as teachers and parents, who exert social pressure in favour of good work. Often, as Turner (1983) points out, work-oriented pupils in less academic schools may use considerable subtlety in conveying to their less work-oriented peers that they are not subservient to the teacher, while those who want to avoid work use equal subtlety to avoid the teacher's pressure. This book is concerned with the part nonverbal behaviour plays in those tactics, and the teacher's response to them.

SUMMARY

Nonverbal communication is potentially important in the classroom because teacher and children may believe the nonverbal rather than the spoken message, and because some messages can be conveyed implicitly by nonverbal means which would be unacceptable if they were sent through more explicit channels. In some cases nonverbal signals may be the only ones available – if a child is working at the other side of the room, or the teacher is working with a class group and cannot talk to individuals.

In this book attention is restricted primarily to behaviour which has specific functions of communication. Room and school layout are also considered, as these are formalisations of individual distance, a communicative behaviour.

The modern classroom differs from most other social settings, and from one-to-one learning situations in preindustrial societies, in the numbers involved and the requirements imposed on them. Teachers, especially, have to use a specific selection of signals to reflect this distinctive relationship.

Chapter 2

Children's nonverbal abilities and their development

Children's communicative skills differ from those of adults. If the teacher is to communicate effectively with her class, she must pitch her communication at an appropriate level. She must also make allowances when they try to communicate with her. Differences between child and adult nonverbal communication interact with the specific needs of communication in the classroom. They also interact with differences related to sex and ethnic background. The issue of children's development of nonverbal skills surfaces repeatedly in the book, and if we tried to deal with all its manifestations in this chapter, it would be as long as the book. In this chapter we therefore discuss some of the general issues, illustrated with examples from particular aspects of nonverbal communication. In later chapters we will deal with specific types of developmental change when they arise in context. Firstly we need to look at why knowledge of children's nonverbal skills and their development might be important.

THE INCREASE OF NONVERBAL SOPHISTICATION WITH AGE

Children start with a range of signals which appear to be innate – in other words they are linked to structures which are specialised for signalling, and appear at such an early age and in such a wide range of cultures that the possibility that they are learnt seems highly unlikely. Some facial expressions are an example, such as the smile and laugh (e.g. Hinde 1987). Thus the eyebrow flash seems to be a universal 'marker', used to draw attention to the next interactive behaviour (Grammer, Schiefenhovel, Schleidt, Lorenz and Eibl-Eibesfeldt 1988 – compare the more specialised 'markers' used by teachers (chapter 4)). The innate nature of these expressions is indicated by the signal structures on the face such as the lips, eyebrows and white of the eyes which are used to make them. Other primates have different facial patterns, which match the rather different range of expressions they use (Hinde 1974).

Figure 2.1 The plus face, from a videotape of an experienced secondary teacher during the first confrontation over homework of the school year. It formed part of a sequence of behaviour to embarrass and make an example of the only pupil who had failed to hand in the work

Even when nonverbal signals have a strong innate basis, their expression and even their meaning may be altered by experience and cultural influences. Children's ability to copy facial expressions improves rapidly between 5 and 9, with further improvement up to an adult level of performance at 13 (Ekman, Roper and Hager 1980). Thus the facial expressions of secondary-school children could be entirely under conscious control, unrelated to true feelings. However, for adults, facial expression is an accurate measure of reported feelings, at least for happiness and negative feelings (Ekman, Friesen and Ancoli 1980). Not all developmental change need be due to experience. Toddlers gaze more than babies, for developmental reasons, but school-age children rapidly avert gaze (Scheman and Lockard 1979). This may be because schoolchildren have learnt that it is rude to stare, or because they have lost the babyish physiognomy which protects toddlers against strangers and with it the freedom to stare at them.

Children's nonverbal abilities   15

Figure 2.2 The minus face (on the right), from a videotape of a disciplinary incident at the end of a secondary music lesson. Note that it is the opposite of the plus face, in terms of head position, gaze aversion and facial expression. This 'principle of antithesis' is common in pairs of nonverbal signals which have opposite meanings but are both innately based

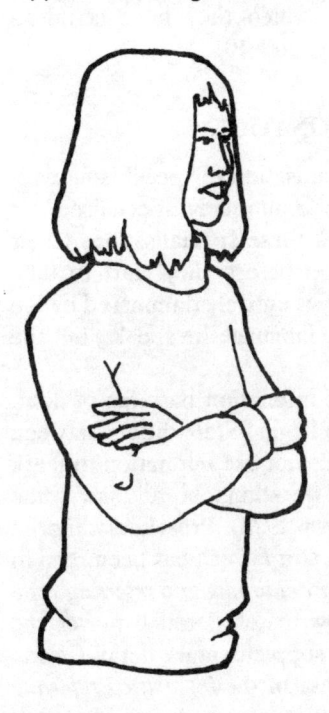

In general, facial expressions move from an initial biologically based state to one which is largely influenced by individual learning and experience. One example, described by Zivin (1982), is the way in which children's use of dominance signals develops. In young children the two signals of dominance ('plus face' – chin up and gaze at the opponent – and 'looking down one's nose', Fgure 2.1) and subordination ('minus face' – chin down, Figure 2.2), which are opposites, as is the case with many innate signals, are used solely in inter- personal disputes. With age, dominant children come to use the chin in non-social situations, for instance, when dealing with a difficult piece of apparatus. They transmit a message of competence to any onlooker, even before any interaction takes place. By contrast unpopular children transmit (a different set of) signals which maximise the possibility of rejection (Putallaz and Gottman 1981). It is therefore possible in principle for other children to assess a newcomer – child or teacher – and treat them appropriately at first interaction. How far children actually do so and how this ability develops is unknown, though even at the preschool, dominance signals do tend to help the signaller get his own way in disputes (Zivin 1982). It is likely that teachers rely largely on skills in signalling dominance which they have acquired through their childhood experience in school (chapter 10).

THE DEVELOPMENT OF SPEECH AND INTONATION

We are the only talking primates, and basic organisation of speech sounds is similar across languages; our throat structure is uniquely specialised for speaking (Aitchison 1983). Newborn babies lack these specialisations (their throats are adapted for sucking) which develop before they start to talk. Despite its innate bases, the final form of speech is entirely dominated by the child's experience which influences not only the language he speaks, but the dialect and the intonation patterns he uses.

Children begin to produce the characteristic intonation patterns of adult speech in infancy, though their use when children begin to talk differs between languages. Finnish children, whose language does not use intonation to mark questions as English does, do not produce questions at an age when English-speaking children can do so freely (Brown 1973). Preschool children (4.5–5.0 years old) are well able, when retelling a story which has been read to them previously, to use the distinction between *proclaiming* and *referring* tone (chapter 5) to mark out which sections are new material which moves the action along, and which are merely descriptive supplementary detail (Wade and Moore 1986). Particularly notable is their use of the *intensified referring* tone, which has a dominant, reminding quality. It is frequently used by adult story-tellers, but would be seen as 'cheeky' if used by a child when talking to an adult. Wade and Moore consider that the fact that the children use this tone as much as adults telling the same story implies they have grasped the conventions of story-telling and realise the dominant role of the story-teller.

This ability to control intonation appears even more clearly in preschool children's use of intonation and different voices when they are playing several characters in an imaginative game, to distinguish between them; 3-year-olds can do this (Garvey 1977). They may be assisted in learning intonation patterns by the very marked intonation range of 'motherese'; children are capable of producing motherese themselves when talking to younger children from an early age (Ellis and Beattie 1986). Teachers, especially those of younger children, use a wide range of expressive intonation when talking to their classes (Boileau 1981).

Ellis and Beattie consider that the main function of motherese is not, as has usually been assumed, to help the child in learning language, as this would require a rich and varied set of examples from which the child could deduce the rules of language. Rather it ensures reliable communication with the child at his current state; its primary function is to get a message across to the child rather than to educate him. Under the more demanding conditions for communication in the classroom (and other similar situations) it is therefore explicable that teachers, even of quite old classes, adopt many of the features of motherese – the emphatic intonation supported by gesture discussed in chapter 5.

THE DEVELOPMENT OF GESTURES

Children's use of gestures also develops with age, though newborn babies gesture in time with their speech (Trevarthen 1977; see also chapter 5). McNeill (1985a, 1986) views gesture as an alternative communication channel working together with speech to communicate ideas generated in the same centre (chapter 5). Therefore the development of gestures reflects the development of the underlying centres. Thus *iconic* gestures, which represent something in the physical world, change with age. In younger children they merge into actual mime of the events the child is talking about, where the child describes a character's actions and simultaneously acts them out. McNeill (1986) gives as an example a preschool child describing a movement and turning his whole body round as he does so, as if following the moving object with his eyes. An adult describing the whole movement would make only a hand gesture, which she would not follow visually. In McNeill's view young children's gestures, like their speech, are initially centred on the self; older children and adults typically have a more detached view, as onlookers to the theatre of gesture which they unfold in front of them.

Metaphoric gestures, which stand for abstract ideas (chapter 5; Figure 2.3), seem to appear somewhat later than iconic gestures (at the age of about 9), as would be expected since they process more abstract concepts which children develop later. As McNeill (1986) points out, children sometimes reveal in their gestures that the apparently adult grammatical structure of their speech cloaks incompletely developed ideas. Thus an adult gesturing while talking about a spider crawling up a pipe synchronises her gesture with the whole phrase, but a 5-year-old synchronises his (much more expansive) gesture with the word 'pipe' alone, suggesting that the whole meaning of the phrase is concentrated on this single word, the others being largely redundant. McNeill also describes the ability of adults to return to a gesture after an aside, such as a subordinate clause (the example he illustrates is of a woman returning to a horizontal gesture demonstrating the power-wires for cable-cars after a phrase describing the pantograph, accompanied by a vertical gesture). In other words the continuing existence of an object in the conversation even when the conversation deviates from it is symbolised by its having the same location in gestural space when it is returned to. This ability of adults reflects the higher-level organisation of their conversation, and McNeill has not

Figure 2.3 Metaphoric gestures (see also chapter 5). Left: 'holding an idea' for inspection by the listeners; right: 'open sesame', signalling that the idea should now be clear. The two signals are usually used in this sequence, the idea being 'held' while the teacher explains it. The teacher then metaphorically opens the gates of knowledge after the explanation

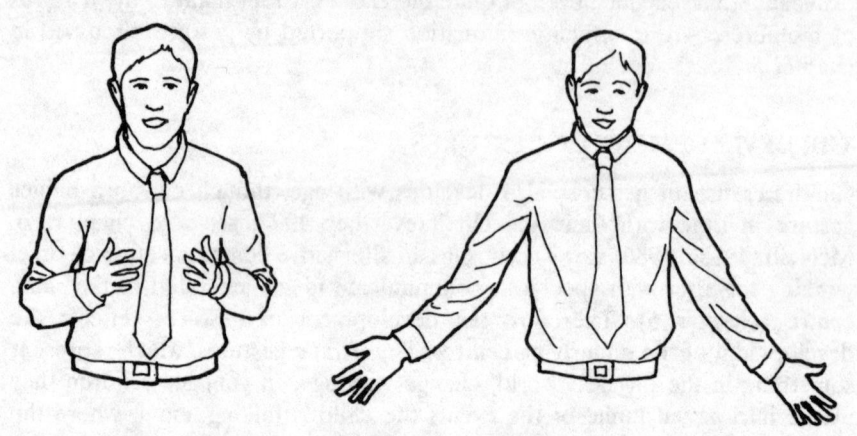

Source: Reproduced with permission from *Pastoral Care in Education* 6 (4): 38

observed it in children as old as 12. (The development of the ability might be linked to formal operations in the Piagetian sense, but there is no evidence on this point.)

An earlier development of conversational structuring is the appearance of *beats* at the age of about 5; these serve to punctuate speech, and they or their equivalents are extensively used in the public speech of teachers (chapter 5). Freedman, van Meel, Barroso and Bucci (1986) consider that beats (which they call *speech primacy movements*) increase progressively from 29 per cent of 4-year-olds' gestures to 82 per cent at 14. Correspondingly *representational* gestures (equivalent to iconix and metaphorix) decrease from 55 per cent to 13 per cent. (The remainder appear to be self-touching movements.)

Overall, it appears that the development of children's gestures continues throughout the primary years, and that children may be at a disadvantage when the teacher is trying to explain relatively complex concepts because, in addition to any difficulties they may have with the words used and the concepts involved, they are deprived, to a greater or lesser extent depending on their age, of the supplementary information and organisation offered by gesture. Little information is available at present, however, as to whether children's comprehension of gestures develops in parallel with their use of them. As we will discuss in chapter 5, teachers do make very considerable use of gesture, at least when talking to large groups of children, but so do speakers to groups of adults (e.g. Atkinson 1984, Bull 1987). There seems to be no evidence as to whether teachers, or indeed other adults, use a gestural form of 'motherese' when talking to children, or whether they tend to suppress gestures when dealing with children at an age where the children themselves do not yet make extensive use of gestures, substituting more direct forms of influence.

SIGNALS OF UNDERSTANDING

Signals of understanding may, like signals of dominance, become habitual. Allen and Atkinson (1978) found that high-achieving and low-achieving 10–11-year-old children tended to signal their characteristic level of understanding regardless of what their actual level of understanding was likely to be. The children were recorded while looking at videotaped lessons, which were either very simple, so that all could understand them, or well above the comprehension level of this age-group. Adults judged that high-achieving children understood more than low-achieving children, though the children's own ratings of their level of understanding did not differ. The judges also thought that children understood more when they had been listening to an easy lesson than a difficult one. The difference was more marked for girls, who are generally more nonverbally expressive (chapter 9). At this age the children were capable of signalling understanding and non-understanding deliberately when asked to do so, so the spontaneous differences related to achievement level occur despite this ability. The difference between ratings of understanding and non-understanding is more pronounced for deliberate than spontaneous behaviour, which may reflect a lack of subtlety parallel to that recorded for dissimulation (see below).

The implications of these results are potentially serious, if teachers use similar judgments as a basis for forming expectations about children they have just met. Ratings of likeability and intellectual ability were both strongly correlated with ratings of understanding. In other words, if children have easily understood with their previous teacher, they will be more likely to look as if they understand with a new teacher. The new teacher will see them as bright, likeable children. Thus the children's expectations will help form the teacher's expectations. Negative expectations about low-ability children will be transmitted in the same way. The raters in Allen and Atkinson's study (1978) were undergraduate students, and different results might have been obtained from experienced teachers. If experienced teachers do understand these signals in the same way (chapters 6, 10) high-ability children who are more rewarding to the teacher are likely to get more praise and attention (chapter 6) than low achievers, perpetuating the process.

Allen and Atkinson (op. cit.) do not cite the actual behaviours involved in signalling understanding or lack of understanding, but Lawes (1987b) suggests several cues can be used by student teachers. Irrelevant behaviours such as playing with objects, hand to mouth and looking around (chapter 4; Figure 2.4), especially in combination, were used successfully to judge that a child had not understood; their absence indicated comprehension. Slow

Figure 2.4 The pupil on the right is putting her pen to her mouth, a sign, if it is sustained, that she is having problems with the work

responses from the children, especially when combined with these irrelevant behaviours, indicated lack of comprehension. On the other hand the students did make several incorrect judgments of comprehension from children's behaviour. They felt that a fast response meant the child had understood, and that facial expressions such as frowning or a puzzled brow (Figure 2.5) indicated lack of understanding: neither set of cues was reliable. In general the student teachers used null cues – the absence of a particular type of behaviour – as indicating that children had understood; they would look for the presence of a behaviour to judge that help was needed. If experienced teachers make similar judgments, there may be potential for overestimating the level of understanding, especially of the less expressive pupils. This may partly account for the inaccurate matching of tasks to children's ability found, for instance, by Bennett, Desforges, Cockburn and Wilkinson (1984).

Figure 2.5 The puzzled frown, expressing worry at lack of understanding. Teachers use this expression in a less extreme form during explanations, to signal to the class that they should be paying attention to an explanation of something which would otherwise be puzzling

DEVELOPMENT OF THE ABILITY TO UNDERSTAND NONVERBAL SIGNALS

Children's skill in interpreting nonverbal communication increases with age and experience of specific situations. Primary children's ability to decode student teachers' classroom messages from video and content-filtered audio messages improves with re-testing (Yerrell, Lovell, Stote and Rosenthal 1986). The children were tested with two teachers, only one of whom had taught them before they were re-tested. Children did not consistently do better with the teacher who had taught them. Yerrell et al. felt that this was because some student teachers signalled in such an obvious way that only minimal practice was needed to decode the signals; no improvement was found with these. Classes who had been taught by a subtle teacher still found it easier to decode an obvious teacher who had not taught them. There was some indication that better decoders had higher self-esteem. It might be worth investigating whether better decoders are able to use this skill to react appropriately – for instance are they the children whom Brophy (1981) describes as good in getting teachers to praise and reward them (chapter 6)?

From ages 6 to 10 individual children's judgments of photographs of teaching situations become more consistent (Norton 1974). This may reflect not only their increasing sophistication, but also increasing knowledge of the cultural interpretations of particular incidents. The latter possibility is supported by increasing differentiation between the judgments of girls and boys, and of ethnic groups. This is discussed more fully in chapter 9.

The increases in children's skill in interpreting nonverbal communication, up to late adolescence, may be related to their general cognitive development (DePaulo and Rosenthal 1979a, 1979b). While 19-year-old students were quicker in identifying whether an expression was pleasant (smiling) or unpleasant than 11-year-olds, if their scores were adjusted to allow for their rapidity in deciding whether a figure was a circle or a square this difference disappeared (Stanners, Byrd and Gabriel 1985). In other words the students showed a similar advantage in both tasks, and there was no specific adaptation in relation to faces. A general skill in decoding nonverbal cues seems to be accompanied by specific skills in decoding visual (especially facial), voice and combined (including discrepant) cues (DePaulo and Rosenthal 1979b). A person who is good at one of the specific skills may not necessarily be good at the others. However, DePaulo and Rosenthal's interpretation, based on the simulated signals of their PONS test, may not apply to spontaneous innately based signals.

There are obviously differences in the way in which individuals signal the same emotions. At the simplest level these can result from differences in facial structure which result in differences of resting facial expression. Thus Ekman and Friesen (1975) illustrate individuals whose faces at rest look somewhat aggressive because of prominent straight eyebrows. A slight smile, which on another face would look affable, looks sinister on them; they cannot readily avoid the sardonic combination of smiling mouth and apparently frowning brows.

Abramovitch (1977) found that preschool children could tell if their own mother was talking to a familiar person or to a stranger, but could not make this distinction for a strange woman, though adults could do so readily. Similarly, whereas adults could tell from a film whether a preschool child (who was strange to them) was talking to a familiar child or his mother, or a strange child or adult, the preschool children could only make this distinction with members of their own class (Abramovitch and Daly 1979). With strange preschoolers, they could not judge either whether the child was talking to a peer or an adult, or whether to a familiar person or a stranger. These studies do not record the signals which discriminate between talk to familiar people and strangers, though they suggest more animation, such as smiling, in conversations with strangers. Recognition of these signals seems only to be possible for these young children when they are familiar with the baseline of behaviour shown by a particular individual. Adults, with their wider range of experience and more sophisticated understanding of nonverbal signals, are better able to separate the signal from the 'noise' of individual variation. This task is probably made harder for young children by their inability to combine information from several channels. Particular interest has been shown in children's ability to detect discrepant or 'leaky' messages.

THE DECODING OF DISCREPANT AND DECEPTIVE MESSAGES

Discrepant and deceptive messages can be detected by older children or adults because the verbal message such as 'Very good' is delivered with, for example, a harsh intonation or frowning face (sarcasm, Figure 2.6). Sarcastic messages, especially, during adult discussions, are reacted to with initial nonverbal signals of uncertainty, followed by threat and withdrawal from communication (Leathers 1979). Such messages are significant in the classroom context not only because the teacher may use sarcasm or irony, but because children may be able to detect the uncertain teacher because she 'leaks' her uncertainty by intonation, hand movements, or pacing or rocking on her feet (Neill 1986b; see also Ekman and Friesen 1969b, Hocking and Leathers 1980; chapter 3). The work of the Woolfolks on secondary children's responses to discrepant and nondiscrepant verbal and nonverbal messages is discussed in chapter 6.

Older children are more skilled in differentiating nonverbal signals (DePaulo and Rosenthal 1979a). This is reflected in their greater ability both to detect such discrepancies than younger children and to produce deceptive messages. They tend to take more notice of the nonverbal component than younger children (Blanck and Rosenthal 1982). Preschoolers attend mainly to the more easily counterfeited verbal message (Volkmar and Siegel 1982). This change does not occur in emotionally disturbed children, who continue to attend mainly to the verbal message (Reilly and Muzekari 1986; also chapter 9).

Older children are also more successful at producing deceptive signals

Figure 2.6 Sarcasm; compare Figure 1.3. The 'devilish' expression shows both a positive smile and a negative frown and poses problems for children who cannot interpret all the elements at once

(Feldman, Jenkins and Popoola 1979). By 13, for mild deception at least, the differences between truthful and deceptive signals are imperceptible. At 19, deceptive signals are more intense than truthful ones, but not in a way which allows detection by adult observers. All three age-groups tested, including the 6-year-olds, were more deceptive when they could be seen than when they thought they could not. The 6-year-olds were already aware of the need to control their behaviour, though they were still ineffective deceivers. There has been a considerable amount of research on deceptiveness in relation to feedback in tutoring and teaching situations, and this is dealt with in chapter 6.

Though girls are initially superior at decoding discrepant messages, they lose this superiority with age, which Blanck and Rosenthal (1982) attribute to the relative social positions of the sexes; girls learn to be 'politely ignorant' of deceptions which might be embarrassing. In other words, because of their lesser readiness to challenge others, they come to be ignorant of cues which would allow them to detect deception, and which, if they used them, would allow them to challenge deceptive members of their group, but at a cost in conflict which they might not wish to bear. However, sex differences do not invariably appear: Snodgrass and Rosenthal (1985), whose methodology was generally similar, found none.

Relevant here is Stanworth's (1983) finding that girls were more sensitive to teacher approval, which they more rarely received than boys due to their unobtrusiveness. Teachers attend to children who are potential disciplinary problems or notable contributors to classroom discussion and are therefore more unpredictable (Garner and Bing 1973, Brophy and Good 1974), and these tend to be boys.

Zuckerman, Blanck, DePaulo and Rosenthal (1980) point out that children of both sexes switch their attention from bodily cues, which are relatively leaky, to the more controllable facial cues, most markedly at about 14–15. They feel this relates to the particular importance of social conformity at this age (see also Neill 1983b). Paralinguistic (audio) cues of liking and being liked also seem more reliable than facial cues, with student subjects, for the same reason (Snodgrass and Rosenthal 1985). People who are especially good at decoding visual cues may rely on them more than is justified by their accuracy. This is a potential problem for the teacher who may have to rely on facial visual signals, either because the class as a whole are silent during whole-class work or because during individual work pupils at a distance cannot be heard above the general level of talk.

SUMMARY

Some types of nonverbal signals, such as facial expressions, head posture and intonation, appear from an innate base in the preschool period. Children's sophistication in using them, and conscious control over their use, increase during the school years. Other types of signals, such as gestures, and the ability to understand nonverbal signals, especially discrepant signals, develop more slowly. For these, nonverbal ability seems related to general cognitive ability.

Children may develop characteristic styles of behaviour, for example for signals of dominance and understanding, which can communicate expectations to others. These styles seem to be the basis from which recruits to teacher training develop their skills, as discussed in chapter 10. Children's nonverbal perceptiveness may decline, perhaps especially for girls, apparently to avoid embarrassment from interpreting messages which a social companion would wish to keep hidden. This could be a potential problem for student teachers.

Chapter 3

Signals of dominance and uncertainty

Dominance signals and hierarchies are of considerable interest in the school situation, for both theoretical and practical reasons. Despite the publicity given to the 'classroom jungle', the large-scale survey and detailed study of inner-city schools carried out for the Elton Report (Department of Education and Science and Welsh Office 1989) showed that serious incidents were rare. The great majority of incidents were controllable; it was their frequency which made them wearing for teachers. Though the Report discussed a wide variety of influences on discipline, from senior school management to parents, politicians and the media, it concluded that teachers' own skills in controlling and managing class groups were critical.

For most children the preschool and school are both the first situations where they have to make their way with large numbers of peers and with unfamiliar adults, and the main arena in which they have to exercise these skills until school-leaving age. From the teacher's point of view the social structure of the class is of importance indirectly, as relationships between the children affect the way they carry out their schoolwork. Dominance also has direct implications for discipline, when the teacher has to deal both with children's own conflicts, and, especially as they grow older, with direct challenges to her own authority. Analysing exactly how individual challenges develop and are resolved has proved as difficult for researchers (Parry-Jones and Gay 1980, Clarke, Parry-Jones, Gay and Smith 1981) as it is for the teachers involved, but it is possible to derive some of the principles involved.

THE NATURE OF DOMINANCE

For the purposes of the following discussion, dominance is defined as a feature of a *relationship*, by which the dominant individual can control the subordinate's behaviour. Dominance may involve actual aggression, or more usually the threat of aggression, but the subordinate may give way without any overt sanction from the dominant (for example a child who moves out of the way when another approaches, or a class which falls silent when the teacher enters the room). Often dominance has been established by initial confrontation or threat, but, as described in chapter 2, both dominant and subordinate individuals may give out signals which indicate their status to a newcomer before any interaction has taken place. One question, dealt with below, is why such signals are often accepted as reliable or 'honest' without being fully tested (for instance when a class probes but does not explicitly challenge a teacher's authority). Since the nonverbal signals used represent the ways in which interpersonal relationships are communicated, much of this and the following chapter will deal with this context of relationships, since it governs the way in which the nonverbal signals are understood.

From the theoretical point of view, dominance behaviour is of interest for two reasons. Firstly, the signals used have an evolutionary history which influences their use in young children, before children's own experience leads to modifications with age. Secondly, there has been a considerable amount of debate on the communication of dominance by animals; whether or not the mechanisms are the same, there is a formal similarity to situations in human behaviour. In other words particular types of behavioural strategies are effective across a wide range of situations, and their effectiveness does not depend on the actual way in which decisions are made. For example if a person plays against a chess computer the better strategies win, however the decisions are taken. In the same way 'chess tournaments' have been run between different computer simulations of animal conflict tactics (Maynard Smith 1982). The animals being simulated may have purely innate rules, evolved by natural selection, or rely partly on learning from individual experience, perhaps at a conscious level (Humphrey 1976). In the human case we can expect a decision to have the same effect whether it is arrived at rationally or intuitively. Thus the 'tit for tat' strategy mentioned by Maynard Smith (op. cit.) closely resembles 'pacing', one method of conflict management recommended by Bowers (1986). Both derive their success from matching tactics to those of the opponent, and from immediately de-escalating when the opponent does, so that conflicts are not escalated unnecessarily.

The formal modelling approach may have relevance, especially to our understanding of why individuals may communicate uncertainty or lack of dominance when this appears to be against their own best interests and we would expect them to avoid doing so because they would find the experience distressing at a conscious level. We will explore some of these aspects after first looking at some of the phenomena which need explanation.

CLASSROOM SOCIAL STRUCTURE

Conflict in classrooms has been going on in much the same form since the introduction of compulsory education (Humphries 1981), as children struggle or negotiate with the teacher and their peers. Each class contains cliques whose values differ (Meyenn 1980; Macpherson 1983): frequently these cliques may be in bitter opposition to each other, and their conflicts create distractions from the lesson and problems for the teacher. Among younger secondary-school children, cliques will almost invariably be single-sex, and draw on social skills which have already had several years of intensive practice in the primary-school playground (Sluckin 1981). Indeed it seems that the purpose of primary-school games, such as the games with rules, many of which have been passed down through generations of children, is not the games themselves, but the social skills learnt through them. Games with rules offer children opportunities for practising manipulating rules, bending them to one's own advantage, countering the efforts of the other side to make use of them, excluding those whom one does not want to play with, and including those whom one does (Sluckin, op. cit.). Once children have developed skill at manipulating rules, they can turn this skill against the teacher. They expect the teacher to conform to the rules for teacher conduct. They are prepared to sanction teachers who do not stick to what the class thinks appropriate conduct, by failing to keep order adequately and not setting enough written work. Discussions, for example, were not 'real work' and classes did not expect teachers to rely on their self-control (Nash 1974).

Furlong (1976) found that while normally a particular group of children were interacting and formed an 'interaction set', sometimes the set might expand to include the whole class, for example if a weak teacher could not cope with disorder (Figure 3.1). At other times a member of the normal interaction set would find herself isolated, when her friends refused to support her, either because the teacher was in a strong position, or because they had become absorbed in work which interested them. Furlong claimed that although cliques have continuity, because they contain children whose

Figure 3.1 Recruitment to an interaction set. The two boys at the front formed the initial interaction set, but the girl's protests (which may be staged) are attracting attention from other pupils

resources and interests are similar, the actual children involved in a particular interaction and their roles are in a state of flux, as each child assesses from moment to moment whether it is worth joining in an activity, especially one such as a confrontation which involves risks as well as potential benefits. A clique or a class, like a fountain, has apparent continuity over time, but this actually reflects a continued dynamic balance between the various forces acting on it. Even at a time of stability there will be fluctuations, and any major alteration in the balance of forces acting may be rapidly reflected in a dramatic change in the patterns of interaction.

This view of the group as the resultant of individual decisions has parallels in the animal literature, where it is now generally accepted that, for instance, subordinate members do not submit 'in the interests of the group'. Game theory, first used in economics, is a way of modelling the behaviour of opponents who behave in a 'rational' way in accordance with their own self-interest (Maynard Smith 1982). Though attempts have been made to apply models of rational economic decision-making to the classroom (Drake 1979), they have not so far been formalised as much as those used in the study of animal behaviour.

CLASSROOM DOMINANCE

Some teachers appear to maintain classroom control almost effortlessly, while others, even after years of experience, seem to make no impression on the chaos in their classrooms whatever their threats and promises. Initial encounters make a major difference to the success or failure of classroom relationships. Walker and Adelman (1976) drew attention to the way in which a classroom develops its own distinctive subculture, but there has been relatively little research on initial encounters. The following account draws on the work of Wragg and Wood (1984) and Moskowitz and Hayman (1974, 1976) as well as Neill (1986a).

Experienced and effective teachers present first lessons which differ markedly from their own later lessons and the first lessons of their more inexperienced and ineffective colleagues. They display in exaggerated form both their willingness to deal severely with any infractions of the classroom order and their more positive side: the ability to offer help, humour and interesting curriculum material. The positive aspects are dealt with elsewhere; here we consider the way in which the teacher capitalises on the class's initial uncertainty as to her methods and standards. Children run risks, to their self-esteem if nothing more, if they expose themselves to a position they cannot cope with. Experienced teachers are skilled at dealing promptly with the initial infractions or disciplinary 'probes' by the class (Ball 1980, Beynon 1985), intercepting them promptly by the low-level tactics which will be discussed shortly; in this way they build up 'case law' which acts as a precedent for future interactions (Wragg and Wood 1984). They also make clear to

Figure 3.2 Clothes offer one way in which the teacher can consciously modify the signals she sends. By meeting her class for the first time with her hands in her pockets she can convey calmer control than if she stands with her hands on her hips, which children tend to see as bad-tempered and unfriendly even when accompanied by a smile (Neill 1989a)

Source: Reproduced with permission from *Pastoral Care in Education* 6 (4): 38

pupils exactly what they should do, as well as what they should not (Anderson, Evertson and Emmer 1980).

The calm approach of the experienced teacher gives the class little initial information (Figures 3.2, 3.3), and their probes are likely to be cautious. If the teacher reacts to low-level challenges promptly, she can avoid using serious sanctions, and this preserves an area of uncertainty for the children. They cannot be sure what she would do about higher-level challenges. If low-level offences attract prompt and mildly unpleasant sanctions, the children are likely to extrapolate about what her response will be to higher-level challenges. This is vitally important since teachers are legally forbidden to use severe sanctions on children (Partington 1984) so that one of the foundations of 'honest' signalling (discussed below), the ability to move from 'conventional' threats to real force, is removed. The teacher's control relies less on the actual sanctions she uses than in producing the responses which would characterise a powerful and dominant opponent. Provided her behaviour is consistent in all respects, the children seem to control themselves

Figure 3.3 A calm posture, displayed by an effective music teacher while dealing with a disciplinary problem. The open posture (compare Figure 3.10) and lean against the cupboard indicate no anxiety about counterattack from the children

via the strength of their perceptions of her behaviour. (We will come to possible explanations for these responses.) Even though, in discussion, they may rationally agree that there is very little she can actually do, they find it virtually impossible to act on this knowledge, so long as they accept the sanctions available in the school system. Though there are a proportion of children who do not respond to this approach, the great majority can be controlled by a calmly dominant teacher. Calmness, fairness, a clear rule structure and a teacher who takes responsibility for enforcing it by appropriate punishment are what children prefer (Lovegrove and Lewis 1982, Lewis and Lovegrove 1984).

We can contrast this strategy with two alternatives which are unpopular with children: the 'strict' teacher and the 'weak' teacher. The 'strict' teacher, whether she starts off strict or is forced into an aggressive posture by the class, runs the risk of getting involved in avoidable escalation (Figure 3.4). A fierce response to an initial tentative probe by a child is likely to be temporarily

Figure 3.4 Angry and sad postures, both from videotapes of a teacher with discipline problems. Such clear displays of emotion are relatively infrequent among adults in other public circumstances

Source: Reproduced with permission from Neill 1986a

effective. If the child is still uncertain of the teacher, his tentative probe indicates that he considers her a high risk. Her strong reaction indicates an aggressive dominance and confirms his view that she is a high risk, so succeeding probes are also likely to be cautious. Meanwhile, as mentioned above, experienced teachers aim to show their positive side, to demonstrate they can reward as well as punish.

However, fierce threat, because it indicates that the opponent has to be taken seriously, is likely to be counterproductive either if the child is making a stronger challenge because the teacher has already indicated her insecurity, or if the teacher persists in using it against low-level challenges. We will discuss in a moment how this judgment may be made from threats which are an 'honest' indication of the perceived risk from the challenger. As a result aggressive teachers may encounter discipline problems; their continued threatening is an indication of how seriously they take the challenges to their authority, and undermines their dominance. For this reason, experienced teachers tend to avoid provoking trouble from difficult children (Stebbins 1970, Bowers 1986). Aggressively threatening teachers also threaten children's self-esteem, and do not permit them to establish their mark on the classroom situation in a positive way, by contributing to the lesson content or by humour.

By contrast, the uncertain teacher may give the children information on her likely reaction by her nonverbal leakage (Ekman and Friesen 1969b), which is more 'honest' than her controlling words, conveying her preference to avoid a threatening situation before any damage is done. Under normal circumstances, outside the classroom, this reaction is likely to be the best one, as it may allow unchallenged withdrawal from a threatening situation. In the classroom, where the teacher cannot escape her responsibilities, it merely gives the class information to which they are extremely sensitive. Their fuller information gives them a better basis from which to mount a challenge, and when the challenge comes it is likely to be at a higher level. High-level challenges will usually be met by threat from the teacher; she will then find herself having to act as a 'strict' teacher.

'HONEST' SIGNALLING

Differences in the signals individual teachers use explain why children 'see through' the uncertain teacher so easily, why they are so impressed by the apparent lack of action of the effective teacher and why the 'strict' teacher often runs into difficulties of control and popularity. The uncertain teacher signals her uncertainty to the class by her intention movements of escape, shown as agitated, jerky movements, as opposed to the smooth movements of the confident individual (Exline 1985). She also shows anxious 'displacement' activities (Neill 1986a, Morris 1977; Figure 3.5). Both are readily detected by children. Some behaviours, such as the head groom, are ritualised developments of the threatening behaviours used by younger children (Grant 1969), and potentially signal suppressed aggression.

A considerable amount of discussion has taken place between ethologists as to whether communication in animal confrontations can be 'honest' (e.g. Dawkins 1986). Either party in a confrontation could 'bluff' by producing impressive threats which are not in fact justified; they might threaten what they could not deliver. We might expect dishonest bluff to be general as an animal which 'honestly' signals how much risk he is prepared to take is 'giving away' information which may allow a rival to win the confrontation – like a bidder at an auction who says what his upper limit will be in advance. Evidence is now accumulating to suggest that high-level threats between animal contestants are more risky as well as more effective (Enquist, Plane and Roed 1985). In other words, as mentioned above, by bluffing an individual may win some confrontations rapidly, but may find himself exposed to dangers which a more cautious strategy might have avoided. We may liken this to an auction in which anyone who bids must risk losing his bid money; in such an auction if everyone declares his upper limit, this allows those who have no chance of success to avoid bidding at all.

Honest communication is most strikingly demonstrated in some species by permanent 'badges' of status (more intense colouring or patterning) which

Figure 3.5 A grooming movement shown by an inexperienced teacher with discipline problems, indicating anxiety. This teacher verbalised her worry about initial encounters with classes

Source: Reproduced with permission from *Pastoral Care in Education* 6 (4): 39

permanently display to all comers what position in the hierarchy an individual is prepared to defend. If these badges are bluff, an individual is permanently committed to them (unlike behavioural bluffing) so they provide a particularly clear test of whether bluff exists. Experiments suggest low-status individuals 'made up' to resemble higher-status ones (i.e. as bluffers) do not rise in status unless they are given hormone injections so that their behaviour alters to greater aggressiveness (i.e. they become 'honest'); they just get involved in more fights with the real dominants which they lose (Huntingford and Turner 1987). High status has disadvantages as well as advantages; there is evidence that high-status individuals have physiological costs which go with their greater assertiveness and success (Roskraft, Jarvi, Bakken, Beeh and Reinertsen 1986). Badges of status are most important in setting the initial tone of interaction between strangers; familiar individuals tend to be more influenced by actual behaviour.

There is some evidence of similar patterns in humans. The more inefficient physiology and greater susceptibility to risk and illness of human males compared to females (Hutt 1972) may be related to their greater assertiveness and willingness to engage in escalated conflict (Huntingford and Turner 1987). The characteristic facial and voice differences (described in chapter 9) appear to be 'badge' signals. In other words, whether for cultural or biological reasons, male appearance confers an initial advantage in assessment of dominance. This can be accentuated when behaviour is brought in as well. Henley and Harmon (1985) suggest that the same nonverbal signals, such as standing close, standing over the other person, pointing at and touching them, were interpreted as indicating more dominance when performed by males, and more sexuality when performed by females. As they point out, and as is apparent from the sample pictures they present, these effects might be partly due to differences according to sex in the way their models posed the signals, with the men tending to give a more consistent pattern of confident behaviour. Similarly Wex (1980) illustrates a wide range of nonverbal signals, such as the 'bouncer' posture, standing with legs apart and arms folded, as characteristic of men rather than women, reflecting the male-dominated nature of society.

An alternative explanation would be that these signals are not inherently sex-typed, but reflect characteristic differences in confidence between the sexes (Cronin 1980). However, whether the differences are due solely to the way in which the signals are received, or also partly to the way in which they are transmitted, the conclusion that women might have to work harder to convey the same authority remains. Beynon (1985) found that conveying authority was a major problem for the women staff at the tough comprehensive school he was studying (and for the quieter male staff, who were denigrated as honorary women). Only one female teacher was accepted, because she behaved like a man (though exactly what she did is not specified). The others were provoked sufficiently to drive them to use physical force or verbal 'showing up' ('showing up' is discussed in more detail in chapter 4). The boys resented these behaviours much more from a woman than from a man, and fiercely condemned the women for reacting to their provocation. This literature suggests potentially severe discipline problems for women. On the other hand, my own study of children's reactions to slides of teachers' nonverbal signals (Neill 1986a) showed no differentiation according to the sex of the teacher portrayed, compared to substantial effects of the particular behaviour patterns shown. This implies, as did the study of the actual behaviour of effective teachers (Neill 1986b), that once interaction begins, the interaction itself dictates the outcome rather than the fixed characteristics of the individuals concerned, such as sex and age, though these may convey an initial advantage (Hargreaves 1975).

The theory of 'honest' signalling can also be used to explain the problem of the 'strict' teacher. As we have seen, the range of sanctions which teachers can use are legally circumscribed, but high-level threats would normally be used, outside the classroom situation, in circumstances where physical violence would normally be the alternative. Indeed, for most of their school careers children, especially boys, continue to use violence in the school or playground (e.g. Neill 1976, 1985; Macpherson 1983). They may indeed be using rough-and-tumble play as a low-risk way of exploring how far peers can physically sustain their claims to dominance (Neill 1985), though this is disputed (Humphreys and Smith 1984). They therefore have ample opportunity to assess from experience how far threats are 'honest' and can be backed up, and indeed develop negotiation skills to resolve playground conflicts without resorting to actual violence (Sluckin 1979). This knowledge can readily be used in dealing with teachers. Indeed, since adults seldom resort to actual violence to solve disputes, their knowledge of the implications of threats may become less accurate from disuse. Children readily discover that repeated and severe threats in the classroom are not backed up by the violence they would imply elsewhere, though they may be cautious in response to an isolated single threat.

ACCURATE READING OF SIGNALS

Receivers of 'honest' signals should be able to assess them accurately; indeed the pressures against bluffing that we have described derive from this. Inaccurate receivers may miss opportunities against weaker opponents or avoid harmless social situations because they see them as threatening, if they misinterpret signals as more negative or threatening than they really are. More seriously for the teacher who is trying to manage the classroom, those who fail to recognise threatening or negative signals may get engaged in confrontations which they have no hope of winning. As the consequences of confrontations may be serious, we may expect normal receivers to readily detect and take note of signals of dominance. This does not mean that teachers have to give a flawless performance. Even the most effective teachers in the behavioural study (Neill 1986b) show signs of stress, such as grooming movements, at times such as transitions between activities (Figure 3.6), when the risk of disorganisation before the children get settled into the new activity is higher (Gump 1975, Kounin 1970). However, the children seemed to discount these signals. Often the signal of uncertainty occurred as the teacher approached the transition to the new activity, and at this point only a minority of children were attending to the teacher; characteristically she would then use a 'marker' (chapter 4) to ensure that she had the attention of the whole class and by this point, when every eye was on her, the stress signals would have disappeared.

Accurate reading of signals underlies normal interaction; children with behavioural problems seem in many cases to have normal decision-making processes, but a faulty perception of the situation so that they underestimate or overestimate the risks in a potential confrontation. In animals, and to a

Figure 3.6 An experienced teacher during a confrontation early in the school year. He is clarifying the way he runs the work, hence the self-pointing gesture, but he is also performing a defensive body-cross with his arm (compare Figures 3.7, 3.8, 3.9)

Source: Reproduced with permission from *Pastoral Care in Education* 6 (4): 39

lesser extent in people (Huntingford and Turner 1987), confrontations lead to hormonal changes which make the winner more assertive and the loser less so. This sharpens what may initially have been a relatively small difference in competitive ability. If a repeat confrontation would lead to the same result, both parties will benefit from avoiding the risk and the hormonal changes serve to modify the participants' assessments in future confrontations. We therefore have a picture of normal individuals accurately reflecting the degree of stress they feel in a confrontation. Those who lack normal awareness of the risks or are aware of them but do not feel the normal level of anxiety find themselves in an unduly high number of all-out confrontations (chapter 9). As a result they frequently experience punishment, become desensitised to aggression (Huntingford and Turner 1987) and come to feel 'picked on' which only increases the problem. Individuals who stress too easily may fail to become engaged in social groups at all because they adopt behaviour which

38 Classroom Nonverbal Communication

Figure 3.7 Two shielding gestures. The teacher's need to read from the book (left) exposes her to the temptation to hide behind it if she is anxious (compare Figures 5.1, 5.3). Holding hands with oneself (right) has been considered to be a way of regaining the security of childhood

Figure 3.8 The self-hold arms-fold (left) is less assertive than the normal arms-fold (right), which in this case is accompanied by a more upright posture and direct gaze

Source: Reproduced with permission from *Pastoral Care in Education* 6 (4): 40

causes them to be ignored rather than included in the group (Trower, Bryant and Argyle 1978) or they may be persecuted because they do not signal their rejection of attacks forcefully enough, even if they have fighting ability (Macpherson 1983).

BEHAVIOUR PATTERNS INDICATING CALMNESS AND STRESS

Dominant individuals look relaxed; blinking and fidgeting lead to less favourable assessment (Exline 1985). Gaze is related to dominance in adults of both sexes (Weisfield and Laehn 1986). Graham and Argyle (1975b) found no interaction between gaze and facial expression (smiling and frowning) which was related to sociability.

Fidgeting and self-comforting actions are characteristic of secondary teachers with less effective relationships with their classes (Neill 1986b, Bull 1983; Figure 3.5). When the less effective teachers were criticising a child, or dealing verbally with a discipline problem, they tended to use more barrier signals (Morris 1977; Figure 3.7), for instance the self-hold arms-fold, indicating a defensive attitude to their classes. (The self-hold arms-fold involves the hands gripping the opposite arm just above the elbow – Figure 3.8. The plain arms-fold, with the hands resting in the crook of the elbow, has a more relaxed appearance and a rather different status, as described below.) They also fumbled and groomed themselves more. These signals undermined the effect of their words. The ineffective teachers used barrier signals more throughout the lesson (Figures 3.9, 3.10), and groomed their clothes more when they were talking about the subject. Effective teachers used more controlling gestures such as the baton signals (Morris 1977; Figures 3.11, 3.12) and palm forward across the lessons as a whole and while talking about the subject, but especially during confrontations. However, even during confrontations they remained calm; they shouted less, used illustrative gestures and animated intonation, and prosocial signals such as the smile (Figure 3.13). In other words they remained involved with the child as a person even during confrontations, and avoided escalating the dispute. Their more interesting delivery of material related to the subject, and more interesting behaviour throughout the lesson, are discussed in chapter 5. Their success seemed due as much to their ability to involve the class positively as to their ability to deal with conflicts and retain them at a level they could cope with.

Secondary-age children respond similarly to pictures of the more extreme threatening or controlling gestures (such as the baton signals, palm-forward fend, hands on hips and shouting) and pictures of actual attacks (such as a teacher swatting a child's head with a book or twisting his head round – Neill 1986a; Figure 3.14). All are labelled 'strict', 'angry' and 'unfriendly', and questions on children's preferences show that teachers described in these terms are strongly disliked. Children at ages between 8 and 17 strongly disliked physical assault (angry touch) in a separate study, concentrating on

Figure 3.9 This teacher patrolling her classroom is displaying one of a range of ambivalent gestures. She combines the defensive body-cross with the aggressive hand on hip (compare Figure 3.2). Her tight mouth corners also indicate slight fear

Source: Reproduced with permission from *Pastoral Care in Education* 6 (4): 12

touch (Neill 1986c). It is likely that the same results would have been repeated if younger age-groups had been tested. The hands-on-hips posture (Figure 3.2) was seen by adults as haughty and inflexible, in a conversational group, by comparison with a range of other postures (Spiegel and Machotka 1974). It bears a resemblance to the threatening postures of many animals, as it involves expanding the apparent size of the body, making the threatener look more formidable. Erect posture, spontaneous and posed (Figures 3.8, 4.11), is related to both self-reported dominance and readiness to take rewards in an experimental setting (Weisfield and Laehn 1986). By contrast postures which reduce size (Figures 2.2, 4.11) stop aggression among 8–12-year-old boys (Ginsburg, Pollman and Wauson 1977). These include not only, as one might expect, head-bowing, shoulder-slumping, kneeling and lying, but apparently 'irrelevant' bending down to tie one's shoelaces!

Two other groups of confrontational gestures received rather different classifications from secondary children. The plain arms-fold was grouped as

Signals of dominance and uncertainty 41

Figure 3.10 A different form of self-touching shown in the first lesson of the school year by a teacher with subsequent discipline problems. The tight grasp on the desk, together with the arms pressed against the sides, give a jerky, unconfident quality (compare Figure 5.1)

Figure 3.11 Palm-forward fend (left) and palm-down movements, both usually used in the classroom to stop or silence children, for instance to nominate another to speak

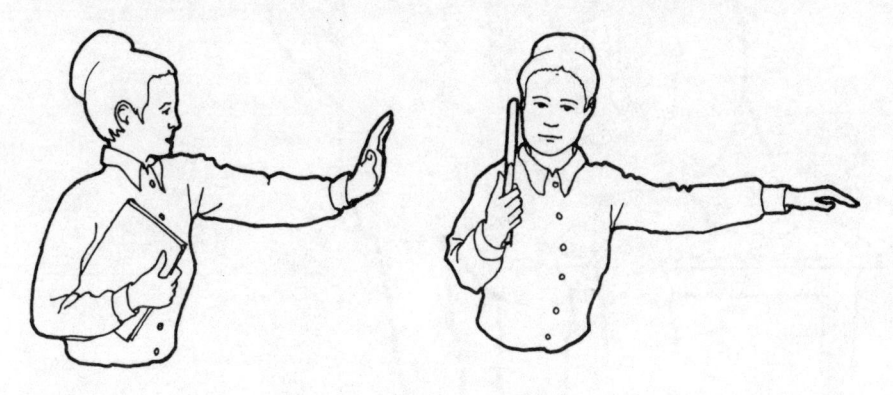

42 Classroom Nonverbal Communication

Figure 3.12 Forward (left) and upward batons. The forward baton is distinguished from a point by its more forceful and rapid movement; in the classroom it usually indicates a specific pupil. The upward baton usually stresses a point which is being made verbally

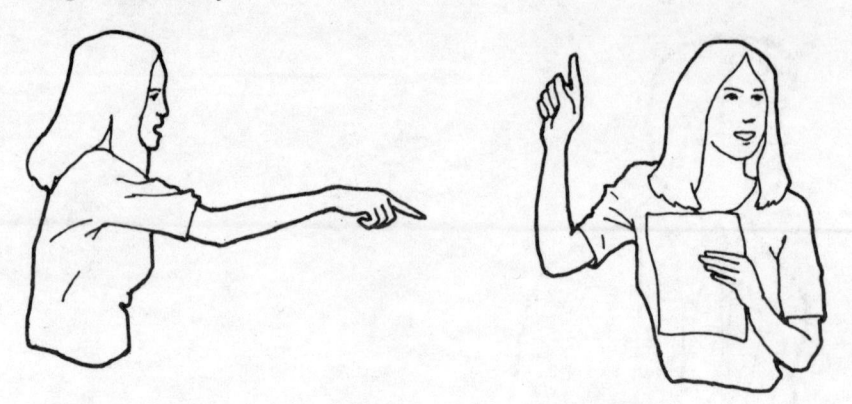

Source: Reproduced with permission from Neill 1986a

Figure 3.13 A teacher with effective class control reprimanding a boy quietly at the end of the lesson. The seated position and slight smile counteract the assertiveness shown by the forward lean and direct gaze. The boy's position is markedly relaxed, which could indicate defiance, but in this case the reprimand was accepted without protest

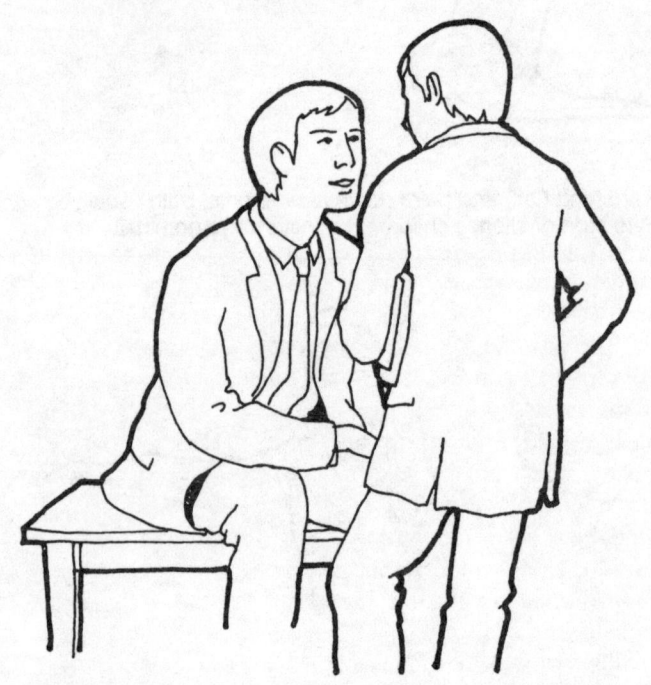

Source: Reproduced with permission from *Pastoral Care in Education* 6 (4): 39

Signals of dominance and uncertainty   43

Figure 3.14 Head-twisting is very unpopular with both the victim and onlookers. It represents a dangerous escalation which the teacher may not be able to sustain if the child resists physically

'serious' with a number of other actions, mostly explaining gestures. Here 'serious' can be seen in relation to the classroom context, as involved with getting children to understand and get on with their work. Another group including the plain arms-fold, but also hands in pockets (Figure 3.2), used by the effective teachers, the plus face (Figure 2.1) and leaning hand on hip (Figure 3.15), were described as 'calm'. These are lower-intensity displays, which appear not to be seen as threatening, and the group shows some resemblances to the observed behaviour of the more effective teachers. In Spiegel and Machotka's study (1974) the plain arms-fold was seen as intermediate; the most submissive posture was one where the hands clasped each other behind the back. This posture was not observed among the teachers, and not tested on the children, but resembles the fumbling and self-holding postures mentioned above in the observations of the more ineffective teachers. Children categorised postures of this type as 'boring', together with others which indicated avoidance or fear of the class: a teacher

44 Classroom Nonverbal Communication

Figure 3.15 This posture combines the assertive hand on hips (Figure 3.2) with the relaxed lean (Figure 3.3); compare Figure 3.9

Source: Reproduced with permission from Neill 1986a

Figure 3.16 While the body posture is the same as that in Figure 1.3, the teacher's absorption in the book completely changes the meaning to avoidance, as opposed to the social meanings seen in 1.3

leaning back against the board (an intention movement of escape) with a sad expression (Figure 3.4), and one looking down at a book on the desk (Figure 3.16). This latter indicates a failure to meet the gaze of the class, again a submissive posture related to Zivin's (1982) 'minus face'. Children require teachers to maintain control over the class (Docking 1980) and here they are rejecting as 'boring' teachers whose behaviour indicates they will be unable to do so.

So far as children's own use of these gestures is concerned, the development of baton signals is unclear, though they are used from middle childhood on. Fumbling and other stress patterns change in their form over childhood; younger children can thumb-suck or cling to an adult, but more ritualised forms of comfort movement are developed with age. Thus the hair-grooming pattern seems to derive from the intention movement of beating down on another child, used by preschoolers (Grant 1969). In older children the actual beat is inhibited with the hand at the back of the head and the child grooms his hair, which is conveniently nearby, instead.

The well-worn piece of teacher advice 'Don't smile till Christmas' has a sound theoretical basis. Though most used as a friendly signal, the smile is by origin a signal of submission, as is apparent if the human expressions are compared with the corresponding facial expressions of chimpanzees and monkeys (Van Hooff, 1972). The human expression has moved closer to the 'play face' or laugh, though there is also a, rarely seen, grin of terror. Uncertain teachers may smile at the class not only when they are being friendly (though less than effective teachers – Moskowitz and Hayman 1974, 1976), but also in a confrontation. When children were shown pictures of teachers in which other nonverbal signals had been held constant while the facial expression was varied, smiling teachers were categorised as less firm as well as being more friendly than frowning ones (Neill 1989a; Figure 3.17). These results confirmed earlier work which had shown that facial expression had a major effect on whether children assessed pictures of teachers positively or negatively, though in this case expression and other aspects of the situation were not varied systematically (Neill 1986a).

The smile is used as an appeasing signal in threatening situations, especially by younger children. If children smile when the teacher is criticising them this can lead to misunderstandings, as its meaning is ambiguous. If the teacher then criticises the child for insolence the child may be pushed into an aggressive defence because his effort to show contrition has been unsuccessful. The appeasing smile can be distinguished because it occurs together with the downcast gaze of the minus face (Zivin 1982) mentioned above; if the child smiles while meeting the teacher's gaze or looks away sideways or upwards, the smile indicates a lack of respect.

Figure 3.17 The change of facial expression (compare Figure 3.2) changes the primary message to social involvement and interest, though the hands-on-hips posture continues to indicate a degree of tension

SUMMARY

Legal and other constraints limit the classroom control tactics teachers can use. Effective teachers respond rapidly, but with low-intensity tactics. This calm but firm behaviour would outside the classroom indicate an ability to escalate the response considerably if required. Classes seem to respond to this implicit possibility despite their knowledge of the teacher's limited sanctions. Excessive threats or signals of uncertainty indicate less ability to maintain control over the situation. Though this 'honest' nonverbal signalling of uncertainty may be a disadvantage in the classroom, and run counter to the teacher's conscious intentions, theoretical models suggest it would have been advantageous in the situations for which it evolved. Uncertainty shows itself in a range of signals, such as grooming movements and smiling. Effectively controlling teachers are more relaxed, but also use both directing and social behaviours.

Chapter 4
Attention – positive and negative

In most classroom communication, control is less explicit and usually relations are more positive than those we have been talking about in the last chapter. In the next three chapters we look at related aspects of such communication. In practice they tend to become interwoven, but for purposes of analysis they are best dealt with separately. In this chapter we look at *attention* – the extent to which participants are involved with or ignore one another. Attention does not of itself signal the quality of the interaction. In the next we look at the ways in which participants signal their *enthusiasm* for the subject matter they are discussing: and in chapter 6 we consider the behaviour which shows their friendly *interest* in each other as people.

ATTENTION AND CHILDREN'S ROLE IN THE CLASSROOM

By comparison with the teacher's, the children's role is restricted, especially in the formal classroom. Their opportunity for legitimate communication is also often restricted, and the nonverbal signals they give are therefore fewer and less clear than those of the teacher. This becomes an even greater problem when dealing with signals for comprehension, for instance; there are few generally understood signals for conveying comprehension by members of a class-sized group. In these circumstances the teacher has to gauge the effects of her actions on often inadequate feedback. However, by middle childhood at least, there is a further complication. Children are becoming aware of how signals can be manipulated, and skilful at doing so (chapter 2). Their chances are improved by the diffusion of the teacher's attention across the class as a whole. They can disguise their true level of understanding, for example if they do not want to be embarrassed by the teacher asking them questions to which they do not know the answer. The same skills can serve them in good stead if they want to subvert discipline without being detected.

Children's ability to use these signals deserves particular attention because they have better awareness of the course of the lesson than the teacher and, at least in some circumstances, considerable influence over the teacher's conduct. Hook and Rosenshine (1979) found that children's views of lessons coincided with those of nonparticipant observers and were more accurate than those of teachers. The teachers were so involved in their teaching that they failed to take in as much information about what was happening as the other two groups. This gives children the possibility to manipulate the course of the lesson – a possibility which they can use to disrupt the teacher's control. More positively, they can encourage the teacher by their responsiveness. This is discussed further in chapter 6.

We look first at the way in which attention is distributed and manipulated, at the subversive applications of this manipulation, and finally at the ways in which attention is used positively to convey liking and interest.

ATTENTION STRUCTURE

The differences in role, age and experience between teacher and class inevitably mean that she will receive a disproportionate amount of attention from the class members compared to the amount she gives to them individually and they give each other individually (on average – friends may, of course, give each other as much attention as the teacher). In many classrooms this is formalised by the arrangement of furniture. This gives a more permanent reflection of the intended relationship between class and teacher (chapter 7), by, for example in the formal classroom, setting the teacher apart and orienting the class to her: the different furniture arrangement of the informal classroom proclaims the different social and educational arrangements which are expected, even if not always realised (Cooper 1981). The effectiveness of these permanent arrangements is largely dependent on the teacher's ability to manipulate the *attention structure* on a second-by-second basis.

'Attention structure' (Chance 1967), the tendency of subordinates to look at dominants more than dominants look at them, is of particular importance in the classroom. Among preschool children, dominant children tend to be the centres of attention of a group, especially when they are showing confident, self-referencing behaviour (Hold-Cavell, Stohr and Schneider 1985). The teacher can, therefore, capitalise on children's tendency to behave in this way. Attention structure is widely distributed cross-culturally and appears to be universal (Hold-Cavell et al. op. cit.). The way in which attention is directed allows judgments of dominance to be made from still pictures or even drawings. Thus Spiegel and Machotka (1974) showed students drawings of two foreground figures and a standing audience (resembling a group of men, such as an army platoon being briefed by two officers). Both the gaze and body orientation of the audience affected judgments of which foreground figure was more important, but gaze had more effect than body orientation. Chance claimed that attention structure was actually the cause of the dominance hierarchy, but the more generally accepted view (Hinde 1974) is that it is merely an indicator, the establishment of the hierarchy being separate, and usually due to overt action. This overt action might be actual aggression, forcing others to act in a particular way, or merely taking immediate confident action from which others may deduce that the dominant individual could assert her authority if required (Zivin 1982; chapter 2). However, the attention structure is an indication that dominance is affecting behaviour even when there is no sign of any dispute. Attention structure is modified by learnt rules; before moving to this we need to consider the setting within which these rules operate.

CLASSROOM SETTINGS AND THEIR IMPLICATIONS FOR ATTENTION

The distribution of attention discussed in the rest of this chapter occurs within a set of cultural understandings of how classrooms should run (Cook-Gumperz and Gumperz 1982). The understandings are rather different in the cases of informal and formal classrooms, but in both cases they derive from the fact that the teacher's time is a scarce resource, which needs to be equitably distributed between children (Merritt 1982). In the formal classroom (Hammersley 1976) the assumption is that the pace of the lesson is dictated by the teacher. One of her major tasks is to ensure that *strategic time* – the organisation of the structure of the lesson – is appropriately mapped on to *clock time* in a way which is grasped by all the participants (Erickson 1982). To ensure that the whole class makes coordinated transitions between *framed* segments of the lesson she will make use of *markers*. These can be stock phrases such as 'Let's have your attention please!' or 'Pencils down, arms folded' whose purpose is purely organisational (Sinclair and Coulthard 1975, Hammersley 1976), or signals such as clapping her hands or switching the lights on and off which the children have come to recognise (Walker and Adelman 1975). Alternatively they may be less ritualised nonverbal signals, such as changes in paralanguage including silence, gaze, posture or position in the room (Erickson 1982, Green and Harker 1982, Gilmore 1985). Such coordinating moves are unlikely to be successful for long unless the teacher can continue to engage children's attention by communicating enthusiasm and interest as we discuss in the next two chapters.

In the informal primary classroom, or in the formal classroom with older children working independently, the teacher often adopts a strategy by which the children work largely on their own initiative, referring to her only intermittently (Merritt 1982). When the teacher is primarily involved with one group she can, during the 'down-time' when they are fully engaged in their activity, afford a side-involvement with other children. As Merritt describes, this 'slotting-out' is often signalled by a change in nonverbal behaviour which distinguishes her words to the secondary group from those to the primary group. She may stand up, turn away from the primary group while remaining seated, or change her intonation. Younger children do not always realise the

Figure 4.1 Leaning back with the hands behind the head (left) is seen as relaxed and superior (Pease 1984). Like yawning, it is a behaviour which polite adult audiences would generally avoid; both can potentially offend the speaker. Their unconcealed use by schoolchildren is therefore potentially subversive

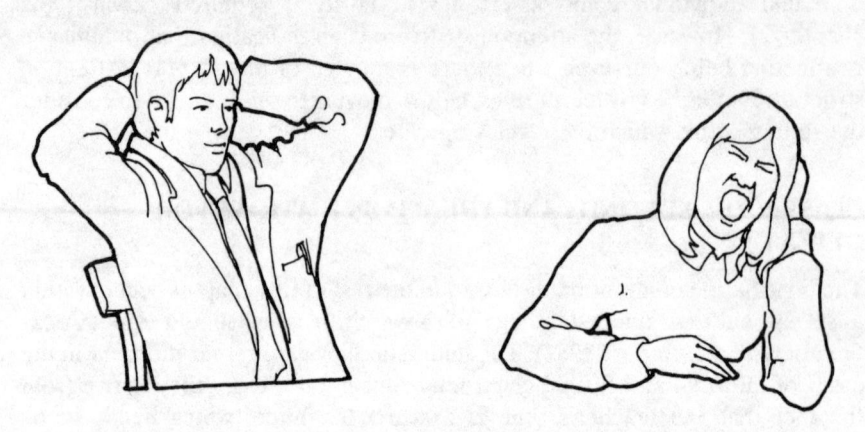

significance of these moves, and continue to try to interact with the teacher when her attention is elsewhere (Merritt, op. cit.), but they are generally effective.

ADVERTANCE

Advertance is the formal display of attention (Chance, Callan and Pitcairn 1973), and involves a comparison between the level of attention which would customarily be expected under a specific set of circumstances and that which actually exists; it emphasises the importance of the participants' understanding of the meaning of behaviour. Participants' understandings become of particular importance in 'showing up' – the exertion of social pressure via challenge to the opponent's self-esteem which is discussed below.

Advertance is an example of the more general concept of 'metacommunication' – communication about how communication is to be interpreted. The rules which govern the manipulation of behaviour in advertance are culturally acquired, and indicate what is expected in a given situation. In normal adult discussion groups Chance, et al. (op. cit.) found that listeners showed 'alert' attention, either focused or unfocused, though they might spend time 'away', gazing into space. The advertance rules for discussion groups indicate that all members should signal their continuing willingness to participate in this way. If they are unwilling to continue they can signal this by increasing the amount of time they spend 'away', and stepping up their use of signals such as fiddling with objects or yawning (Figure 4.1). The current speaker needs to be very subtle in interpreting advertance if she is not to become unpopular by failing to pick up signals from her peers that she is

Figure 4.2 A confrontation in which the boy is more relaxed than the teacher in terms of posture, facial expression and gaze. The normal rules of advertance would imply that the teacher, as dominant individual, would be more relaxed; compare Figures 2.2, 3.2, 3.13 and 4.3

boring them. Psychiatric patients did not follow these normal rules and spent longer times 'away' or 'huddled', avoiding interaction, by not facing the rest of the group or the speaker, or curling up with their head buried in their arms. Their illness displays itself in an inability to maintain a normal social relationship by giving other people the attention they expect. Normal adults may behave in this way, for instance under the stress of grief, but there are cultural rules which prohibit the use of these signals in polite adult society, and small children who break these advertance rules, by burying their face in their mother's dress, or staring concentratedly, are often reprimanded for doing so.

Older children in classroom contexts can manipulate advertance to avoid contact with the teacher like the psychiatric patients, but in this case the mental upset affects the teacher! They may withdraw completely, chat to friends, rock back on their chairs, or reach the point of challenging the teacher directly by describing the material as 'boring'. Secondary children are skilled at the metacommunicative use of a wide range of signals (Turner 1983; Figures 4.2, 4.3); for example, asked to close a door, a girl flounced across the room instead of walking directly; Licata (1978) gives other examples of this 'subversive obedience'. Normally schoolteachers, like many managers in many

Figure 4.3 Advertance can be conveyed by clothing as well as posture. The creative rearrangement of the school uniform accompanies an extremely relaxed posture, which would be challenging if directed against a teacher

other organisations, use instructions whose implicit meanings are usually only spelled out to new children (Edwards and Furlong 1978). This offers plentiful opportunities for 'working to rule' by taking instructions literally, a frequent tactic in the 'showing up' discussed below. The basic problem from the teacher's point of view is that children have learnt the necessary skills to use advertance effectively to regulate interaction, but, like the mental patients, they do not have the inhibitions against their use which normal polite adults show. In the children's case this is probably due to their still regular use of the more extreme type of social sanction in interacting with peers – overt expressions of boredom or dislike. If the teacher fails to 'switch gear' from the way she would respond in adult groups when dealing with children she is vulnerable. The children's signals of interest are important, of course; they are an immediately accessible form of feedback which the teacher can use to ensure she is carrying her class with her. Inexperienced teachers, especially,

Figure 4.4 Postural echo (chapter 5) has been claimed to indicate the empathy characteristic of friends who are on the same wavelength, though this is not universally accepted (Bull 1983). Such behaviour might indicate that the pupil is trying to establish an over-friendly relationship with the teacher

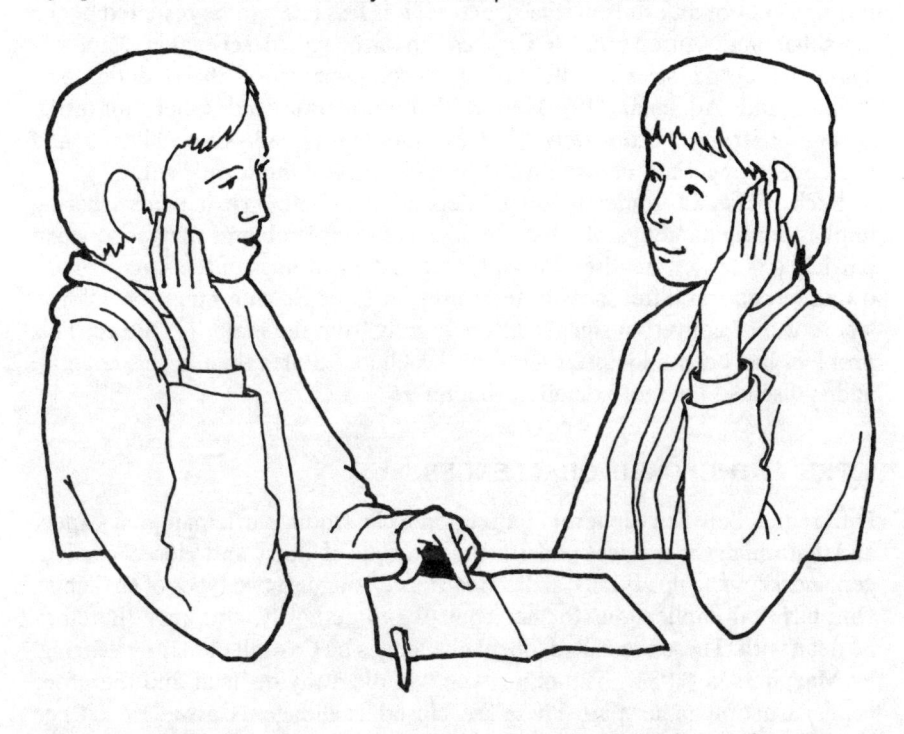

may fail to recognise that classes can use this feedback to manipulate them and run into problems when they try to get the class to like them. Children's abilities to manipulate the rules of friendly interaction are applied in an informal secondary setting, which deprives them of their usual route to controlling the teacher via regulating attention and noise level (Denscombe 1980). Where the ethos of the school encourages friendliness and equality, children use this by trying to encourage social conversations and divert teachers from talking about work (Figure 4.4).

SUBCULTURAL AND CULTURAL DIFFERENCES

Children are well aware that individual teachers differ in what they will permit and, especially in secondary schools, will modify their 'personae' from classroom to classroom (Galton and Willcocks 1983). In secondary classrooms, much of this difference may depend on the way in which the teacher represents her conception of classroom order through her speech. Teachers who represent themselves as enforcing an external system of rules may be able to deal with challenges better than those who rely solely on their personal authority (Torode 1976). If a teacher defines physical punishment (legal at the time Torode was writing) as the rule-governed result of an infringement of an external rule structure, it is less likely to be resented by the class than undisguised escalated aggression of the type described in chapter 3. Though Torode stresses the linguistic components of these definitions, Walker and Adelman (1976) show that intonation and other nonverbal signals contribute extensively to these subcultures, allowing children and teachers to negotiate personal relationships outside the formal rules.

Such personal understandings depend on both participants sharing implicit understandings of what the signals mean. Problems may arise when participants have unrealised but different understandings of the same signals, owing to cultural differences in their use; for example with minority children whose use of nonverbal signals differs slightly from the majority culture. This problem has been addressed more in the United States than in this country, and is discussed in more detail in chapter 9.

'OPEN' AND 'CLOSED' CHALLENGES

Differences between the level of attention a classroom participant may expect and that which she receives underlie the concepts of 'open' and 'closed' challenges, and 'showing up'. Firstly, skilled teachers distinguish two types of challenge. One has real implications for her control and authority, and must therefore be dealt with. These are called 'open' challenges by Caswell (1982) or 'stirring' by Macpherson (1983). The other type will die away by itself and therefore needs no action on her part. These are 'closed' challenges (Caswell op. cit.) or 'mucking about' (Macpherson op. cit.). Secondly, what are often apparently innocent actions may be understood by the participants as being challenging or insulting; 'showing up' injures the self-esteem of the party who is 'shown up'.

Many challenges to the teacher are overt open challenges, and represent the forms of confrontation which have been described in chapter 3. More difficult to interpret are concealed challenges. Behaviourally Caswell (op. cit.) has distinguished concealed open challenges from closed challenges by the greater vigilance which participants show; typically this takes the form of a 'flick check', where pupils *rapidly* look to see where the teacher is, and as rapidly look away again (Figure 4.5). The flick check is a scan for danger, like the vigilance patterns of animals; it has parallels with the scanning behaviour shown by diners in restaurants (Morris 1977, Wawra 1986)! The rapidity of the movement minimises the chance that it will be noticed; the rate at which flick checks occur increases just before an illicit action, to ensure it is not noticed, and again afterwards, to check for any response. By contrast, according to Caswell, children engaged in closed challenges tend not to check the teacher's whereabouts or do so much more slowly and casually (Figures 4.6, 4.7, 4.8, 4.9, 4.10). The teacher is therefore more likely to notice 'closed'

Attention – positive and negative   55

Figure 4.5 Both the close huddle and the flick check towards the teacher suggest that the group may be engaged in an open challenge to the teacher

Figure 4.6 The rules may forbid throwing rulers, but the boys' lack of effort to hide their activity from the teacher suggests this is a closed challenge, which could be ignored without serious consequences for classroom control

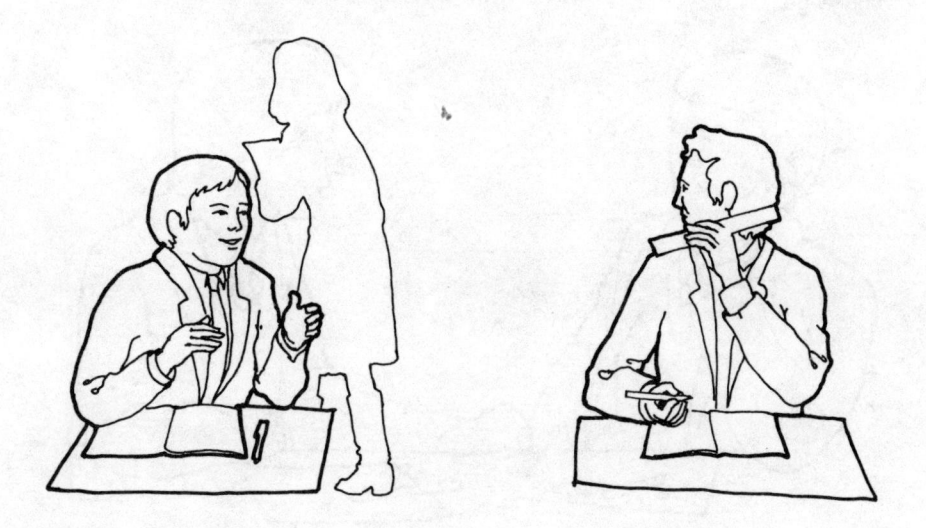

challengers watching her than open ones. Open challenges may be concealed in a variety of other ways, capitalising on the complexity of the classroom situation, which increases the chances that deviance will go unobserved. Conversations may be concealed by the participants hiding behind books or bags on their desks, or by speaking *sotto voce* (Figure 4.7). The noise level in

56 Classroom Nonverbal Communication

Figure 4.7 The concealed conversation indicates an open challenge; there are also indications that the boys are beginning to attract the attention of others who may join the interaction set (compare Figure 3.1)

Figure 4.8 By contrast, this unconcealed conversation would be legitimate in many classrooms; but even if it is not related to the work it is only a closed challenge

most classrooms allows such conversations to be inaccessible to the teacher. Miming, facial expressions and gestures may be used to communicate to sympathisers without teacher intervention (Beynon 1985), provided a sufficient degree of vigilance is maintained by flick checks. Funny voices and tapping with and dropping objects are auditory challenges which are difficult

Figure 4.9 Concealment of a different kind. Hand to mouth conceals a smile or conversation, while the coy look of the girl in the foreground allows her to keep an eye on the teacher without overtly looking. The pens in their hands suggest, however, that this is only a mild closed challenge

for the teacher to locate. Licata (1978) describes this as 'tight-roping', and it can shade into 'boundary testing' where the disobedience is performed in a way which makes it difficult to deal with; Licata gives an example of an American school library which suffered from 'cattle stampedes' where, as the tapping built up, it was improved by 'a few adolescent "moos" thrown in for atmosphere'. In all these cases the challengers in the class have superiority over the teacher; they know that her order is being subverted but she is either unaware, or aware but unable to do anything about it. Whether or not she is aware of her humiliation, she is being 'shown up'.

SELF-ESTEEM, STATUS AND 'SHOWING UP'

'Showing up', or social humiliation, may be unintentional or inevitable, though in the majority of instances it is being used as an intended tactic. According to Woods (1975) it is the punishment most frequently used by secondary teachers at least, rather than any of the range of formal punishments open to them. Despite the concern expressed by the Elton

Figure 4.10 The boy's indignant protest suggests his self-esteem has been threatened. He might have been accidentally and inadvertently shown up; but in the video it was clear that the indignation was simulated to try to get the teacher on the defensive and show her up

Source: Reproduced with permission from *Pastoral Care in Education* 6 (4): 11

Report (Department of Education and Science and Welsh Office 1989) about humiliating punishments, it seems unlikely that this will change, because of the importance of self-esteem to adolescent pupils especially (see below). As mentioned in chapter 1, pupils may take decisions primarily on their social consequences; hence, as the Elton Report mentions, corporal punishment has been found to be ineffective, largely because pupils can get kudos from enduring it. To be outsmarted carries no such kudos, especially when non-attributable nonverbal signals are used, making a riposte difficult.

A participant is 'shown up' by their accepted rules of communication being broken, so that they do not feel they are being treated in the way their self-esteem demands. As Woods (op. cit.) mentions, teachers may offend children's self-esteem when, for example, they need to choose athletics teams quickly and offend adolescent girls who dislike or are embarrassed by athletics as there is no time to discuss their feelings. Equally, Delamont and Galton (1986) feel teachers may be forced to disregard children's feelings when safety is at issue. Normally experienced teachers of adolescents are aware of their pupils' need for self-esteem and can take it into account in their reactions, either positively to create rapport (Watts and Bentley 1987; see also chapter 6), or negatively (Figure 4.10).

Children indulge in showing up as well as teachers, and most classes contain at least one child who is skilled at delivering the ambiguously insulting remark with a calmly smiling face. Central to 'showing up' is the awareness of both participants of the real meaning as opposed to the apparent meaning of interactional moves. Thus Beynon (1985) describes boys shouting out loudly that a neighbour has attacked them. An effective teacher would be 'with it' and able to nip such behaviour in the bud (Kounin 1970). However, the boys have colluded to ensure that the shout happens when the teacher is engaged elsewhere (concealed open deviance). They thereby minimise the chance that she will be able to challenge the interpretation of the situation which they present, and they make sure not to assist her in her enquiries. If she investigates the disturbance she gets nowhere; if she ignores it she is failing in her duty to keep order. Either way she is demonstrably not a member of the group of effective teachers.

The problem is that, in informal adult social groups, such challenges serve a similar function to the physical rough and tumble used by adolescents (Neill 1976, 1985). They test out the relationship and status within it by enabling people to push each other to the limits of what is acceptable. If adults blow up every time their friends say something teasingly insulting about them, they would soon have no friends. The smile with which such insults are delivered is a 'play face' which indicates that they are not to be taken at face value (in an informal social group – compare Figure 4.9). Inevitably, inexperienced teachers tend to apply the same rules in the classroom; but the classroom is not an informal adult group. Experienced teachers, therefore, disregard the smiling face and take the insult at 'nonface' value. One solution, as Woods (1975) and Beynon (1985) describe, for the teacher who is skilled at repartee, is to give better than she gets, so that the child is hoist by his own petard. This has the advantage that on the surface amity is retained and the course of interaction is not disrupted, but it is a high-risk strategy. If the child can cap the teacher's response, he will have won a substantial victory because the teacher has taken him on, on his own ground, and lost. If the child loses, he may bear a grudge because of the importance of maintaining self-esteem. As Lasley (1981) points out, the teacher who is skilled at 'facework' can often deal with potential disruption by treating it as a legitimate work-oriented move. For example, she can provide a pencil for a boy who has not got one, and disregard his lethargic movement to get it. Thus honour on both sides is satisfied. The boy has got the attention he wants and has been able to show his resistance; the teacher has kept the interaction overtly entirely work-oriented.

AN ETHOLOGICAL APPROACH TO SELF-ESTEEM

The ethologists Barkow (1980) and Weisfield (1980) have tried to account for the functional importance of self-esteem. They suggest that self-esteem acts as an index of successful peer relations; the conscious feelings can act as a 'proximate index' of successful behaviour which is easier to monitor than its ultimate purpose: preferential access to resources. In other words anyone who behaves in a way which satisfies their needs for self-esteem will automatically ensure that they are maintaining a social position which will help them in getting what they need. Social and competitive success would in evolutionary terms have been especially important at adolescence: in traditional societies with low geographical mobility adolescents would have been able to establish their position with considerable permanence at the start of adult life, when relative status would have had its maximum value (Neill 1983b, 1985). This implies that adolescents would be particularly prone to take decisions in terms of their effects on self-esteem, and they would not only be vulnerable to effective threats to their own self-esteem, but liable to challenge the position of peers and the teacher in order to increase their status.

Weisfield (1980) points out that high self-esteem makes individuals more willing to assert themselves and take risks, seek out competitive encounters, and behave in a way which encourages both the individuals themselves and others to overestimate their ability. Low self-esteem has the reverse effects. Self-esteem may be conveyed by nonverbal signals without explicit verbal statement. Weisfield and co-workers have found that dominance signals such as erectness and openness of posture and chin-up carriage of the head are related to status as assessed by peers in high-school children (Weisfield and Linkey 1985; Figure 4.11) and willingness to claim rewards in an experimental situation (Weisfield and Laehn 1986). Ambiguous nonverbal signals are used to communicate self-esteem and authority as they allow both teacher and pupils to assess how the other side will react without committing themselves in the way that a verbal statement would.

SIGNALS OF CHILDREN'S INTEREST – GAZE

This ambiguity is partly due to the inaccuracy of observable attention as a predictor of understanding (Peterson and Swing 1982; Figure 4.12). Relative to teachers (chapters 5 and 6) children's use of nonverbal signals to convey interest during class sessions is limited; as listeners they have, like other listeners, a relatively limited range of signals compared to speakers. We will discuss in chapter 5 the way in which diffusion of responsibility among members of an audience reduces the amount of feedback they give to the speaker, and the effects this has on the speaker. Given that children in a class do not give the regulatory signals characteristic of a single listener, their signals to the teacher reduce to fairly static displays, such as gaze direction, concentration expressions and posture.

Peterson and Swing (1982) videotaped children at the top of the primary age-range (fifth and sixth grades) during a mathematics lesson and related their achievement on the individual work at the end of the lesson to their observed level of attention and to responses to a series of questions in

Figure 4.11 Subordinate (left) and dominant postures, distinguished by the erectness, stably planted feet, hands in pockets, raised chin and direct gaze of the boy on the right

stimulated recall interviews. The children were shown the recordings of themselves after the lesson and were asked whether they were attending or not. Their self-reported attention was a better prediction than their observed attention; children who looked as if they were attending closely reported in some cases that they were worrying about whether they would be able to do the problems at the end of the explanation or were thinking about something else rather than taking in the explanation. Peterson and Swing also found that achievement was related to children's reports that they had understood the material, and to reports that they had used specific strategies related to solving the tasks, especially when these strategies related the new material to what they already knew. Peterson and Swing considered teachers would do better to ask children about their interest and understanding than to deduce it from watching them, especially as even 6-7-year-olds were capable of simulating attention.

Figure 4.12 This girl's behaviour gives few clues as to what is going on in her mind. If there was something interesting outside, the teacher might judge that she was watching that rather than concentrating. Otherwise she might be daydreaming or she might be disengaging herself from her surroundings to think about her work. She would not necessarily give an accurate answer if asked, partly because she may not be fully aware of her behaviour. The teacher will probably come to a conclusion based on her preceding and following behaviour, and how long she continues to gaze like this

Sustained gaze is, as mentioned in chapter 5, the normal response when a number of listeners are attending to a single speaker. Its effect is increased when listeners show the concentration frown (Ekman and Friesen 1975; Figure 2.4). This frown seems to help listeners see clearly, but to the mind of an anxious teacher it is likely to be taken for an anger frown. The concentration frown is indistinguishable from mild forms of the angry frown, since there is an overlap in form.

Lawes (1987b) found that student teachers could reliably judge the amount of attention shown by 10-year-olds from their direction of gaze. Children who looked at the teacher were judged as attending; those who did not look at the teacher, especially if they were involved in irrelevant behaviour such as fiddling with objects, were judged inattentive (Figure 6.2). Both judgments were equally accurate. Lawes's students did not have any accurate way of judging which sections of the lesson the children found interesting or boring. They tended to judge that sections where the children looked at the teacher evoked more interest than those where they did not, but this did not relate to the sections the children said they enjoyed most. Students' perceptiveness was also linked to their own abilities, and this is discussed more fully in chapter 10.

SUMMARY

The attention of a group will normally be on the individual who has a controlling role. In an informal group attention will shift to the individual who is currently talking, but in a formal classroom attention will normally centre on the teacher. The teacher needs to be able to regulate children's attention, especially to ensure smooth transition between activities. Incipient control problems will first show themselves as disruption to the attention structure.

Advertance is the formal display of attention, relative to a socially expected standard. Children may challenge the teacher by displaying an inappropriate level of attention. Alternatively challenges may be furtively concealed. Teachers as well as pupils use 'showing up' to challenge the opponent's self-esteem by acting in an insulting or denigrating way. In all these instances nonverbal signals are extensively used because their ambiguous nature makes it more difficult for the recipient to challenge them. It may therefore be better for the teacher to judge children's attention and interest by asking children directly rather than by trying to deduce it from their nonverbal signals.

Chapter 5

Conveying enthusiasm

Because learning is largely a voluntary process which the teacher cannot check directly (since the children have voluntary control over how much they reveal about what they have learnt verbally or in writing), much of the teacher's task consists of 'selling' ideas to the children. In other words she must present material in ways which arouse their interest or enthusiasm, and deal with their responses in ways which convey her interest in them and their efforts. In this chapter we discuss primarily the ways in which teachers – and children – convey enthusiasm, while in the next we look at prosocial behaviour and the ways in which the teacher, especially, can convey her liking for her class and her appreciation of their efforts.

Obviously this is the ideal picture; in some types of teaching, such as lectures to large groups, there is virtually no opportunity for any sort of feedback to individuals (though the design of the teaching course may often include work with smaller groups, in practical work or seminars, which will allow an opportunity for more individual contact). In other cases there may be a 'conspiracy of busyness' such as has been described in primary schools, where the teacher provides a mass of low-grade and non-challenging tasks on work-cards, and so long as the children stay apparently productively engaged in these, they do not get challenged to do hard thinking. However, this routinised learning may allow errors in children's thinking to persist because thorough discussion which would illuminate children's understanding or lack of it never takes place (Bennett, Desforges, Cockburn and Wilkinson 1984).

PERSUASIVE BEHAVIOUR IN TEACHING

Persuasive teachers, like other speakers, also assist their audience by signalling how their speech should be responded to by using gestures, and to a lesser extent facial expressions (Figure 5.1). Children are highly sensitive to teachers' nonverbal signals, and, by secondary level, will describe them spontaneously with accuracy (Watts and Bentley 1987) as well as being readily able to assign pictures to categories (Neill 1986a). Watts and Bentley give a 16-year-old's description of enthusiastic teachers:

Figure 5.1 The forward lean, open posture and direct gaze round the class make this a more confident presentation than that shown in Figure 3.10. Teachers tend to stand, or sit on desks, to talk to the class as this gives them visibility and authority

> Well ... I suppose ... they're quick ... you know, they have little excited body movements.... Their eyes light up when they talk to you. Their speech is fast. They smile a lot, and joke. They seem ... well sort of fast, somehow ... their hands move quickly, they use their body a lot when they're talking ... they're not well ... still.
>
> (Watts and Bentley 1987: 130)

Such teachers show their enthusiasm by structuring their speech more clearly to compensate for the lack of feedback which a single listener would give to show that he was taking in the structure of the argument. It is notable in classroom recordings that, at secondary level at least, confident children begin to gesture if they find themselves in the same position as the teacher, having to structure a complex argument to the rest of the class, or if they are trying to make a point to an unresponsive (and therefore probably unpersuaded) teacher. Normally, as we shall see, teachers signal their response to children's contributions extremely clearly.

At the secondary and university levels, videotape-based studies suggest effective teachers convey more enthusiasm nonverbally than average or ineffective teachers (Willett 1976, Neill 1986b). At the early secondary level this occurs especially during educational talk, as well as over the lesson as a whole. Willett also found that effective language instructors on university courses made more use of nonverbal signals to focus student attention on important points, demonstrate or illustrate points they were making, and encourage students by approaching them. Average teachers were more likely to use directing or threatening signals, or to show anxious signals. This contrasts with the effective teachers in Neill's study, who used more controlling behaviours than the ineffective ones (Figure 5.2). The difference is due to the disciplinary role of the secondary teachers, who were working with 13–14-year-olds. College teachers have a more egalitarian relationship with their students, and a disciplinarian attitude on their part is likely to reflect

Figure 5.2 An effective experienced secondary teacher using a hand chop to symbolise cutting through to the solution of a difficulty. This example is taken from a discussion of discipline and organisation, but the same gesture was used in dealing with academic problems

insecurity. Consistent with this, Willett found that the effective instructors rated themselves more highly than their students rated them, while the average ones rated themselves lower. The effective instructors therefore show a more confident self-esteem.

The skills required to communicate enthusiasm and interest in a teaching situation differ somewhat from those used in everyday social interaction, and this can cause problems for inexperienced teachers. This may create counter-productive anxiety. Bower's (1980) experiment, while imperfect in many ways, suggests that a tense posture leads to poorer outcomes with otherwise identical instruction (Figure 3.10). He assessed how much 16-year-olds recalled from seven-minute lessons on economics presented in a range of sitting postures from tensely rigid to languid floppiness. Differences were small, but the tensely rigid posture did worse than any other.

Differences between the social situations in informal social interaction and classroom interaction

The two major differences between the classroom and informal social situations are the inequality of the relationship between teacher and taught and the greater numbers involved in most teaching situations. To appreciate the differences we need to look first at normal conversations between adults. There are also differences, especially with younger classes, due to the children not having fully developed the use and appreciation of nonverbal signals which normal adults possess (chapter 2).

Social interaction between adults will be the inexperienced teacher's normal knowledge background. It is also the most fully researched setting. There are differences between interaction among adult peers, among children, and between adults (for example mothers) and children.

In normal social interaction between adults approximate equality of status exists, and even in hierarchical situations (with the exception of organisations such as the army) conventions of respect and consent are maintained. Typically, group size is small. The resulting pattern of interaction is displayed in Kendon's (1970) early description of a conversation. Though some members of the group speak more than others, control of the topic of discussion passes from speaker to speaker. Listeners encourage speakers by giving them their attention (Figures 4.4, 6.1), and by various nonverbal signals, discussed more fully below. These patterns of behaviour convey that all members of the group have an equal right to make a contribution, provided other members of the group continue to signal their consent. If an individual wants to stay as a member of the group, he must modify his contribution if the others signal that he is beginning to bore them, or he is speaking about a topic which is unacceptable for some reason. Good relationships are related to interactional skill in married couples (Noller 1984) and among child friends (Foot, Chapman and Smith 1980).

Even in young children acceptance into a group depends on conforming with its existing interests; Putallaz and Gottman (1981) found that popular primary children joined groups by making contributions relevant to the groups' ongoing activities, so that they were willingly accepted as useful companions. Unpopular children, by contrast, tended to try to reorient the group towards themselves and their interests; as a result they were usually rejected. Mutual regulation by the interactants is therefore a critical factor of cooperative informal groups at all ages.

The teacher's problem is that she is constrained by the curriculum (even if the topic is one she chose herself) and can therefore allow the children only a certain amount of freedom to direct the conversation. As Walker and Adelman (1975) discuss, genuine 'freewheeling' conversation, where the teacher exerts no control over the direction in which talk develops, is extremely rare in classrooms. Indeed, some children may be highly suspicious of such discussion, which they do not regard as 'real work' (Nash 1974). Such children, according to Nash, regard the teacher as having broken the classroom contract by which she provides material and they learn it; they therefore feel justified in disrupting her lessons.

The teacher therefore has to dominate the interaction, and to ignore feedback from other members of the group, in a way which would not occur in a normal social conversation. The deviation may be very slight, in a small group discussion, or extensive, in a formal lecture. Such deviations are not exclusive to teaching – they occur in other situations where group members have unequal power, such as parent–child interaction, or cross-sex interaction (Henley and Harmon 1985), as well as in business conferences (Turk 1985) and political speeches (Atkinson 1984). The types of signal used in normal social interaction therefore have to be modified when the teacher expresses enthusiasm for her subject and her children's contributions.

REGULATORY SIGNALS IN SOCIAL INTERACTION

Normally, whether standing or sitting, a conversational 'social distance' is adopted, greater closeness conveying intimacy, while to hold a conversation at a distance is unsocial, unless there is some obvious reason. The question of distance is dealt with in more detail in chapter 7. Close friends, especially, but any conversationalists who are 'on the same wavelength' may signal this by adopting matching or, more usually, mirror-image postures. This 'postural echo' (Figure 4.4) also contributes to liking; people who adopt similar postures because they are seated in similar chairs like each other more under experimental conditions (Maxwell and Cook 1985; see also Bull 1983). It is rare in classrooms, where less intense and more impersonal signals are normal (see chapter 6).

In order for conversations to mesh smoothly, listeners have to be able to tell when it is appropriate to take over from the speaker, despite the fact that normal spontaneous speech is full of repetitions and pauses as the speaker organises his thoughts to move on to the next topic (Chafe 1980). Speakers normally 'fill' pauses with sounds such as '...er...' to indicate that they intend to continue to hold the floor (Beattie 1983); if they are searching for an appropriate word they may indicate, often by an expression of puzzlement, that their silence is not to be taken as an indication that the listener may take the floor (though if the listener supplies the missing word, this may be accepted – Goodwin and Goodwin 1986).

To a considerable extent, as might be expected, turn-taking is dependent on the verbal content, but, of the available cues, the combination of falling intonation with a drawl on the stressed syllable, with the termination of any gestures which are being made, seems to be the most effective indicator to a listener that a speaker wishes to hand over the floor (Ellis and Beattie 1986).

Speakers may accompany their speech by gestures, which may illustrate or duplicate what is said. Most of the gestures made during conversations are *illustrators* and *regulators* in Ekman and Friesen's (1969a) terminology (discussed below). This is certainly also the case for teaching, where there are even fewer of the third class, *emblems*, than in normal conversation. Kendon (in McNeill 1987) suggests a continuum, with *pantomiming* intermediate between gestures (illustrators and regulators) and emblems.

Emblems are gestures which are consciously used and have a verbal equivalent, such as the V-sign; most of them are insults (Morris, Collett, Marsh and O'Shaughnessy 1979) and are therefore more likely to be used appropriately by the children rather than the teacher! Their importance in the classroom is negligible. Pantomiming is much more frequent in the classroom; it involves demonstrating an action, with, according to McNeill (1987), a standardised imaginary object. Pantomiming is allied to Ekman and Friesen's (1969a) *pictographs* (which draw a picture of their referent). Like emblems, pantomimes and pictographs may substitute for speech, and the pantomimer can describe what she is doing. Pictographs have been shown to assist the communication of shapes, especially complex shapes, between adults (Graham and Argyle 1975b).

The other two types of gestures, illustrators and regulators, mostly operate at a low level of consciousness; they are less used when the hearer cannot see the speaker (Cohen and Harrison 1973, McNeill 1987) and increased to compensate when there is interference with speech (McNeill 1985b). Users are less likely to be able to specify exactly which gestures they have used if they are questioned immediately afterwards. Illustrative gestures, as their name implies, amplify the context of speech, while regulators punctuate it (Ekman and Friesen 1969a). These are described in more detail below.

Gestures may also serve to direct the listener's attention; if a speaker wants to recall the listener when they know the listener's gaze has been directed away by a previous topic in the conversation, or the speaker wants to avoid listeners being distracted by an event extraneous to the conversation such as someone joining the group, they may transfer the meaning from speech to gesture. The listeners are then forced to attend to them visually, or they will lose the thread of the conversation (Goodwin 1986). On the other hand, body-focused gestures such as putting the hand to the mouth, which cut off the stream of communication, may indicate that the listener can take over. As discussed below, gestures of this type seem to be used to regulate pupil listeners' attention by teachers, in association with more overt signals.

All these gestures, and related facial expressions, by the speaker are synchronised appropriately with speech during informal interaction (Ekman and Friesen 1969a, Kendon 1970). Bull (1987) found that movements which peaked simultaneously with the main vocal stress were seen as emphatic by speakers and listeners. Listeners also signal their involvement with the speaker by synchronising their movements with the structure of the speaker's speech (Kendon 1987; see also Bull and Brown 1977, who suggest that such movements occur mainly with statements which introduce new information into the discussion) as well as producing confirmatory noises such as 'ah-h'm'. These movements in time with speech appear even in young babies, who synchronise their gestures with their own prespeech and move in a similar way to adults when spoken to (Trevarthen 1977). The same sequencing patterns appear in gaze 'conversations' in early babyhood (Jaffe, Stern and Peery 1973). They appear to be part of the innate pattern of human adaptation to speech (see also Aitchison 1983).

These listening behaviours are strikingly absent in most large audience groups. It is not impossible for large audiences to produce highly interactive feedback to the speaker; Atkinson (1984) describes a speech by Martin Luther King punctuated by the frequent and enthusiastic response of his audience. However, even for audiences accustomed to the southern black congregational tradition, it is likely that the area within which such response was seen as appropriate would be strictly limited. The intense and charismatic interaction between King and his audience would be inappropriate for a factually based discussion.

When speakers are looking, they tend, if involved with what they are saying, to synchronise their blinking with the 'punctuation' of their speech, so that they can monitor the listener's reaction to their speech (Robertson 1989). They thus hold their audience with their gaze and command attention to the point they are making. By contrast, listeners blink more regularly without relation to the structure of the speech they are listening to. Their blinking rate reflects the physiological function of blinking in keeping the eye lubricated and oxygenated. Blinking during speaking deviates from optimal physiological requirements. In the same way speech interferes with the normal physiological functions of breathing (Aitchison 1983); again effective communication takes priority. Ineffective speakers blink during their speech without synchronisation, breaking the contact between themselves and their audience. Excessive blinking during speaking is seen as a signal of uncertainty in a public speaker (Exline 1985).

In ordinary conversations speaker and listener exchange roles at intervals, and nonverbal cues make some contribution to ensuring that the conversation runs smoothly, without too much overlapping speech and the consequent necessity for participants to stop to sort out the interference. Kendon's (1967) initial suggestion was that this regulation was largely performed by gaze. More dominant or involved speakers tend to look at their listeners more (Dovidio and Ellyson 1985). This is consistent with the teacher's scanning of her class. Kendon claimed that speakers tend to look away while composing their next section of speech, to avoid interference with speech production, and to look back when it has been composed, while listeners look more steadily, but break gaze when they are looked at. The periods of mutual gaze, when their eyes meet, are usually short, unless communication is intense – for example if conversational partners are strongly attracted to each other. More recent research (reviewed by Ellis and Beattie 1986 and Bull 1987) suggests the position is more complex. Thus Hadar, Steiner and Clifford Rose (1985) suggest listeners' head movements differ according to function, with short linear movements used to show synchrony with the speaker (especially when the speaker is hesitant) and longer linear 'anticipation' movements indicating a wish to take the floor. Both are distinguished from the rhythmic nodding or head-shaking indicating 'yes' or 'no'.

However, the position may be more indeterminate. Rutter, Stephenson, Ayling and White (1978) suggested that the patterns of gaze simply allow the participants to be seen by each other, and that conversations could be coordinated perfectly well without them. Turn-taking is as efficient, or indeed more so, over the telephone; people may use nonverbal signals when speaking face to face to deal with speech overlaps, and be more careful to avoid them when this buffering system is not available. However, it is doubtful that synchronisation could be effective in a multi-party interaction, as in the classroom, without visual signals. The gaze patterns may help interactants to assess each other.

Bull (1987) reports that changes in posture indicate the type of conversational move which the participant intends to make next; people turn their head towards their conversational partner, or raise their head, before making a request (though the former also predicts statements of material new to the conversation ('offers') and reactions to what the other speaker has just said), and they look away from the other before replying. The use of posture to indicate willingness to contribute is formalised in the schoolroom, into the raised hand posture which new infant-school children soon learn.

THE REGULATION OF INTERACTION IN THE CLASSROOM

When a teacher is speaking to pupils the patterns of normal adult conversation are interfered with in various ways. Part of this interference is due, especially with younger classes, to children not yet having developed the adult range of nonverbal signals and responses, part to the inequality of status between teacher and pupil mentioned above, but the most serious interference, except in small-group work, is due to the teacher–pupil ratio. This causes interference which is not unique to teaching, but has parallels in other public-speaking situations.

The large number of listeners disrupts the normal signalling between conversational partners we have discussed, especially if, as in the teaching situation, there is an expectation that one speaker will dominate the proceedings and will nominate. In this case the listeners do not have the usual prospect that they will suddenly have to take over speaking, and there is less need for them to signal in the usual way that the speaker continues to have their attention, and that they are not about to try to take over the floor. As a result the speaker finds she is getting none of the feedback which she is used to. Listeners in a class or similar large group do not nod, move in synchrony with the speech or produce conversational noises as an individual listener would. In addition, because the speaker's gaze is distributed over many of them, each receives less than would an individual listener, and therefore, if attentive, tends to look more. Though a listener may look away if gazed at by the speaker, in accordance with the normal pattern for limiting mutual gaze, the effect is that the teacher tends to find, if she looks round the group, that each pupil she looks at is already looking at her. As mentioned above, sustained gaze can imply hostility; this impression is accentuated by the lack of apparent responsiveness (again negative in a one-to-one situation) and, if the class are really involved, by their concentration frowns.

Any situation where one person is the 'observed' and the other the 'observer' causes discomfort to the observed, especially if female (Argyle, Lalljee and Cook 1968). Feeling 'observed' could be by virtue of the situation (for example being an interviewee) or, experimentally, by altering visibility; even dark glasses would convert the other person into an 'observer'. Speaking to a class-sized group is therefore potentially a disquieting experience, as the asymmetry makes the class 'observers'. It may be even more so in a lecture theatre, where the raked seating gives the class the added intimidating feature of superior height (chapter 3).

Like other speakers, some teachers may respond by fixing their gaze on an individual, restoring a one-to-one situation by ignoring the rest of the class; alternatively they may avoid the gaze of the whole class by looking at the board or their notes. Either of these tactics, especially the latter, which looks like a submissive posture (Figures 2.2, 3.16), conveys lack of enthusiasm and competence. More effective speakers scan their audience, and this is very noticeable among effective teachers where the scanning assists them to check comprehension and incipient disorder.

The second response to lack of audience feedback is to compensate by increasing the signal, by modifying and reordering the spoken content and by using more expansive gestures than would be appropriate in one-to-one or small-group conversation of the same intensity. Much of the spoken modification is directed towards the need to ensure that the attention and comprehension of the whole audience keep in step, in the absence of cues of comprehension, as mentioned above. In the case of political speeches, which are prepared, and given to a usually responsive audience, suitable phrasing, such as the use of 'lists of three' and 'contrasts' ('Never in the field of human conflict has so much been owed by so many to so few'), gives the whole of the audience time to realise that they should respond, usually by applause (Atkinson 1984). Speakers who fail to phrase their speeches correctly suffer embarrassing silences when their punch-line is delivered at a point when the audience do not expect it. Alternatively the audience may decide to clap when the speaker has not yet finished, and the speaker will have to explicitly stop them.

ACCENTUATING PARALANGUAGE

The teacher lacks the politician's advantages of preparation and a responsive audience, and therefore has to rely more on 'marker' phrases (Sinclair and Coulthard 1975) or signals (chapter 4) and confirmatory questions('Do you all understand what I want you to do?') together with a loud and measured delivery. However, these methods are too explicit for continued use, so she has to rely heavily on structuring her message by intonation, facial expression and gestures so that the class knows how to deal with it (Neill 1986b). She also needs to show the assertiveness described in chapter 3; hesitancy and speech nonfluency give a weak impression (Exline 1985). Evidence on how children perceive hesitation by teachers is not available, but for courtroom witnesses, hesitation is interpreted both in terms of what the listener (in this case counsel) expects, and relative to the witnesses' behaviour at other times in their appearance (Walker 1985). Other types of inappropriate behaviour – in the court context, interrupting counsel – lead to hesitations being picked on and seen as evidence of insincerity. Variations in hesitation could also lead to the longer hesitations being seen as evidence of uncertainty. The only sort of hesitations which were seen as important were unfilled pauses; filled pauses were not noticed. This parallels the importance of filled pauses for holding the floor during informal conversations, mentioned earlier. It is likely that similar processes underlie teachers' use of markers to fill pauses while they are getting the attention of the class and organising transitions between segments of the lesson.

In speaking, the teacher can use 'proclaiming tone' (where the tone of the voice falls) to indicate that she is presenting new information and 'referring tone' (where it falls and rises again) where the information is already known, either because it has been covered previously, or it is common knowledge (Brazil, Coulthard and Johns 1980). In a typical lesson development, this would guide the class as to where they need to pay close attention because the argument is moving forward. However, the choice of tone is under the control of the speaker – for instance politicians, when interviewed, may use referring tone when making a contentious point, implying that it is common knowledge among reasonable people. Teachers are more likely to use proclaiming tone when referring to aspects of their theme which have already been covered once; by presenting an apparent novelty repeatedly they increase their chances that the class will actually take the information in. Important sections of the message may be emphasised by speaking slowly and emphatically, while 'filling' material is skimmed through rapidly (Robertson 1989). Effective teachers are more likely to employ this emphatic intonation while actually talking about the subject material than ineffective ones (9 per cent versus 4 per cent; Neill 1986b). Their intonation is more varied in other respects too; they use more animated intonation (with a wide range of stress and pitch – 23 per cent versus 5 per cent) and joking intonation (7 per cent versus 1 per cent) while talking about the subject, while ineffective teachers use more neutral intonation (71 per cent versus 41 per cent).

GESTURES AS A FRAME TO IDEAS

As mentioned above, most gestures used in teaching situations are *illustrators* or *regulators*. So far as illustrators are concerned, McNeill's (1985a) classification is probably the most useful in looking at teachers' gestures. McNeill classifies illustrators into two types. *Iconix* are gestures which are icons of a physical object or movement, corresponding to Ekman and Friesen's (1969a) deictic (pointing) movements, spatial movements (depicting a spatial relationship) and kinetographs (depicting an action). *Metaphorix* are gestures which are icons of an abstract idea, corresponding to Ekman and Friesen's *ideographs*. *Beats* (corresponding to Ekman and Friesen's *batons*) are gestures which help to regulate conversation.

In McNeill's view (which is by no means universally shared – Ellis and Beattie 1986) gestures originate from the same central mental processing as speech, and are then processed in parallel with speech. They may carry part of the information, which is not duplicated in the speech, or alternatively indicate the nature of the point made or how the audience should respond to it. As mentioned above, a range of movements, including head, leg and body movements as well as gestures, which peaked at the same time as the main vocal stress were seen as emphatic (Bull 1987). Speakers and listeners, however, mentioned hand and arm movements predominantly when asked to identify emphatic movements; Bull did not have the evidence to tell whether movements of the other parts of the body were actually influential at a subconscious level. Bull identified a wide range of movements which were used in this way, but did not feel there were any particular movements which communicated emphasis. However, he did not analyse speech content, and it is likely that what is seen as an emphatic movement depends on the context. In other words emphasis is conveyed by appropriate combinations of words with gesture, not the use of a small subset of gestural 'adverbs'. It is also likely, as Bull points out, that temporal synchronisation is a critical factor, and here there may be a vestige of the infant's sensitivity to movement rather than shape. Babies are extremely responsive to movement patterns, such as the characteristic movement patterns of facial expressions, which they can recognise in an extremely abstract form, with only the critical points of the face identified by points of light (Pitcairn 1985). With age the visual system moves to analysing displays such as faces more in terms of shape rather than movement, but it would not be surprising if the synchronisation of movements was still influential.

Iconic gestures (Figure 5.3) refer to physical objects (for example sketching out cable-car power wires and the cable-car pantograph in the air – McNeill 1986) or movements (such as a spider running up a drainpipe – McNeill 1985a). McNeill (1987) suggests that subject content can be transferred between speech and gesture in two ways. Firstly, complexity can be transferred in either direction; if it is impossible to use gesture, speech may become more complex, while if speech is interfered with, gesture may increase (this may be

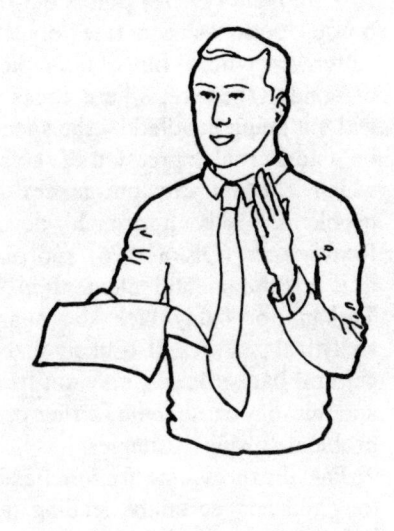

Figure 5.3 Two iconic gestures used in lessons on physical geography. The air punch (left) accompanied a description of boulders crashing down the bed of a river in spate. Note the concentration frown, signalling that the class need to listen carefully. The air chop (right) illustrated an explanation of river valleys cutting through hills

the explanation for increased gesturing under the more stressful teaching situation). Secondly, listeners may pick up information from a speaker's gestures which they subsequently report in speech. McNeill found that gesture could override speech where the two gave contradictory messages.

In the classroom iconic gestures are frequent in many subjects (for example demonstrating the sinuous line of the First World War trenches across Europe, a boulder-laden river cutting down through rocks, or the structure of a mathematical equation). They merge into pantomimic demonstrations with impromptu apparatus (for example using two exercise books to demonstrate mountain uplift when plates collide, or bending two boys, back to back, when talking about the bimetallic strip) and thence into formal diagrams or demonstrations with apparatus.

Metaphoric gestures represent abstract ideas physically (for example moving the hand to two positions while talking about a mathematical 'dual' – McNeill 1985a), and are most represented in teaching by *conduit* gestures signalling to the class what kind of idea is being presented to them. A question may be represented by a cupped hand, needing filling, while one hand may press against the other to symbolise that something is 'packed with meaning' (McNeill 1985b). Teachers hold up ideas for the class to 'look' at (Figures 5.4, 2.3), sometimes between finger and thumb to show the precision with which the idea needs to be 'grasped' (Figure 5.5); as the explanation proceeds the idea may be offered on cupped hand for the class to 'pick up' (Figure 5.6), or the teacher may 'open the door' for the class on the new knowledge (Figure 2.3). McNeill (1985b) points out that this use of conduit gestures which symbolise ideas as concrete objects which can be manipulated may be culture-specific, as film of nomadic Turkana shows them using a different type of conduit gesture, where ideas seem to be able to move autonomously, without being handled by the speaker. The Western gesture pattern seems to be a nonverbal expression of the analytical, heuristic approach to knowledge which concentrates on general strategies of wide application to novel problems. This approach developed in Western cultures after the Renaissance (Olson 1976) and distinguishes them from traditional cultures; it is a fundamental element in Western education (Gladwin 1970). The Turkana probably lack the analytical modes of thought as well as the analytical gestures. It is likely that younger children, or children from certain cultural backgrounds, may not be familiar with conduit gestures of this type, and this may cause them further problems in recognising and learning abstract problem-solving strategies.

Facial expressions are less flexible in their range, but may be more salient to children; certainly smiling and frowning seem to affect children's judgments more than gestures (Neill 1986a, 1989a). During explanations, concentration (Figures 5.3, 5.5) and puzzle frowns (Figure 2.4) are commonly used to signal when children need to pay attention to a problematic section of the teacher's explanation. No evidence is available as to how much effect these

Figure 5.4 In this variant of the 'holding an idea' posture, the idea is being held more closely than in Figure 2.3. The variant might be expected to accompany an earlier section of an explanation, when the idea is being introduced

two expressions have on the class. There is some restricted evidence for the posture most commonly used by enthusiastic teachers: the forward lean, which is an intention movement of approach (Morris 1977). It therefore signals the intention to decrease interpersonal distance, which intensifies any communication (chapter 7). Children tended to see it as a positive signal (Neill 1989a). Facial expressions and forward leans are used in the same way in one-to-one conversations, but would normally be well developed only in very intense interactions; as with gestures, they are more developed in the one-to-many situation to compensate for the lack of feedback.

However expressive and enthusiastic the presentation, it is unlikely to be effective if the verbal explanation is not clearly structured and matched to the rate at which children are likely to be able to take in the information. Thus Roehler and Duffy (1986) found that the most effective teachers reduced their level of assistance progressively after giving children a full explanation and demonstration of the skills that were being practised. Children were therefore able to take over direction with an already existing knowledge of how to

78　Classroom Nonverbal Communication

Figure 5.5 The air purse (left) is a vacuum version of the precision grip (used to hold the chalk in the right hand) and is frequently used, for example, by mathematics teachers. Note the concentration frown. Teachers count off points (right), especially when summarising an explanation involving a sequence of stages

Figure 5.6. The palm-up gesture (left) offers an idea in a non-dominant way and was seen by children as cheerful and friendly (Neill 1989a). The palm-side gesture symbolises reaching out to the audience

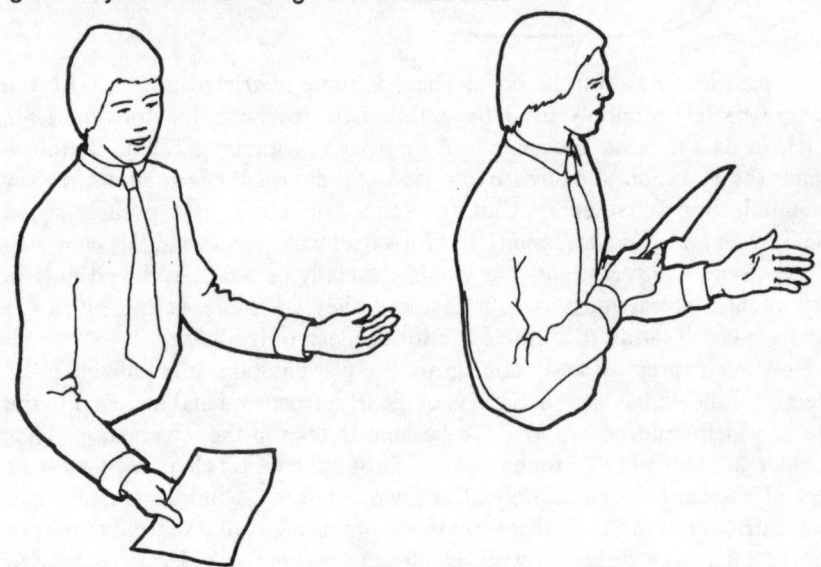

Source: Reproduced with permission from *Pastoral Care in Education* 6 (4): 37

perform the task. This matching between teacher and learner is not unique to the classroom, and is often shown better by untrained teachers (Wood 1986). Wood recorded the tactics mothers used when helping their preschool child solve an experimental puzzle. The more effective mothers matched their level of assistance to the child's progress, reducing their prompts if the child was succeeding but returning to giving more specific assistance if it was apparent that the child was encountering problems. Greenfield and Lave (1982) describe a similar transition of responsibility between teacher and learner among illiterate Mexican Indian women teaching their daughters traditional weaving methods. Greenfield and Lave consider that formal education differs from informal education in traditional societies in the lesser relevance of what is being taught to the learners and their lesser social motivation. Responsibility for ensuring learning therefore falls to the teacher rather than to the learner. The enthusiastic behaviours described in this chapter are one necessary response to this situation; the prosocial behaviours described in the next are another.

SUMMARY

Enthusiastic instructors use more marked nonverbal signals, such as gestures and range of intonation, than would be normal in informal social interaction. This appears to be due to the inequality between teacher and taught and the speaker's need to compensate for the lack of feedback characteristic of most large audience groups.

Gestures appear to parallel and supplement verbal output. In some cases, especially *iconic* gestures which refer to objects or movements, they carry part of the meaning. *Metaphoric* gestures, which refer to abstract ideas, often indicate how the listeners should respond to an idea. Thus the development of a teacher's argument may be supported by gestures, facial expressions and intonation indicating the development of stages of the argument, and where potential problems arise. These contribute to the clear structuring of the material which is necessary for the children to learn readily.

Chapter 6

Showing interest and friendliness

In the previous chapter we considered how the teacher could enthuse her class about the material she was teaching them. However, her ability to show interest in their responses and in them as persons is equally important. Nonverbal signals are particularly influential in other situations where one person shows interest in another, such as counselling, due to their vivid persuasiveness. They make the counsellor appear more friendly, trustworthy and knowledgeable (Robbins and Haase 1985).

The signals used are rather different in the whole-class situation, and when talking to children on a one-to-one basis. Particular attention has been paid in the research literature to the ways in which teachers convey their differential expectations of good and poor performance by individual members of their classes (e.g. Brophy and Good 1970). This area received very active research after the pioneering work of Rosenthal and Jacobson (Brophy and Good 1974) and it was rapidly realised that expectations can be transmitted nonverbally. Stein (1976), for example, found that teachers were more likely to smile, nod, lean towards and look at high-ability 6–8-year-old children and to frown, shake their head and not look at low-ability children. She also found that teachers were more positive to younger children.

This was one of the greatest spurs to investigating the ways in which teachers can encourage or discourage their pupils. Brophy and Good (1974) reviewed the extensive literature which developed after Rosenthal and Jacobson's initial publication on teacher expectations and concluded that, though experimental studies had frequently failed to demonstrate expectations (probably because the subject had become so well known that teachers became suspicious of researchers trying to alter their expectations), naturalistic studies had clearly demonstrated expectations. Naturalistic expectation effects were greater in behaviour than in longer-term outcomes. Experimenters then turned their attention to the way in which expectations were conveyed in one-to-one tutoring situations. After looking at this literature we will see to what extent the results apply to normal classrooms. Children are active and influential participants too, so we then look at their ability to convey their interest and expectations to the teacher.

STUDIES OF POSITIVE AND NEGATIVE COMMUNICATION DURING TUTORING

Typically tutoring studies used undergraduate students as tutor to a child, usually the same child for all tutors. The tutors were briefed to expect the child to be either bright or dull. Chaikin, Sigler and Derlega (1974) used this paradigm, with 10-year-old boys as tutees. Tutors were more encouraging to 'bright' boys than average or dull ones; they leaned forward rather than away and met the boy's gaze more (both behaviours indicating more involvement) and nodded and smiled more (both positive behaviours – compare Figure 6.1). Allen and Feldman (1976) report somewhat similar results from 11-year-old children tutoring 8-year-olds who were consistently successful or unsuccessful. With successful tutees the tutors nodded more and sat more erect, and

Figure 6.1 Nominating a child to answer in the classroom. The teacher's forward lean and smile are expressions of interest which are also seen in one-to-one situations, such as tutorials. However, she has had to indicate clearly which child is to answer by moving close and pointing. She has also bent her head because she is standing; in one-to-one situations interest might be expressed by a head cant (Figure 6.5)

fidgeted, pursed their lips and shook their heads less. However, the tutors seemed to be more involved with their less successful tutees; they leant and reached forward more and gazed at them more. These differences are probably due to the child tutors feeling under more stress to get the tutee to perform correctly than the student tutors, who could explain failure as due to their child's lack of ability.

Feldman and Prohaska (1979) found that undergraduate students were rated more highly as teachers by judges viewing videotapes of a one-to-one tutoring situation if the person they were teaching behaved positively to them. (The judges could not see the tutee.) The tutors also rated their own lessons more highly. However, measurable differences in the tutor's nonverbal expressions of interest (facing towards the tutee, eye contact and forward lean) were slight. A matched experiment in which the tutees believed the tutor was effective or ineffective showed slightly greater effects on nonverbal expression of interest. However, only one individual behaviour showed a significant difference; tutees tended to lean more towards teachers they had been told were effective. Again tutees rated their lesson more highly with an 'effective' tutor, but they actually learnt more on only one of the tests used. Feldman and Prohaska's paper title 'The student as Pygmalion' reflects their belief that the learners have as much effect on the classroom process as the teacher, but as they point out, caution has to be exercised in extrapolating from this limited evidence to the mainstream classroom.

Experiments of this type suggested that expectations could be transmitted to children in a fairly damaging way. They were therefore followed by similar experiments to see if tutors could conceal their negative expectations. (By this time Ekman and Friesen's (1969b) work on leakage was well known.) Feldman, Devin-Sheehan and Allen (1978) report that 8- and 11-year-old tutors leaked their true feelings when asked to say 'good' whether their child tutee performed correctly or not, and this could be detected by other 8-year-olds. They found that the tutors leaked their true feelings when the tutees consistently performed poorly, by smiling less, and raising their eyebrows, staring, pausing more often and making a negative mouth movement.

As might be expected from chapter 2, adults are better at avoiding leakage. Feldman (1976) used other undergraduates as raters of the nonverbal responses of student tutors, working with high-school children. The tutors could conceal their like or dislike of the tutees when they could see them, though they showed their feelings when the tutees were behind a one-way mirror. Tutors who liked their tutees were much more enthusiastic when they answered correctly than when they did not; those who disliked them showed a similar lower level of enthusiasm for both correct and incorrect answers. This suggests that children whom the teacher dislikes will get little information to guide them from her nonverbal feedback. We shall see a similar lack of feedback to the teacher from low-achieving children shortly.

Sullins, Friedman and Harris (1985) used a similar methodology. They found that the tutor's ability to monitor her own behaviour was critical. Expressive teachers who had low awareness of their own behaviour transmitted their expectations clearly; but those who were self-aware tended to be more positive to tutees for whom they had lower expectations. Sullins et al. thought that this was due to the tutors' wish to be seen to be fair to all their tutees. However, they thought that in the normal classroom situation teachers would be monitoring their behaviour less carefully than in the experiment, so that their true feelings would come through. It is unlikely in most classrooms that teachers' verbal comments will be as unrevealing as in these experiments, where the words used were standardised between conditions. However Silberman (1969) found that teachers were able to suppress overt display of their affection for particular children and rejection of others. He relied primarily on verbal and intonational expressions. Concern about a child was expressed more clearly. Children were able to detect and report teachers' different treatment of individuals. Concern was much more acceptable to children than affection or rejection, which were seen as favouritism. It therefore seems likely that teachers are reasonably successful in concealing the feelings which would be unacceptable to children and in maintaining the requirement for professional fairness. The feeling of concern, which they express more overtly, is an acceptable part of their professional role.

THE EFFECT OF PUPILS' FEEDBACK

It is important to stress that both parties have a powerful influence on the way classroom communication develops. Children's ability to use these signals deserves particular attention because they have better awareness of the course of the lesson than the teacher and, at least in some circumstances, considerable influence over the teacher's conduct. Hook and Rosenshine (1979) found that children's views of lessons coincided with those of nonparticipant observers and were more accurate than those of teachers, due to the teachers being so involved in their teaching that they failed to take in as much information about what was happening as the other two groups. This gives children the possibility to manipulate the course of the lesson – a possibility which they can use to disrupt the teacher's control, as discussed in chapter 4. More positively, they can encourage the teacher by their responsiveness. Klein (1971) primed university students to change their responsiveness to visiting lecturers at quarter-hour intervals; they were to be either positive (smiling, nodding, looking at the teacher, taking notes and responding when requested), neutral (i.e. to adopt their customary behaviour in lectures) or negative (frowning, looking out of the window, slumping in their seats, talking and disregarding the teacher). It seems the students' neutral behaviour was encouraging, since little difference was found between the lecturers' behaviour in the positive and neutral conditions. In the negative condition the lecturers' performance deteriorated; they tended to be more directive and critical and to give fewer illustrations of what they were talking about. Klein felt that the effects of negative student feedback were stronger than those of positive feedback, and potentially damaging to pupils' interests. The unfortunate lecturers were unaware of what the students had been doing to them!

Similar results were obtained with student teachers by Jenkins and Deno (1969). They taught a small group of first-year students, most of whom were confederates of the experimenters and had been told to act either in a happy, interested way, smiling, nodding, with attentive eye contact and taking notes, or in a negative way, avoiding all these signs of interest. Students who had taught the positive groups rated their own lessons as more enjoyable and productive of learning than those who had had negative feedback. They also felt they were more effective, and that the type of teaching they had been engaged in was useful to first-year students. This study did not include direct observation of the participants' behaviour, but a study by Bates (1976) did.

Bates trained 11-year-old boys to give positive feedback (smiling and high eye contact) or negative feedback (no smiles and low eye contact) to students who were tutoring them in mathematics on a one-to-one basis. Positive feedback resulted in more positive nonverbal behaviour by the student tutor, who also rated the boy more favourably. Bates concluded on the basis of extensive analysis that this was a genuine effect, but he found considerable variation between individual boys and between different sections of the experiment. Female students were more positive than men overall, in line with other work (chapter 9).

SIGNALS OF ENTHUSIASM AND INTEREST – POSTURE

Adults adopt different sitting postures to signal different levels of interest (Figure 6.2). In addition to body posture, fiddling with objects and looking at them rather than the teacher are reliable signs of disinterest (Lawes 1987b). There is some evidence that self-directed movements, such as grooming or fiddling with objects, indicate stress, especially social stress in children. Ten-year-old children show them more frequently when talking to an unfamiliar adult than when doing mental arithmetic (Kenner 1984). This matches the situation in adults (chapter 3; Figures 3.1, 3.5). Teachers therefore have to be careful that their interpretation of these signals is the correct one.

In experiments where students were asked to listen to videotaped talks a forward alert posture and legs drawn back signalled interest while a backward lean, legs stretched out, dropping the head or propping the head on the hand indicated boredom (Bull 1987; Figure 6.3). Students also decoded these postures, shown as drawings, in the same way, though there were certain highly complex interactions which Bull (op. cit.) found it difficult to explain.

Figure 6.2 Attention is on fiddling with the pen, not work. The boy's attitude to the lesson is indicated by his feet casually propped on the next chair, and the fact that he has not bothered to take his outside coat off. In a formal, teacher-centred lesson this would show serious inattention; but it was photographed during individual work (compare Figure 4.11)

Source: Reproduced with permission from *Pastoral Care in Education* 6 (4): 13

These may result from the signals only being used in certain combinations, so that other combinations are not readily interpreted. It is certainly the case for facial expression that only a small proportion of the different permutations of facial movements which could theoretically occur are actually used (Ekman and Friesen 1975). It is not clear from the comparison of this work and that of Lawes (1987b), cited previously, whether adults actually use a wider range of behaviours to indicate interest or boredom than 10-year-olds. Alternatively Lawes's student teachers might have been using a narrower range of cues than Bull's students viewing adults, so that only a narrow range of the actual behaviours shown by the children figured in their judgments of attention.

Since a continued high level of attention is tiring to maintain, adults normally adopt relaxed postures in any extended lecture or discussion and this falls within the customary advertance rules. Secondary-school children not only behave in this way, but may break the adult display rules. This can cause problems to inexperienced teachers.

Despite their ability to encode and decode interest through posture, Bull's subjects seemed to be largely unaware of these postures at a conscious level.

86   Classroom Nonverbal Communication

Figure 6.3 The head prop is frequently shown by adult audiences after a talk has gone on for some time, especially if it is monotonous. Secondary children may use it to manipulate the teacher through the advertance rules (compare Figure 4.1)

Figure 6.4 This pattern is more defiant than that shown in Figure 6.3. The fist is acting as a barrier in front of the face and there is a direct stare without the head being lifted. Tension is also indicated by the force with which the head leans on the fist, distorting the cheek. The lowered head is defensive (compare Figure 2.2) and the boy would probably hold his ground against a teacher who approached

They were unable to describe the postures they could adopt to indicate interest or boredom. Conscious realisation that posture signals interest, and willingness to challenge inappropriate postures when children adopt them, are important steps towards effectiveness as a teacher (Robertson 1989). Since silence and a low level of participation are normal for secondary pupils, they use posture to indicate that they are in a nonparticipant 'sulk' (Gilmore 1985; chapters 4 and 9). Children show an inappropriate level of engagement by staring defiantly at the teacher (Figure 6.4) or inappropriate disengagement by completely ignoring her and becoming involved in their own 'side' activities (Figure 6.2). Adults can behave in these ways, to show 'dumb insolence', for example in the army, but such behaviour (and the willingness to explicitly correct it) shows a social distance which is incompatible with normal informal social relationships. Whether children can manipulate their use of these postures in a way which adults cannot, in line with other evidence on the increase of 'politeness' with age, perhaps deserves investigation, as does the development of these signals in younger children.

THE EFFECT OF THE CLASSROOM SETTING ON PROSOCIAL BEHAVIOUR

Just as teachers tend to exaggerate their signals during speaking relative to a normal one-to-one conversation, they also tend to give much more intense listening signals, as well as verbal encouragement (very often by repeating the correct section of what the child has just said) and evaluation of the response. Like teachers, children may be anxious when responding in front of a large number of class-mates, and they may in addition be more anxious because, unlike when being questioned in normal conversation, the teacher normally asks questions to which she already has the answer, and has the right to evaluate the children's answer (Edwards and Furlong 1978). In addition, as Watts and Bentley (1987) point out, especially in areas such as science, the development of knowledge will often involve the rearrangement or destruction of children's existing concepts. Children tend to bring to such areas common-sense or popular understandings of concepts such as 'energy' (Solomon 1983), which are incompatible with the scientific usage of the same terms. As Watts and Bentley say, 'cognitive assault' of this type is only likely to be acceptable if the teacher can provide a supportive atmosphere, both by showing her own enthusiasm, as mentioned above, and by being trusting and supportive of the children's efforts. Doyle (1983) describes the 'piloting' tactics which children use to extract themselves from such situations, which have both high ambiguity and high risk to their self-esteem. If the teacher were to use any of the relaxed listening signals which children frequently employ, the answering child would almost certainly dry up.

The first thing the teacher can do is to exaggerate the listening signals described in the previous chapter, to compensate for her greater distance from

Figure 6.5 The head cant is used to express interest from early childhood onwards, and by non-teachers as well as teachers. However, it is not mentioned in the literature on tutoring situations, though this generally lacks descriptions of the exact behaviour seen

the child, compared to normal conversation, and the inhibiting factors described above. In normal social interaction, gaze and proximity (Argyle and Dean 1965), facial expression and posture (Waldron 1975) signal positive feelings. In adults facial expression has a much greater effect than posture (Waldron op. cit., Graham, Ricci Bitti and Argyle 1975) and the same applies to children's assessments of teachers (Neill 1989a).

Facial expressions are also used by teachers when listening to children's responses, to encourage them to respond. Common expressions are the concentration and puzzle frowns, though smiling is used to encourage children to respond (Figure 6.1). Some teachers make considerable use of the head cant, an expression of interest which first appears in preschool children, who use it to show sympathetic involvement with another child (Figures 6.5, 7.2). Intense gaze and forward lean is also characteristic, emphasising the normal tendency of the listener to look more at the speaker than vice versa (chapter 5). In some cases teachers may further emphasise their involvement with children's answers by adopting poses such as the 'wicket-keeping' pose shown in Figure 6.6. These nonverbal patterns are characteristically accompanied by verbal encouragement, such as repeating the relevant part of

Figure 6.6 This 'wicket-keeper' posture would be seen as theatrically exaggerated in most informal situations, but may be appropriate when responding to children's answers in class. It shows in accentuated form many of the features seen in Figure 6.1

the child's answer and offering clues to what would be a correct response (Sinclair and Coulthard 1975). However, these verbal moves can interfere with the children's need for silence to compose their answers.

As mentioned above in chapter 5, pauses occur in normal conversation when the speaker is processing the next part of what they are about to say, and speakers use a variety of devices to hold the floor during these pauses. Pauses also occur when children respond to teachers, but it is more difficult for children to employ floor-holding tactics, probably due to a combination of factors – their absorption in trying to deal with difficult ideas, their relative inexperience as conversationalists, and the superior status of the teacher. Rowe (1974) found that most teachers tended to interrupt children when they were pausing to process the next part of their response; on average teachers intervened after only 0.9 seconds, while children tended to pause for up to 2–3 seconds when left to their own devices. As a result children were prevented from giving as full and complex responses as they would have been capable of, and felt frustrated. Rowe trained teachers to extend their wait time, and found that children, especially low achievers, were more willing to respond, that responses were more confident, and that there were more higher-order responses, involving speculation, inference, suggestions as to how problems could be solved or explored, and so on. She felt that this represented a more genuine dialogue between children and teacher, with the children having more control over their own learning. Teachers who allow children time to think are seen as more considerate and helpful. Keith, Tornatzky and Pettigrew (1974) did not record wait time, but found a similar relationship between encouraging behaviour and children's response. Student teachers who smiled more often and longer had classes where individuals and groups thought for longer, answered more often, discussed more and responded more spontaneously.

It may in fact be that the intense listening behaviour – and for that matter some of the intense explaining behaviour – discussed above is a compensation made necessary by the fact that teachers tend to make the classroom a threatening and unrewarding place by their rapid-fire control of dialogue. One notable feature of first lessons by experienced and effective teachers is their use of the first lesson to build up a relationship (Moskowitz and Hayman 1974, 1976, Wragg and Wood 1984), often using one-off material which does not relate too strongly to what will be covered in the rest of the year, but which is related to the class's own experience and therefore makes it easier for them to gain confidence by making contributions. Many of the effective teachers observed in Neill (1986b) also did this; they also used a mixture of self-deprecating and pupil-directed humour. Pupils find this sociable and interesting (Ziv, Gorenstein and Moris 1986). Self-directed humour on its own is seen as weakness, pupil-directed humour alone as stern.

PRAISE

One of the most salient effects of teachers' status relative to their classes is teachers' power to evaluate and praise children's work and behaviour, while the reverse would be seen as impertinence. However, Brophy (1981) concluded that the effectiveness of praise in encouraging achievement in ordinary classrooms, as opposed to in specially manipulated situations, had been much exaggerated. He felt this was due to a number of factors, especially that praise tended to be given for a number of reasons, some of them social, which were not closely related to achievement. (Brophy accepted that praise might well improve the social atmosphere of the classroom, but felt that where praise did improve achievement, this might be due to a context of positive relationships rather than to the praise itself – Figure 6.7.) Furthermore, in praising disliked children, for instance those who are troublesome, immature or dependent, or children of other races (see also chapter 9), teachers tend to cancel out their verbal praise by negative nonverbal signals, making the recipients aware that the praise is insincere.

Showing interest and friendliness 91

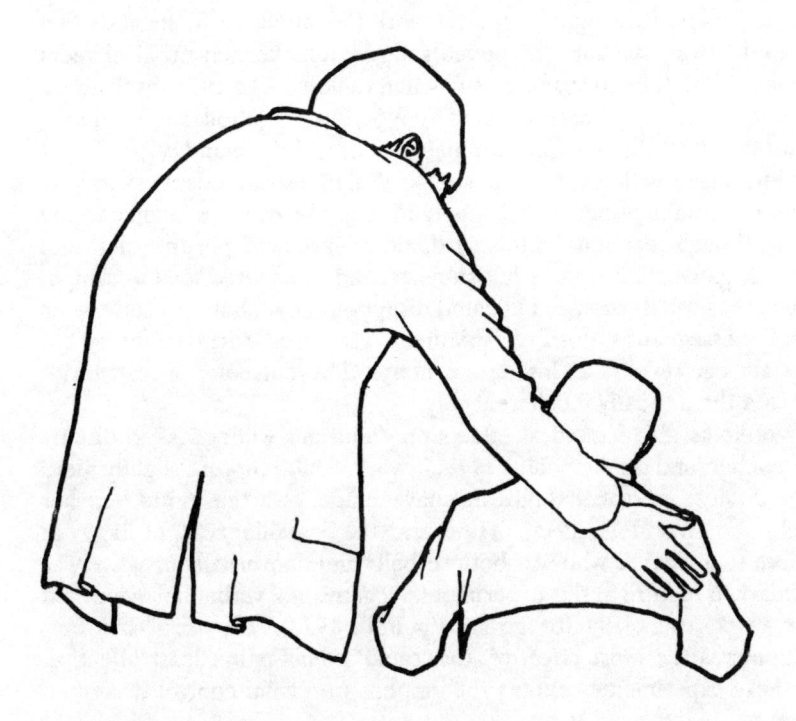

Figure 6.7 Touch used in a first lesson to show appreciation of good work, but also helping to build up a warm relationship

The significance of contradictory verbal and nonverbal messages (chapter 2) is explored in the Woolfolks' work, dealt with shortly.

One of Brophy's most striking conclusions was that some children are highly successful at eliciting teacher praise, particularly when they bring work to show the teacher. These children rewarded teacher praise by reacting to it very positively – smiling and beaming proudly. (These nonverbal rewards would have been more acceptable to the teacher than a corresponding verbal response, which would have seemed smarmy or cheeky.) Brophy concluded that here the children were reinforcing and controlling the teacher's behaviour, the reverse of the formal situation. Other reports (Garner and Bing 1973) confirm teachers' preference for outgoing children.

The Woolfolks' experiments explored the relative effects of verbal and nonverbal feedback on children's achievements and attitudes. Their use of student teachers and fixed vocabulary test scenarios, for experimental control, casts slight doubt on the validity of an important series of experiments (Galloway 1974). The teachers delivered either verbal praise or criticism, each accompanied by either positive (nod, smile and pleasant intonation) or negative (frown, headshake and angry tone) nonverbal signals. Woolfolk and Woolfolk (1974) found that perception of a female teacher and attraction to her were affected by both verbal and nonverbal signals. To their surprise praise accompanied by negative nonverbal signals was preferred to criticism accompanied by positive signals. In later work (Woolfolk 1978) suggests that the former is 'firm but fair' (or possibly sardonic), the nonverbal element suggesting control; the latter suggests fawning timidity. The 1974 results were replicated for two more female teachers by Woolfolk, Woolfolk and Garlinsky (1977), but the effect did not apply for male teachers. Friedman (1979) did not find sex differences with a somewhat similar design, using students as judges; his results for combinations with happy and angry faces were similar to the Woolfolks', though reactions to the 'sardonic' (angry face, positive message) were more negative with these adult subjects. Sad faces were seen as sympathetic when the verbal message indicated disappointment, but apathetic when the verbal message was positive. Friedman also used surprise faces, but without clear-cut results, as his design lumps different emotion categories together in a theoretically incoherent way.

The Woolfolks also looked at effects on children's willingness to discuss with the teacher, and on the quality of their work. Children were slightly more willing to disclose personal topics in conversation with the 'timid' teacher (Woolfolk and Woolfolk 1975). However, the unwillingness of boys to self-disclose to a teacher who was both verbally and nonverbally negative was the only marked feature in this experiment. Negative nonverbal behaviour led to better work, especially for girls (Woolfolk 1978). The 'firm but fair' combination was the most effective, the 'timid' combination least effective. Overall, these experiments support the emphasis on calm control described in chapter 3.

SUMMARY

Much of the work on signalling interest and enthusiasm has been done in one-to-one tutoring. Both tutor and tutee can send positive or negative signals. The signals used include gaze, posture, and movements such as nodding. Much of this work has used adult tutors and tutees, but some experiments have used children down to primary age. Concern has been expressed that potentially damaging expectations can be signalled. Adults are better able to control the signals they send than children, and experienced teachers may be able to conceal their expectations to some extent under classroom conditions.

As in the case of conveying enthusiasm (chapter 5), teachers' signals of interest are accentuated relative to normal social interaction. Effective teachers also wait longer for children to compose their answers. This may compensate for the stress imposed on children by speaking in public. Successful performance is rewarded by praise; children who are rewarding to the teacher (usually by nonverbal signals) receive more praise. 'Firm but fair' praise accompanied by negative nonverbal signals seems most effective.

Chapter 7

Interpersonal distance and classroom layout

The concept of interpersonal distance or 'personal space' was largely originated by Hall (1966), who drew parallels between the regular spacing out of humans and many animals, most obvious when sitting or standing in lines. Hall distinguished between intimate distance, when people were in contact or nearly so, which (except in tube trains, lifts and similar crowded spaces) usually characterises close personal relationships; personal distance (within easy arm-reach), which characterises friendly interaction; social distance (within which it would be possible to touch at a stretch) which suits more impersonal interaction; and public distance (beyond touching range). Hall's clear-cut distinctions have not been entirely supported by subsequent work, and preferred distances differ between cultures and with age, but the general pattern he described still has validity and is of considerable value in interpreting classroom processes and layouts. Not only do teachers move around classrooms, altering interpersonal distances, and, usually, controlling children's movements, on a minute-to-minute basis, but the layout of the classroom reflects the types of relationship and interaction which are expected on a more permanent basis. For example, the status of the teacher is reflected in most classrooms by her position separate from and facing the children. This reflects the tendency of subordinates in a hierarchical organisation to maintain a greater distance from superiors, even in informal interaction (Dean, Willis and Hewitt 1975). At the end of the chapter we will discuss position in the classroom as a temporary or permanent reflection of the interpersonal dispositions of the participants.

INTERPERSONAL DISTANCE

It has been suggested that interpersonal distance is a biological universal, but this has been challenged on the grounds that acceptable distance varies with age and culture. Interpersonal distance tends to increase with age (e.g. Baxter 1970), at least up to puberty (Willis, Carlson and Reeves 1979). Differences can occur even between closely related subcultures, such as the Hispanics of Costa Rica and Panama in Central America (Bull 1983). American blacks maintain smaller distances than whites and touch each other more, especially in later childhood (Jones and Aiello 1973, Willis and Hoffman 1975, Willis and Reeves 1976, Willis, Reeves and Buchanan 1976, Willis, Rinck and Dean 1978, Willis et al. 1979 – Baxter (1970) however found that they maintained greater distances than whites in a zoo setting). They seem to compensate for this by facing each other less directly (Jones and Aiello op. cit.). They are also more likely to touch teachers (Heinig 1975). American Jewish girls get touched less than Catholic or Protestant ones (Jourard 1966). Preferred distance is therefore clearly influenced by cultural experience, and this may create problems in the multicultural classroom. Though there may be biological foundations to interpersonal distance simple functional requirements (such as avoiding bumping into others – which apply to other species as well) may be sufficient explanation (e.g. Sundstrom and Altman 1976). Closer approach gives interactions a higher intensity, since it is a prerequisite for extreme positive and negative behaviour – affection and aggression (Sundstrom and Altman op. cit.).

Figure 7.1 Directing touch; the boy has been 'easy riding' by sharpening his pencil too long. Though it is light, the hold to both shoulders allows the teacher to steer the boy exactly

Source: Reproduced with permission from *Pastoral Care in Education* 6 (4): 38

TOUCH IN THE CLASSROOM

Touch is the most extreme stage in the reduction of interpersonal distance and therefore has the effect of intensifying any interaction even more than close approach. Among other aspects, it has considerable power implications. Teachers touch children, especially in the primary school (Evans 1979b), but, except at the youngest ages where touch is still used for comfort, children rarely touch teachers (Figure 1.2). If children are in close proximity to the teacher, some messages can be expressed more directly, for instance by simply moving the child as required, showing or taking objects and so on. Much of teachers' touch is directed towards control, especially for boys (Evans op.cit., Heinig 1975), and involves touches to the arm and shoulder (the normal areas for low-level social touches among adults – Jourard 1966, Heslin and Alper 1983, Goffman 1979; Figures 7.1, 7.2). With young children the head is also touched (Bevan and Wheldall 1985), partly because it can be reached conveniently: but touch to the head has as a result a rather demeaning quality, and is unpopular among older children (Neill 1987). Heinig found that all areas except the genital region were touched by the teachers of

Figure 7.2 Friendly touch in a first language lesson; the teacher is about to engage the girl in foreign-language conversation and her head cant (Figure 6.5) shows her interest

Figure 7.3 Ostensibly sympathetic touch used as a punishment; the teacher is 'showing up' the boy by giving him extra work to be done, in front of the class. Being held closely in this way would be acceptable in the infant school, but not by this age-group

10–12–year-old summer-school children, but the relative accessibilities of different areas seemed similar to those mentioned above, with children's faces rarely being touched. Children usually touched teachers to get attention, on the hand, arm and back. This agrees with children's reports of their friendly touches to teachers in Neill's data.

The relative 'touchability' of different areas of the body remains the same for different types of classroom touch, but some kinds of touch are more acceptable than others (Neill op. cit.). Friendly and sympathetic touches are the most popular type among 6–10–year-olds (Norton 1974) and older primary and secondary children (Neill 1986a), but they are less frequently used than controlling touch (Figure 7.3) both by teachers of infants (Evans 1979b) and those of older children (Neill, pers. obs.). All children in the Neill (1986c) study disliked aggressive touch most, but rough-and-tumble, or playfully aggressive, touch (Figure 7.4) was also disliked by some girls.

Figure 7.4 Playful touch during a first lesson; the teacher was re-establishing her relationship with a class she taught in the previous year. Here she is attracting the attention of a boy who has set his work out wrongly; immediately afterwards she tapped her forehead against his, scowled at him, reprimanded him but allowed him to continue as he had to avoid spoiling his book. She was thus interacting in the way a dominant member of the boy's own age-group might

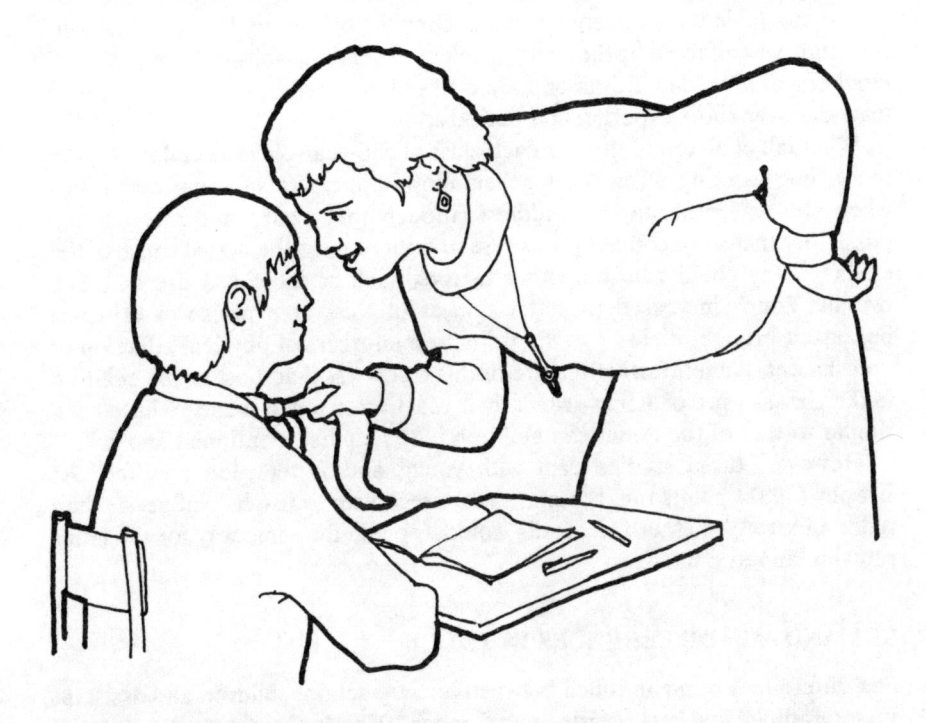

Source: Reproduced with permission from *Pastoral Care in Education* 6 (4): 13

There is some direct evidence of the effectiveness of touch in classroom situations. Clements and Tracy (1977) found that, with a small group of emotionally disturbed 9–11-year-old boys, encouraging touch (the teacher resting her hands firmly on both the child's shoulders), alone or in combination with verbal encouragement, were more effective in improving attention to, and performance in, arithmetic than verbal encouragement alone, though as they point out, their results should be interpreted with caution because of the small number involved. Kazdin and Klock (1973) obtained a similar improvement in attention to work for 11 out of 12 in a mixed-age class of retarded elementary children when smiling or affectionate touch were added to verbal praise.

Verbal reprimands alone were less effective than if the teacher grasped the child's shoulders firmly and made eye contact, by insisting on it, if necessary (Van Houten, Nau, MacKenzie-Keating, Sameoto and Colavecchia 1982). In line with the argument above that touch is the most extreme form of reduced interpersonal distance, Van Houten at al. also found that reprimands delivered from a close distance (a metre) were more effective than those delivered from further away, and that reprimands delivered in this way to one of a pair seated at a table were effective in controlling the behaviour of both. However, this study was affected by the same problem of generalisability related to small numbers, as Wheldall, Bevan and Shortall's (1986) study which used only four teachers over short experimental periods.

Wheldall et al. found that for each class of 5–6-year-olds the children spent more time working when the teacher adopted a policy of using touch only when she was praising the children (though they could not rule out the possibility that a concomitant decrease in criticism was the actual cause of the effect). They could rule out other factors, such as increased use of touch overall. Touch increased the effectiveness of classroom praise or criticism because it brought it closer to the primary reinforcers of physical affection or punishment. An interesting feature of this study was that most of the children in the classes were of Asian origin; their reaction to touch seems to have been similar to that of the American children in the studies mentioned above.

However, these studies deal with young and/or retarded children. As Brophy (1981) points out, these are more receptive to teacher influence than older children; whether the results would apply in the same way for the latter remains undetermined.

SEX AND AGE DIFFERENCES IN TOUCH

Sex differences occur in touch between nursery-school children and assistant undergraduate teachers (Perdue and Connor 1978). In their study, Perdue and Connor found that the differences were strongest in males, and they attributed this to stronger sex-role socialisation experienced by boys. Both male and female teachers touched children of their own sex more than those of the opposite sex, but only male teachers touched children differently according to sex. They were more likely to give a girl a helpful touch, and a boy a friendly touch. There were no corresponding differences shown by the female teachers. Similarly boys touched male teachers more than female teachers; girls made no differentiation. Boys also touched male teachers more than girls did; they did not differ in the rate of touching female teachers. Boys were more likely to touch a female teacher by accident, but they were as likely to touch a male teacher in a friendly way as accidentally. Here girls showed the opposite pattern but more weakly; they touched male teachers accidentally, but female teachers as often in a friendly way as accidentally. It seems possible that teachers differentiated their use of touch because they saw it as a rather intimate form of communication. Perdue and Connor considered that the helpful touch girls received from male teachers was likely to reinforce them in dependency. They also felt that girls would be reinforced in dependent, contact-oriented behaviour because most preschool teachers are female and girls touch and are touched by them more.

Willis and colleagues (Willis and Hoffman 1975, Willis and Reeves 1976, Willis et al. 1976, Willis et al. 1978) have conducted an extensive series of studies of touch between children of different ages in cafeteria lines, a situation chosen because, unlike the school classroom, for instance, it is similar across ages. Their studies showed that there was a decline in touch between children until the age of 14 or 15 when the incidence of touch levelled off or increased slightly towards the adult level. Many of the touches recorded were accidental or casual. Children came into contact merely because they were already close to each other. Correspondingly, of course, if children become less tolerant of touch with age, they will stand further away to avoid accidents. The youngest children and the college students were more likely to touch in a personal or affectionate way than those in middle childhood.

Neill (1987) found that between the ages of 8 and 17, children's expressed views about touch in public places from people who were not close friends or relatives followed broadly the same lines as those of Willis and co-workers: a decline in the general acceptability of touch with age, levelling off after 14 (Figures 7.5 to 7.12). By 17 the pattern of preference closely resembled that reported for adults, in that boys were much more willing to be touched by, or to touch, females than males; females were not very willing to be touched by either sex, though their willingness to be touched had increased from a low point at 14. The change towards the adult pattern occurred between the ages of 11 and 13; 9- and 11-year-olds of either sex showed similar responses to touch from touchers of either sex. However, the adult pattern was foreshadowed in that the 9- and 11-year-old girls were much less willing to be touched on the chest than the boys (as were the older girls from 13 up). Otherwise patterns of preference across body areas held good across all groups of children, and all types of touch (friendly, comforting, directing, rough-and-tumble (horseplay) and aggressive) despite very different actual levels of acceptability.

By the adolescent years, children have absorbed the very rigid but normally unstated rules as to where touch is acceptable and what type of touch can be accepted. For instance, boys are well capable of harassing girls by apparently accidental touches which are not accidental, as both sides are only too well aware (Mahony 1985). On the other hand, a number of guides to assist in teaching young children, who have not yet fully absorbed the rules, what are acceptable and non-acceptable types of touch, have appeared in response to the current concern about sexual abuse of children (e.g. Baldwin and Lister 1987, Wachter 1986). Such guides may be necessary because children are generally less well aware of the appropriate rules for some types of behaviour, but also because they may be bad especially at interpreting the behaviour of strangers (chapter 2).

100 Classroom Nonverbal Communication

Figures 7.5 to 7.12 Plots of children's responses at 11 and 17 to questionnaires about touch in a classroom or public situation. Shoulders, arms and to a lesser extent the back are the most acceptable regions for touch – even angry touch. Eleven-year-olds of both sexes make little differentiation according to the sex of the other person, and their own sex has rather little effect. The odd group out are the 17-year-old boys, who make a strong differentiation according to the sex of the other person in a way which the girls of the same age do not

ELEVEN YEAR OLD BOYS
MALE TEACHER

friendly   angry   comforting

rough-and-tumble   directing   touch teacher

L
OK
P
A

Interpersonal distance and classroom layout 101

Figure 7.6

ELEVEN YEAR OLD BOYS
FEMALE TEACHER

friendly

angry

comforting

rough-and-tumble

directing

touch teacher

L
OK
P
A

102 Classroom Nonverbal Communication

Figure 7.7

ELEVEN YEAR OLD GIRLS
MALE TEACHER

friendly　　　　　angry　　　　　comforting

rough-and-tumble　　directing　　touch teacher

L	
OK	
P	
A	

Interpersonal distance and classroom layout 103

Figure 7.8

ELEVEN YEAR OLD GIRLS
FEMALE TEACHER

friendly

angry

comforting

rough-and-tumble

directing

touch teacher

L	
OK	
P	
A	

104 Classroom Nonverbal Communication

Figure 7.9

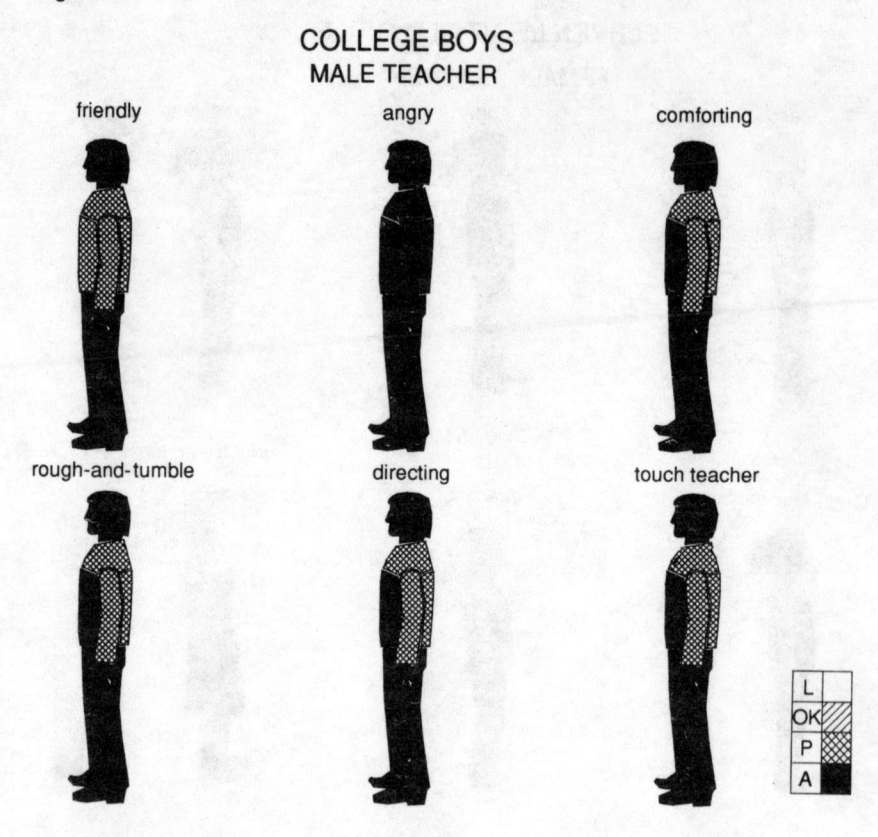

COLLEGE BOYS
MALE TEACHER

friendly

angry

comforting

rough-and-tumble

directing

touch teacher

Figure 7.10

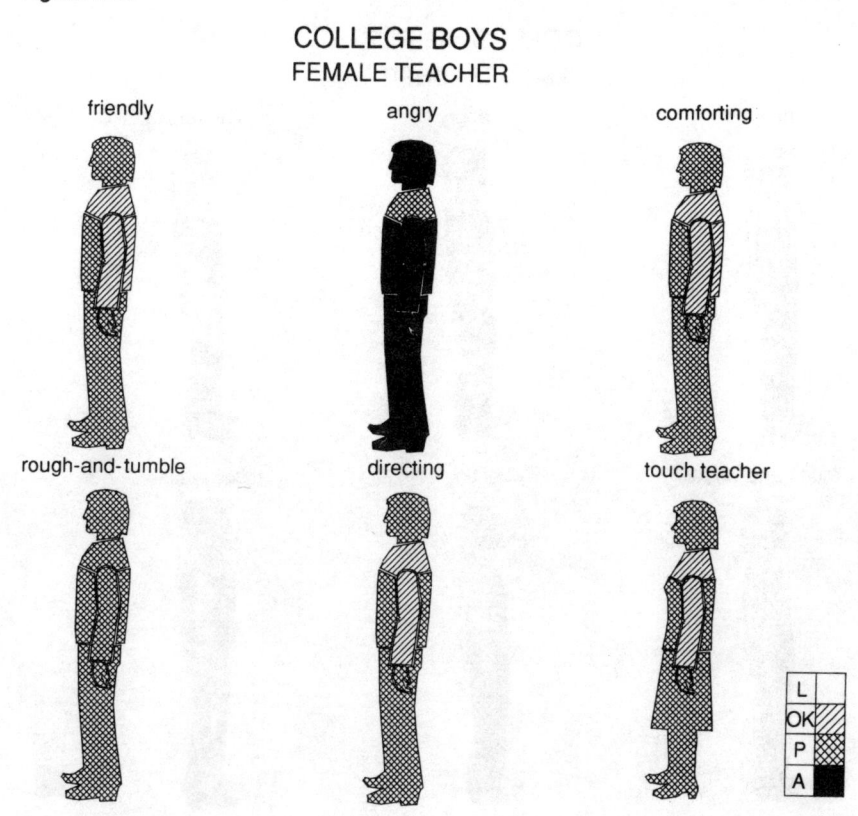

COLLEGE BOYS
FEMALE TEACHER

friendly   angry   comforting

rough-and-tumble   directing   touch teacher

106 Classroom Nonverbal Communication

Figure 7.11

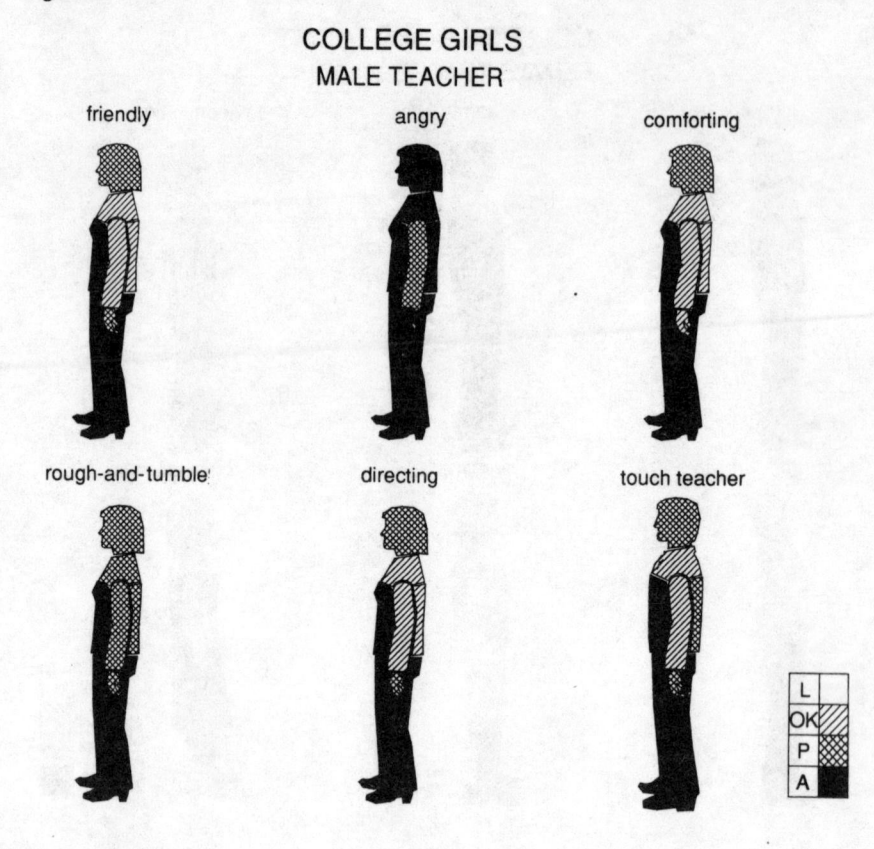

COLLEGE GIRLS
MALE TEACHER

friendly

angry

comforting

rough-and-tumble

directing

touch teacher

L
OK
P
A

Figure 7.12

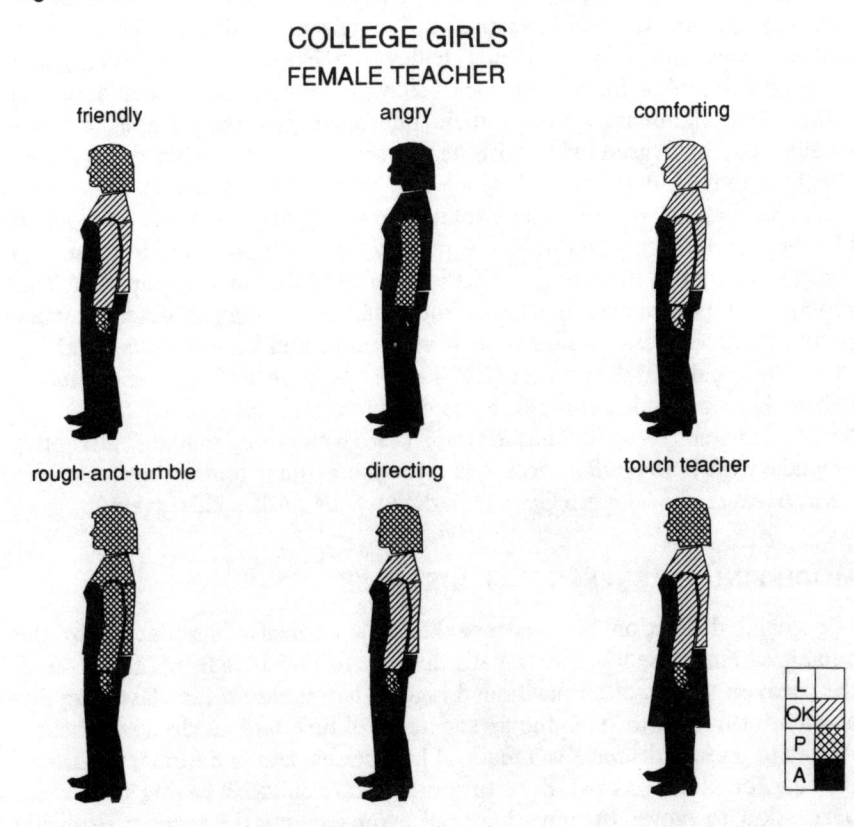

COLLEGE GIRLS
FEMALE TEACHER

friendly · angry · comforting

rough-and-tumble · directing · touch teacher

L	
OK	
P	
A	

Between adults, touching and invading personal space, as well as pointing and standing over the other person, were seen as increasing dominance in an additive way, especially for men (Henley and Harmon 1985). Henley and Harmon found that for women such behaviours tended to be seen as sexual rather than dominant (though their published pictures suggest that the women may have used submissive head postures, such as chin down (Zivin 1982), or looked up to the men which may have given this effect).

Women are attracted to controlling men provided they are competent (Touhey 1974). Men who direct a woman by touch are preferred to those who direct her verbally, though this effect is reversed if they are incompetent. This research underlines male teachers' caution about touching adolescent female pupils: good teachers' combination of dominance and warmth risks attracting them. As Henley and Harmon (1985) say, it is more difficult for women to behave in a way which is accepted as dominant and this is likely to apply to female teachers as well. Thus Beynon (1985) mentions that the disruptive secondary boys he studied accepted only one of their female teachers, Mrs Bear, because she 'is more like a man the way she pushes kids around'.

MODIFYING INTERPERSONAL DISTANCE

The social distinction between speaker and audience is reflected by the audience being close together but at a distance from, and in front of or around, the speaker, who is often positioned higher than them. In the classroom this is often formalised through the arrangement of furniture, as discussed below. Ability to control distance is a mark of high status, and in a formal classroom the teacher alone has the right to move freely, children having to ask her permission to move. In more informal arrangements the teacher explicitly gives permission for children to move or it is implicitly permitted (Denscombe 1980). By controlling distance, the teacher can regulate the quality of the interaction; particularly she can increase the salience of rewards or threats by approaching children closely, as mentioned above.

Teachers usually approach groups or individual children when they wish to help them, for practical reasons in ensuring good contact with minimal distraction to other members of the class. Miller (1979) suggests that closer approach promotes better learning by small groups, right down to intimate distance, but his report is very brief and does not provide evidence to back up his claims. Since erect posture is threatening (chapter 3) teachers often sit down or kneel when they want to approach children in a non-threatening way, for instance to discuss work (Figure 7.13: note that the brow-raise may also be a non-threatening signal – Keating 1985). The reduction in relative height (the opposite of 'standing over') may serve to reduce the threatening effect of close proximity (Figure 7.14). Alternatively, a teacher may use approach as an encouraging or disciplinary move; in the latter case she may merely 'drift' to the problem area with no overt signal of having noticed the potential

Figure 7.13 Kneeling close indicates non-threatening helpfulness, though the teacher's freedom to move round the room gives him a status which the boy lacks

Source: Reproduced with permission from Neill 1986a

disruption there. Her mere presence would be seen as increasing the risk to a point where conformity is the better option. As mentioned in chapter 5, leaning forward, as an intention movement of approach, may emphasise the teacher's enthusiastic attention to a child as he attempts to make a contribution; but the same movement, with a frowning expression, is a definite threat (Figure 1.3; Neill 1989a).

POSITION IN THE CLASSROOM – OVERALL PATTERNS

A number of investigators have tried to assess the significance of position in the classroom, and the earlier work is reviewed by Weinstein (1979). Two problems arise in such an assessment: whether differences in interaction related to position are the results or the causes of the differences in position adopted, and analysing the actual relationship between position and amount of interaction. We may deal briefly with the second problem first, as the available literature does not indicate that a level of statistical sophistication

Figure 7.14 Here the roles are reversed from Figure 7.13. The girl's close approach, standing over the teacher (behind, so he is at a further disadvantage), challenges his authority. This is accentuated by her hand on hip lean (compare Figure 3.15)

has been used comparable to that exerted on, for instance, the searching patterns of animals, which have some formal similarities in terms of being a distribution of effort in a two-dimensional space. For example, Gray (1984a, 1984b) describes a sophisticated computer-aided tracking system for recording teachers' movements round the classroom, and a case study of its application to dance teaching. However, this system does not yet seem to have produced any statistical account of classroom movement.

Reid (1980), working with biology teachers, contrasted behaviour between periods when the teacher was within four feet of the blackboard and when she was in the body of the room. This factor had more effect than any of the the others Reid studied, such as the age or sex of the teacher, size of class, type of syllabus, or personality. Teachers using the blackboard-confined style lectured their classes more, and used pupils' responses for further talk of their own. When teachers were itinerant, they accepted the children's ideas more, and were more likely to receive further contributions from the children. Children were more likely to be working constructively, especially for prolonged periods. In Reid's view, itinerant teachers were more encouraging to their pupils, and gave their pupils better evidence that their ideas were valued. They might also, because they are closer to their pupils, receive nonverbal feedback which indicates the pupils' understanding. By contrast the more isolated teacher at the board is dependent on what the pupils say, which may more often be unsatisfactory.

However, these comparisons were made within the same lessons, and may reflect different segments of the lesson (Gump 1975). Children would be expected to behave differently during a theoretical explanation and written or practical work. Ideally we need a comparison between the same teachers, using board-bound and itinerant styles with the same material.

Reid gives some information on changes in student teachers' behaviour (during theoretical teaching only) after their tutor had counselled them to move around the room more. This suggests that the students moved around more and also adopted a more indirect, sociable style. As Reid points out, the quality of the data is inadequate for a statistical analysis and the students' behaviour might have changed in any case as they gained experience. Further work in this area would seem well worthwhile.

We may consider a teacher in a standard box classroom as having 25 to 30 positions into which she can distribute her 'effort', such as looking children in the eye, asking them questions or, in individual work sessions, going round helping them with their work. For simplicity, we can compare this problem with two theoretical situations in the animal literature. The first, comparable with the teacher going round the room, is searching behaviour (e.g. Huntingford 1984). Here the most efficient strategy is one which searches the area evenly, with modifications to allow a longer stay in more productive areas. Applying this analogy to the teacher, we might expect her, on the simplest model, to quarter the classroom, distributing her attention equally, within the limitations of chance. The substantial deviations from equal attention to each child which do occur (Garner and Bing 1973) indicate that the teacher is responsive either to children's immediate demands, or, as in Garner and Bing's study, to her own view of the children, presumably relying on her experience of their demands. Since the same pattern of unequal attention seems to occur across a range of ages and teaching styles (e.g. Jackson and Lahaderne 1967, Boydell 1978) it seems likely that factors related to individual children and the teacher's view of them are the overwhelming influences on relative amount of attention, and that position in the classroom has nothing like so large an effect. In other words, an attempt to apply the 'searching strategy' model, with its assumption that the teacher's next move around the classroom is primarily predictable from her existing position, seems likely to prove wasted effort.

A second simplified model from animal behaviour initially seems likely to be more productive; this could be termed 'searching from a centre'. A simple example would be a bird searching from its nest. Other things being equal, effort would be concentrated in areas near the nest. The resulting pattern has a superficial similarity to that found by Sommer (1969), Adams and Biddle (1970), Turner (1982), Koneya (1976) and others (e.g. Weinstein 1979), where, in a formal classroom with the usual teacher base at the front, most attention is given to children at the front and in the centre of the room. Adams and Biddle describe a triangular or abbreviated kite-shaped 'action zone' with the base at the front row, tapering to a point at the middle of the back of the room, and Turner (op. cit.) found a similar pattern.

The overall picture is one consistent with proximity, modified by direction of gaze, largely accounting for the amount of attention individual children get. One influence on this distribution is the teacher's usual orientation, since, as described below, children whom she faces are likely to get more attention than those off to one side. An unpublished study by Whittle (pers. comm.), for example, indicated that in a classroom where the teacher's desk was in one corner, the main axis of the 'action zone' was obliquely across the room, reflecting the usual direction in which the teacher faced from her desk.

A circular or semi-circular pattern, often on the floor, around a seated or standing teacher is often adopted where space permits, and is not peculiar to schools. Morris (1977) illustrates both General Montgomery and a South American Indian chief addressing their warriors in this pattern! Turk (1985) suggests that, for business talks, semi-circular or horseshoe-shaped seating arrangements should always be adopted, with a single row of seats or a double row if numbers require; but that a rectangular block of seats should only be permitted as a last resort if the lack of space in the room permits nothing else. However, school classrooms tend to lack space for economic reasons and fixed seating more often tends to be arranged in a block with the seats all facing the speaker. Though this means that some members of the group are further away, they have better eye contact and a better view of any visual aids used. There does not seem to be any unequivocal research evidence on the relative effectiveness of the different arrangements (Weinstein 1979).

WHAT CAUSES POSITION EFFECTS?

Action zones of the type described by Adams and Biddle may be specific to the formal classroom, where the position of the teacher is predictable, and there is therefore differentiation between the experience of children in different parts of the room. Comparisons between classrooms in the same school suggested action zones occurred in formal but not informal classrooms (Turner 1982). This raises the question whether the pattern observed by Adams and Biddle (1970) is due to children choosing seats to match their existing preferences for amount of interaction with the teacher or their behaviour changing to match their position.

The available evidence suggests both factors play a part. Koneya's (1976) approach to the problem was through short-term experiments with newly formed groups of students, so that class habits had not yet had time to crystallise. Base-rates for talking were established during a brief class discussion in a circle. Koneya assumed, perhaps optimistically, that this would give an unbiased estimate of readiness to verbalise. The students were then given a short break to indicate their preferred seats on a plan of a conventional row-and-column classroom. High verbalisers marked more preferences for central seats than low or moderate verbalisers. The discussion then resumed with the students randomly seated in a row-and-column room. Students in the central front 'action zone' talked more. This applied overall and to the moderate verbalisers (the central two quartiles of the whole group) but not to the low verbalisers. Koneya's interpretation is that low verbalisers wish to avoid talking under any circumstances, even when placed in a 'star' position. The differing preferences and the effect of different seating positions should therefore be seen as more related to the negative choices of the low verbalisers than the positive preferences of the rest. Moderate verbalisers, Koneya felt, could participate effectively in a star position, but would normally avoid doing so. On the other hand he felt that a back seat might be aversive and frustrating for a high verbaliser.

High verbalisers are also likely to be the most dominant individuals, and central seats in university classes are the most strongly defended if someone else takes them during a break (Haber 1980). Haber found that their original occupants were more likely to ask for them back, whereas occupants of side and back seats were more likely to move elsewhere, or leave the class, sometimes with a group of friends. Back-seat occupants were more likely to be abusive. Side seats, and seats occupied by women, were more likely to be taken over than central seats, as their occupants were less dominating. Seats occupied by blacks were seldom taken, probably because potential invaders were afraid of a strong defence and accusations of racial prejudice.

University classes show rather different patterns from most school classes (except for academically oriented classes) as the central group of students is more strongly committed to learning (chapter 1). They are also the highest achievers (Griffith 1921). Peripheral students, especially those at the back, seem to do worst, apparently because they are more likely to be distracted. The peripheral situation itself seems to be critical, as the same seat can attract a relatively low score when it is a peripheral seat in a small group, and a higher one when it is a central seat in a larger group being taught in the same room.

In conventional secondary box classrooms the most dominant and disruptive children in what tend to be anti-school oriented classes tend to choose the seats furthest from the teacher, obliquely across the room when the teacher's desk is on one side (Macpherson 1983). Here they are free to indulge in whatever distractions from work are appropriate. Macpherson reported that closeness to the teacher was in roughly inverse relation to position in the dominance hierarchy (and therefore roughly in proportion to school-orientedness). Children at the back had a particular advantage because they could observe what those in front of them were doing, could attack or tease them relatively unscathed because of the difficulty of turning round to resist or counterattack without attracting the teacher's notice, and could readily watch those in front and tell on them if they misbehaved, without being easily watched themselves. When the teachers tried to overcome this by moving their base to the opposite corner where the dissident section of the class was, the dominant children sometimes counter-moved by displacing those in the front corner of the room, so the seating pattern was neatly reversed. Similar patterns of behaviour are probably widely distributed.

So far, the indication is that children choose positions to match their own characteristics. However, both Schwebel and Cherlin (1972) and Moore and Glynn (1984) have found that experimentally moving primary-school children (in America and New Guinea respectively) affects children's behaviour. Moore and Glynn found that teachers had no explicit theory for assigning children to seats at the start of term, but tended to give attentive pupils seats at the front of the room. Over half the pupils would have preferred front-row seats, more than there was room for. Children who moved forwards were seen as more attentive and likeable by their teachers, and tended to spend more time engaged in work, though the latter difference was not significant. Moore and Glynn exchanged children from areas which received a high rate of questions (which were closer to the teacher in five out of six pairs) with children from low-rate areas. Children received more questions when they moved from a low question-rate area to a high-rate area (and vice-versa) in ten out of twelve cases. This effect was similar in both classrooms. Moore and Glynn's analysis compensated for temporal variations in the overall level of the teachers' behaviour, a potentially confounding influence in studies of this type. In both studies the alterations were of fairly short duration (less than three weeks) and it is possible that the effects might have worn off with longer exposure, though there is little evidence of this in Moore and Glynn's longitudinal profiles. It is of course possible that the results of such manipulations would be different with secondary children.

In a circular or similar arrangement, such as a university seminar, those facing the tutor make more contribution than those sideways on or facing in the same direction (Sommer 1969, Caproni, Levine, O'Neal, McDonald and Garwood 1977). In Caproni et al.'s study, the students did not systematically choose positions so that the same students always occupied seats which gave them more eye contact with the teacher than others, even though there was a folder which marked where the teacher was going to sit when the students chose their places. Caproni et al. therefore considered differences in the amount of talk between positions reflected the effect of seating position, rather than the effects of individual students. On the other hand studies such as that of Hiers and Heckel (1977) indicate that students who wish to dominate a discussion will choose more visible seats. As with the choice of seating position in the room, work with secondary children might give rather different results.

ROWS AND TABLES

One of the characteristics of the progressive classroom has been a move away from ranks of desks all facing the teacher to groups working at tables. This move accompanied that towards open-plan classrooms (chapter 8) and reflects the same child-centred philosophy. As well as reducing the teacher's influence, the tables should position the children at an ideal distance for cooperative interaction (Sommer 1969). Sommer's work was based on questionnaires, but indicated that people preferred to be at a 'personal' distance for cooperative work. Given the same size table children preferred different positions to adults (side by side or on two sides of a corner, whereas adults preferred to be face to face) because their smaller size made their personal distances smaller than those of adults. However, more recent studies have shown that these apparently suitable provisions for cooperative interaction are not always actually effective in producing it. Little cooperative work was seen in the ORACLE study of primary classrooms (Galton, Simon and Croll 1980), and a follow-up study and survey of the literature suggested many problems in using group work effectively (Galton 1989). Bennett, Desforges, Cockburn and Wilkinson's (1984) detailed study found that most interaction among groups of infants was at a low level – requesting materials and so on. When children did try to assist each other their help was often misleading.

Large-scale studies of primary classrooms have shown little use of collaborative group work, in which the children are genuinely working together rather than in parallel at the same table (Galton 1989). One reason is the dominance of the teacher. Galton found that children preferred, given the choice, to work in a situation where they could be sure of feedback from the teacher as to whether their answers were correct. They also felt that only written work was 'really' work. They appeared to be concerned that they might be wasting their time in a group discussion.

Bennett and Blundell (1983) and Wheldall, Morris, Vaughan and Ng (1981) have assessed the effect of experimentally changing table-based groups in primary classrooms to row-based arrangements. In both cases they found that attention to work and work performance improved in the rows, and similar marked improvements were obtained by Wheldall and Lam (1987) with special-school children. These studies suffer from fairly short intervention periods, but Wheldall and Glynn (1989) claim, on the basis of these and other studies with longer intervention periods, that alterations in classroom seating are a potent way of influencing classroom operation.

The most interesting of these other studies is Wheldall and Olds's (1987) alteration of seating arrangements by sex. In one class where children normally sat at segregated tables they were required to sit with boys and girls side by side. The children spent more time on task as a result. In a second class in the same school where children normally sat in mixed tables they were required to segregate; time on task fell, though interpretation of the results is complicated by the teacher's increased use of criticism and her change of working practices to include worksheets. Time on task was about 90 per cent in mixed groups, and 75 per cent or less in segregated groups. This applied whether these groupings were the class's normal way of working or the experimental alterations. This suggests that the study is measuring a real phenomenon and not merely short-term changes related to the experimental alterations, though it would be valuable to have results from more classrooms.

Social interaction between group members seems to be the critical factor in these studies. For junior-school children, tables encourage interaction because the face-to-face arrangement makes it easier than side-to-side seating in rows. Since at this age children mainly talk to same-sex peers, mixed-sex tables discourage interaction. All these studies tested conventional 'formal' work, and different results might have been obtained with project work, for instance.

However, another study, reported very briefly in Wheldall and Olds's (1987) paper, gives a contradictory result for a secondary class of 13–14-year-olds, and indicates that we need comparable material across a range of age-groups. This class were normally seated with sexes mixed (it is unclear whether this was in rows or tables). On-task behaviour, which averaged slightly less than 80 per cent in mixed seating, rose to 91 per cent in single-sex seating. Very little detail is given, and the paper does not mention or explore the discrepancy between the results at the primary and secondary ages. There may be real differences between pre-pubertal and post-pubertal children. For example the latter may be more prone to flirtation and sexual harassment (chapter 9). If so, mixed tables would lead to more interaction which interfered with work, as opposed to less in the case of the younger classes.

THE SOCIAL PROCESSES UNDERLYING GROUPING EFFECTS

Streeck's (1983) detailed analysis of a group of five 7–9-year-olds illustrates some of the difficulties of getting successful group work. It also shows the nonverbal signals which could be valuable in indicating from a distance to the teacher how the group is performing. The children were working on a peer-tutoring task assigned by the teacher, where one child had been given a task to explain to the others. Much of the interaction was concerned with negotiating the tutoring task without upsetting the existing relationships between the two boys and three girls in the group. This process worked most smoothly where the tutoring child was a girl who was a dominant member of the peer group; she was able to use her rank to insist on the distinction between her roles as peer and tutor. With other children the tutoring task posed a threat to the existing order of the group and the more powerful members of the group often resisted direction from a tutoring child who normally had low status. The current status of relationships between the group members, as Streeck illustrates, was clearly signalled from minute to minute by their positions and postures. When the dominant girl was explaining the task to the rest of the group, all formed a single cluster with her workbook as its focus. When the girl was acting as tutor to one or two of the others, she and her tutee formed a coherent group, while those children who already understood were dissociated as they continued with their work. For much of the time the dissociation between boys and girls was indicated by their working in separate clusters at opposite sides of the table; at the point where they were involved in a dispute over interpretation of the work, the clusters drew together and glared at the opposition. Once the task was completed, the members of the group lazed back and began to look around the room. This opened up the boundaries of the group, thus signalling to other members of the class that they were available for interaction.

As well as these major postural shifts, Streeck (1983) describes complex second-to-second changes, especially when one of two friends monitored the other moving to talk to a third party. Every time this happened, the status quo was restored by other group members blocking off the child who had moved: they masked their face with their hand or leant their head on their hand, on the side towards her. This cut-off of communication forced her to return to her original position. These finer-scale patterns, though of significance to the children's interaction, would not be readily apparent to a teacher briefly glancing at the group. However, the major shifts are potentially valuable as indications to the teacher whether the group is working together as she intends. It will be apparent from this brief description, and is even more apparent from Streeck's account, that the salience of interpersonal relationships to children is potentially a major influence on the success of their work in informal classroom settings.

All this evidence is not to say that children cannot be encouraged to work successfully in groups (Tann 1981). Children who found it difficult to contribute in whole-class discussion could be highly effective in the more intimate atmosphere of a group. Often leadership and organisational qualities were brought out by the group situation. Boys' groups, especially, were helpful to their weaker members, who did much better than in the class situation, and were particularly effective in discussion. Mixed groups were less successful, especially with older children (11-year-olds in a secondary school, as opposed to 10-year-olds in a junior school). This is consistent with the problems Streeck (1983) observed. The success of group work was critically dependent on the mix of individuals in the group, and the match of the task to their abilities. It was more difficult to get this correct in the secondary school. As cooperative group work can improve social relationships, especially between children of different races (Smith, Boulton and Cowie 1989), and reduce bullying (Smith and Ahmad 1989) at least in the middle school, ensuring the conditions for success seems a justifiable use of teacher time.

SUMMARY

Seating patterns and classroom layout represent individual distance in a petrified form. Individual distance is normally largely controlled by the teacher. Touch, the most extreme reduction of individual distance, shows this; only the youngest children are normally permitted to touch the teacher, but she can touch them. Individual distance increases with age, and touch correspondingly decreases in acceptability. Classroom touch is mostly to the neutral areas of arm and shoulder, as for other social situations. Touch increases the effect of both praise and criticism. Similar effects can be achieved by moving closer to children.

Children in the central area of a conventional box classroom, or facing the teacher in a ring or horseshoe arrangement, participate more. Most evidence suggests that this is due to children making seat choices to match their preferred level of participation. Those who wish to be involved sit centrally; shyer children choose peripheral seats. However, there is some evidence that if children are moved, their participation level changes to fit the area to which they have been moved, at least over the short term. Thus a nonparticipating child will participate if moved into a central area.

Primary children work better when seating is rearranged from tables to rows and from single-sex to mixed-sex groups; these rearrangements seem to decrease conversation which interferes with work. Detailed studies of group interaction indicate considerable time can be spent on negotiating social relationships and this can interfere with task performance. However, groups can be academically productive, and improve social relationships, if teachers can get them to work satisfactorily.

Chapter 8
The use of space

In this chapter we consider mainly the spatial arrangement of classrooms and school buildings, but some related issues are included. The design of school buildings has attracted attention because it has been thought to offer opportunities for the educational establishment to exert unobtrusive control over the way schools operate (Evans 1974, 1979a, Cooper 1979, 1981). The classic box classroom appears to offer the teacher a well-defined territory, which she can mould to project her own image through suitable choice of equipment and wall displays (Delamont 1976). This is equivalent to the 'stage' settings used in other contexts, described by Goffman (1972) in his dramaturgical model. Goffman indicates that people, especially when their work involves performance in front of a customer group, control the setting to assist their performance, while keeping the customers out of their backstage areas. Goffman contrasts the elegance aimed at in the hotel dining room with what goes on in the kitchen, and the classrooms and staffroom of a traditionally built school parallel this. Staffroom 'news' (Hammersley 1984) tends to be about and to the disadvantage of patrons (pupils) in the same way as kitchen conversation, and school staffrooms tend to be as notoriously squalid as hotel kitchens.

MESSAGES CONVEYED BY SCHOOL BUILDINGS

The possibility that the form or layout of classrooms can convey messages about the type of education which is expected has been raised by a number of authors (e.g. Getzels 1974, Proshansky and Wolfe 1975). The Elton Report (Department of Education and Science and Welsh Office 1989) emphasises the importance to school discipline of cared-for buildings, in which damage is promptly repaired and children's work attractively displayed.

The Elton Report assumes school buildings send 'messages' about the kind of education provided inside to those who enter them. There is some evidence for this view (Weinstein and Woolfolk 1981). Weinstein and Woolfolk assessed the reactions of student teachers, non-teacher students and 10-year-old children to slides of primary classrooms. Sets of slides of two or three classrooms were used to illustrate each of four categories of room: an orderly tidy informal open-plan classroom; an orderly formal box classroom; a disorderly open-plan classroom and a disorderly box classroom. Both sets of students rated teachers in the open classrooms as kinder and more inventive; they also expected pupils to be happier and more involved and teachers to be more organised, but these differences were small and not statistically significant. They rated neat classrooms significantly more highly than messy ones for all four categories, as did the 10-year-olds. However, the 10-year-olds did not differentiate between the open and box classrooms. Weinstein and Woolfolk suggest this may be because the adults have stereotypes of the kind of education which happens in the different types of school, while the children in their sample came from a progressive school working in box classrooms. It would be interesting to compare the opinions of children across a wider range of school experience.

THE OPEN-PLAN SCHOOL AND TERRITORIALITY

The general feeling that the traditional school design favoured teacher-controlled education led to the building of open-plan schools being encouraged when educationalist opinion moved towards child-centred methods (Cooper 1979, 1981). The desire to build schools more cheaply may also have been a contributory factor (Maclure 1984), though, especially at the secondary level, building in provision for future flexibility, which may never actually be used, increases costs (O.E.C.D. 1976). The discussion which follows concentrates on primary schools, as open-plan design has been relatively little adopted for secondary schools. The literature on open-plan secondary schools does not investigate the influence of design on behaviour in a systematic way (McMillan 1983, Denscombe 1980). As Cooper (1979, 1981) indicates, the aim of the Department of Education and Science through its Building Bulletins was to encourage the building of schools where children could move freely to investigate whatever learning experiences were relevant at the time – in other words the children were seen as the main user group rather than the teachers. Building Bulletins 53 and 56 (D.E.S. 1976, 1978; see also D.E.S. 1987) give examples of this type of approach; we will investigate how effective open-plan schools actually are later in the chapter.

One possible factor underlying the desire to give children more freedom of movement was the concept of territory, which had some currency at the time through popularised works drawing parallels between animal and human behaviour (e.g. Ardrey 1967). However, there is no evidence that territory, in this form, is relevant to classroom behaviour. For most of their evolutionary history humans have been group-living hunters, and, if they defended an area, would have done so as a group like other group-living predators (Taylor 1988). Taylor suggests that territorial customs could have evolved culturally, as patterns of behaviour which are generally advantageous to the groups involved. Such cultural evolution would normally rapidly lead to changes in territorial customs to fit new circumstances. However, following Boyd and Richerson's model of cultural evolution, Taylor considers that territorial customs may show cultural inertia, persisting when they are no longer functional. If we apply this to the classroom situation, for example the 'stage settings' described above, teachers' views on what is an appropriate physical setting for their work are likely to be linked to their concept of the profession. Control over use of space is linked to professional autonomy. This may account for the problems in getting teachers to work together in open-plan spaces, mentioned below, as dilution of individual control over space represents dilution of autonomy.

THE CONSEQUENCES OF OPEN-PLAN DESIGN

'Open-plan' design covers a range of types, from conventional classrooms, but lacking doors so free movement is possible between them, to completely uninterrupted space with a free line of vision between areas. There are also great variations in the size of open areas, which in primary schools can vary from linked pairs of classrooms to the entire school (Bennett, Andrae, Hegarty and Wade 1980). No agreed way of measuring openness has yet appeared, though attempts have been made to devise an index of openness (Neill 1982a, Neill, Denham, Schaffer and Markus 1977). This index, based on an index for assessing the outside shape of buildings, is the ratio of the perimeter of a circular space of the same size as the area available to the children (i.e. the minimum possible perimeter the space could have had) to the actual perimeter, including partitions above child height and excluding doors which could be opened. The resulting index gives high values for undivided playrooms (which approach the circular space). Buildings divided into small rooms between which children can move freely and modern subdivided open-plan designs have lower values of the index but the values are similar for the two types of design. Since it takes into account only the building plan, it is primarily oriented to the visual effect of the layout. Other approaches, such as the Early Childhood Physical Environment Scales (Moore 1987), have used rating scales, in this case a combination of five-point ratings on ten scales. These cover the spatial enclosure of activity areas, their separation from circulation paths and their visual openness to other parts of the playroom; their appropriateness in terms of size, storage and completeness of equipment to small-group activities; the overall degree of softness and flexibility in the space; and the variety of seating and working positions, and amount of resources. This scale covers a wider range of aspects of the provision, but with some apparent degree of overlap between scales.

Open spaces are likely to cause visual and auditory distraction, and to make communication more difficult through higher noise levels. An extreme example of this is described by Stebbins (1973), who studied schools in Jamaica, where formal teaching of large classes was carried out in buildings where classrooms were only partially walled, to allow for ventilation in the hot climate. The complete openness of the rooms allowed children (as well as dogs and birds, which caused far less disturbance) to enter or leave the class more or less at will, or carry on conversations with children outside. With the large numbers of children involved, teachers tolerated these disruptions because it was not really practical for them to catch and discipline the miscreants. Though Stebbins's observations were not conducted on a systematic basis, he felt that some of the problems resulting from this lack of definition of the boundaries of the school itself were recurring in the open-plan Canadian school he studied, where children had similar free access between spaces within the walls of the school. Problems can occur even in the corridors of conventional schools, if freedom of movement causes traffic jams and disputes result (D.E.S. and Welsh Office 1989).

A large enclosed space creates a relatively hostile acoustic environment for the purposes of teaching. This problem did not occur in the open Jamaican schools, where sound would have been dispersed in the open air! The acoustic qualities of the building relate primarily to the volume of the spaces and the surfaces used; the following outline is based on D.E.S. Building Bulletin 51 (1975). Carpeting can reduce the impact noise from children's feet and the movement of furniture, and was recommended by the Elton Report (D.E.S. and Welsh Office 1989); it was also felt it gave a less institutional atmosphere, and that carpeted spaces were therefore treated with more respect by children. Open buildings are noisier than subdivided ones of the same size, given similar furnishings and surface finishes (see also Durlak, Beardsley and Murray 1972).

Firstly, larger-volume spaces have a longer reverberation time; in other words, a sound, once produced, tends to echo round for longer. As a result, successive sounds, such as footfalls, tend to overlap and produce higher total noise levels, whereas in a small space the first sound would have died away before the second one was produced. Even if no more noise is being produced in the larger space, the small one will be quieter; but the occupants of the larger space are likely to compound the problem by raising their voices to make themselves heard. Larger rooms often have higher ceilings than smaller ones for reasons of aesthetic balance – a low ceiling over a large area gives a cave-like atmosphere, even when rooflights can be used – which further increases their volume, and therefore their reverberation time.

Secondly, walls, even of light construction, attenuate sounds much better than empty space. Low partitions, such as are used in many open-plan classrooms, are not so effective, even if their light construction does not make them acoustically transparent, as sound gets over them by bouncing off the ceiling. They can, however, partially alleviate one of the major problems described by the D.E.S. Building Bulletin: the effect of this increased noise level in restricting the types of teaching which can be effectively carried out in open classrooms.

This problem arises because the teacher's voice is attenuated at a rate which is proportional to the square of the distance from her, so the further members of large groups cannot understand sufficiently unless background noise is low. Whole-class teaching therefore requires good acoustic conditions. As D.E.S. Bulletin 51 indicates, if several teachers are talking to class groups, they will distract each others' pupils unless the teaching area is very spacious so they can be well separated. Spacious open buildings are likely to be more expensive than buildings with walls which will give the same amount of acoustic separation in much less space. Even at a fairly high ambient noise level, small groups can work effectively, since all members are close to one another. In fact a highish level of background noise (especially 'white noise' of the type produced by ventilating or heating fans) may actually be beneficial for small-group or individual work, as it will mask other conversations, which would be potentially distracting in, for instance, a very quiet library. Unfortunately, much of the evidence now available suggests that individualised work can be less effective than whole-class methods, as discussed in the next section.

Weinstein and Weinstein (1979) compared reading performance under noisy and quiet conditions in an open-plan classroom and found that the higher noise level caused no deterioration of standard of work, by children of a range of abilities, relative to the quieter conditions, though the work was carried out more slowly. This was a carefully conducted study, in that the work was introduced by the teachers as part of the children's normal work, was carried out over a period of three weeks, and used naturally occurring noisy and quiet periods of the day, which were assigned in a balanced design to the various conditions. The quiet periods were at a very low noise level (averaging 47 dBA) and a normal conversational voice would have been intelligible at 9 metres; the noisy ones averaged 60 dBA, so that conversation would only have been intelligible at less than 2 metres, though this noise level is less than that occurring in some educational settings (Weinstein 1979). As Weinstein and Weinstein point out, their study school was in a good area, with cooperative children, and results might have been somewhat different elsewhere. Noise is also likely to interfere with individual work less than work which involves listening to talk. However, Weinstein's (1979) review suggested that even severe aircraft noise seemed to have a limited effect on school outcomes, though she felt the cumulative effects might be more severe than the short-term ones. Acoustics may not be the most pressing concern for teachers. When Cooper (1985) surveyed teachers' opinions in ten primary schools of a range of open-plan and enclosed designs, heating, ventilation and lighting attracted more comment, mainly critical, than acoustics, though Cooper does not relate comments to particular types of design.

ASSESSING THE EFFECTS OF BUILDING DESIGN

The potential limitations on teaching style imposed by open-plan schools illustrate one of the problems of assessing their effectiveness. The ORACLE study (Galton, Simon and Croll 1980) found no difference in the effectiveness of teaching in open-plan and conventional box classrooms once differences in the proportions of different teaching styles had been allowed for. The less effective styles tended to be more common in the open-plan classrooms, and these styles were adopted predominantly by the younger teachers. There are several possible explanations for this situation. As indicated above, talking to the whole class, which appears on the evidence of ORACLE and other studies to be the most effective method at least for the transmission of complex ideas (Galton and Simon 1980, Mortimore, Sammons, Stoll, Lewis and Ecob 1988), may be impractical in open-plan schools. Teachers who would have used it in other buildings may be forced by experience to use other methods. Alternatively, teachers who prefer class-teaching methods, which go with a generally more formal approach, may avoid applying for jobs in open-plan schools as they do not feel they can teach satisfactorily there. As discussed below, if appointed they may try to persist in methods which do not match the space in which they find themselves; Bennett et al. (1980) found that buildings were frequently being used in inappropriate and ineffective ways. A third possibility is that, as at the time of the ORACLE data collection (the early 1970s) open-plan schools tended to be newer, they may have had a disproportionate number of younger staff. In this case, experience might be expected to improve performance in open-plan schools. The lack of specific training for working in open-plan schools (Bennett et al. 1980) is also likely to have been a contributory factor. This situation illustrates a general problem in assessing the effect of building design, that of distinguishing the effects of different buildings from those of their different staffs (see also Moore 1987). As we shall see below, attempts have been made to overcome this by experimental studies in preschools, which offer greater possibilities because they are not linked to the statutory education system; but difficulties remain in any such attempt.

One major problem is the tendency for staff to develop traditions in the way they use buildings, often contrary to the intentions of the architect, most clearly seen in residential institutions (Rivlin and Wolfe 1972, Wolfe and Rivlin 1972). These traditions may persist even when changed circumstances, such as a change in the number of children in the institution, make them no longer appropriate. Traditions interfere with the most obvious way to assess building effects – by making short-term changes, within the period in which staff, children, curriculum and weather would be expected to remain the same. Were it possible to get instantaneous reactions to such changes, differences between conditions would in theory be a pure reflection of the effects of the various conditions. As we discuss below, such experimental changes have more often been tried in preschools, but there too they may fail to have effects merely by virtue of their short-term nature. Staff may continue to use the building according to their established traditions, or they may avoid making adaptations which they would have to make if they knew the changes were going to be permanent. A permanent wall or partition, which the staff know they can do nothing about, may have greater effects than an otherwise identical temporary partition. However, once an experimental condition has been implemented long enough for other historical changes to take place, it becomes necessary to separate the effects of the experimental change from the other co-occurring changes, and problems of analysis become very much more difficult (Cook and Campbell 1979).

Traditions of use appear in their strongest form in the way in which some staff continue to use open-plan facilities in the same way as traditional box classrooms. Staff may use cupboards or screens to divide off spaces while retaining the overall open-plan ethos, with children being able to move freely between the spaces: but there are several examples of staff using dividers to convert open spaces into defined private areas, each a box classroom without walls. Angus, Evans and Parkin (1975) give Australian examples. In some cases teachers used one of a pair of open-plan areas as a store, and prevented children moving freely round the other; one teacher carefully rearranged the trapezoidal tables she was provided with to make rows of desks facing the blackboard. Children's movement was restricted, often clustered round the teacher (see also Rivlin and Rothenberg 1976, in America). English teachers in areas which were intended to be used for team-teaching worked individually (Cooper 1979), forbidding children to cross the demarcation lines between them. Canadian teachers had a similarly conservative attitude to innovative buildings (Durlak and Lehman 1974).

In Cooper's view (1981) much of the problem arises because open-plan schools were built with a view to the children as the main 'clients', the intention being that the teachers would be forced by the logic of the building design to operate in a way which allowed the children to learn in the way which the educational authorities thought desirable. Cooper's view that this is a dubious proposition is supported by evidence from Galton et al. (1980) that when classes change teachers the behaviour of the class changes to conform to the teacher's style rather than vice versa. In other words the intentions of the architects and the preferences of the children are likely to be ineffective against the preferred methods of the teachers. Bennett et al.'s (1980) case studies confirm this; they included a pair of identical buildings which were being used in quite different ways. In one the teachers taught formally and on a whole-class basis, with the children's movement being strongly controlled, in line with the teachers Cooper studied. In the other a much more informal organisation was adopted, with a stress on interpersonal relationships, parents heavily involved with working with the children, and children having considerable freedom to choose which activity to do at a particular time. Overall these results suggest that the direct influence of building design, as opposed to the influence of building design in conjunction with staff traditions or philosophies of use, is relatively weak, and, as we shall see below, the work from preschools tends to confirm this.

Furniture layout changes are subject to similar problems to those discussed for room design; a lengthy period of change is necessary to avoid novelty effects. The problem can to some extent be mitigated by the use of time-series analysis, as in the case of a careful study by Weinstein (1977), which followed suggestions on the potential usefulness of layout changes by Proshansky and Wolfe (1975). Weinstein carried out an analysis of existing use of the various activity areas available in an open classroom; some areas were under-used, while others were overcrowded. As a result, children's range of learning experiences was restricted. The teacher was aware of this pattern of use and dissatisfied with it, but her verbal attempts to redistribute the children's activity were ineffective. In the light of her observations, and the teacher's and children's comments, Weinstein modified the furnishings and arrangement of the activity areas. After a settling-in period of three days, analysis indicated that usage of the areas available was much more even, and most of the desired changes in use had occurred, particularly a widening of the range of activities children carried out in areas which had previously only been used in a restricted way. This result was especially striking since there was little overall change in the children's behaviour, though where changes had occurred they had been positive; large physical activity, fidgeting and passive behaviour disappeared and were replaced by more educationally valuable activities.

Weinstein was well aware that changes might be due to the teacher rather than the physical alterations; she therefore did not involve the teacher in her alterations, and monitored the teacher's verbal behaviour before and after the alterations to satisfy herself that it did not change (though she gives no details of the categories she used to record the teacher's behaviour, or the frequencies of these categories). However, since the changes were consistent with the teacher's policy, the children may have been sensitised to use them, or they may have believed that the teacher instigated them, and some synergy between the teacher and the experimental changes is probable. Pre- and post-alteration observation periods were also rather short, at ten working days each. These factors may account for the differences between this study and work such as that of Cooper (1979), mentioned above.

This conclusion is supported by the outcome of a second study by Weinstein (1982). This assessed the effect of the introduction of privacy booths, enclosed carrels which would allow a child to carry on with work without visual distraction or being bothered by other class members. When first introduced into the classroom these were extremely popular, and an extra booth had to be provided, but within a month of their first introduction use had declined dramatically as the novelty wore off. Weinstein's (1979) review of the previous literature, which was rather inadequate at that point, had suggested that privacy was of limited importance in schools.

Space-arrangement factors have attracted most research interest, but there have been some studies looking at other aspects of open-plan schools. As mentioned in the previous section, effective acoustic separation between groups depends on adequate space, whereas space in many open-plan schools is restricted. Clift, Hutchings and Povey (1984) took advantage of the reduction of primary-school numbers at that date to compare the responses to a standard questionnaire of 11-year-old children in two pairs of schools: a spacious pair with about 2.3 square metres of space per pupil, and a space-restricted pair with about 1.2 square metres per pupil. Attitudes to social aspects of the classroom situation (i.e. attitudes to their own class and their classroom image, conformity and relationship with the teacher) were more positive in the more spacious schools. These attitudes were felt to be the most likely to be affected by the classroom situation, including the availability of space. By contrast, more general attitudes (attitude to school, interest in school work and views on the importance of doing well) and more personal attitudes (anxiety, social adjustment and academic self-image) were not affected. As Clift et al. point out, the results are of a rather tentative nature, especially given the very different pattern of responses between the sexes which they obtained compared to previous uses of the questionnaire. There is also no observational evidence that the differences in attitudes were in fact accompanied by differences in behaviour.

Overcrowded spaces could have the further effect of seriously increasing distraction where children have freedom to move around. Distraction does not appear to have been studied in detail, by systematically comparing children's concentration spans under different circumstances and checking what the apparent causes of distraction are. Such observations should be possible in principle, though laborious observation would be needed to capture the original cause of each period of distraction. The problems, discussed above, of teasing out which of a range of possible causes is the main contributor to an effect, would be equally salient for distraction. Some less detailed work in this area has been carried out. Bennett et al. (1980) conducted case studies which followed individual children for extended periods of the school day. They showed that some children spent protracted periods engaged in work, while others were constantly distracted. Their account stressed organisational factors, such as the amount of time spent in transition between activities (Gump 1975) in schools which used the open-plan layout to move children between areas for different activities, even when the areas were not specialised for the relevant activity.

RESEARCH ON PRESCHOOL DESIGN

Preschools offer the possibility of controlled experiment because, as attendance is not compulsory, their organisation and children's attendance can be manipulated by the researcher more fully than in statutory-age education. However, full control requires a unit set up by the researcher and there is relatively little research using this expensive option. The research of Smith and Connolly (1980), which investigated space among other influences on preschool children's behaviour, is an example, but this research covered only the amount of space, rather than layout.

Normally a larger preschool will not only have more space, but more equipment and more children and staff, making it impossible to separate the influence of these confounded factors. Smith and Connolly were able to partition a large hall so one third, two thirds or its whole area was available (in all three cases an open rectangular space was available to the children, so there was no specific investigation on the effect of variation of the layout of space or equipment). They also had three identical sets of play equipment which could be set out one, two or three at a time. All nine combinations, ranging between one set of equipment in the whole space and all equipment in a third of the space could be tested. The manipulations were continued over two and a half terms, so that staff and children were well habituated to the experimental variations, although individual conditions were changed on a daily basis. This leaves the possibilities that staff may have adapted to the 'average' of the various conditions used, or they may have tried to keep conditions as constant as possible between the three conditions, in line with the widely held belief among staff working with children of this age that they need constant conditions. It is not clear whether staff acted in either of these ways, which would have tended to reduce the effects of the environmental manipulations, though their comments indicated that they tended to prefer to work in the less crowded conditions.

The effect of the amount of space was slight, and less than that of amount of equipment within the range of 25 square feet per child (the legal minimum at the time) to 75 square feet per child. Overall, in a free-play situation, children were more vigorously active when they had more space; they ran and chased more, while in the smaller spaces they made more use of the climbing frame and touched each other more (apparently unintentionally, as there was no other corresponding change in social behaviour). A briefer study with an even smaller amount of space (15 square feet per child, below the statutory guidelines) showed more effect. The children tended to engage in static rather than active play, were more aggressive and less sociable – the increased stress seemed to lead to them spending less time in group play and talking less. However, the crowding involved was extreme, to the extent where staff found it quite difficult to move around. (The programme of research also included studies of changes in the number of staff, in the structuring of activities and in the staff–child ratio which are outside our brief here.)

Other work with preschoolers confirms the suggestion that equipment has more effect on their behaviour than playroom spatial arrangement (Neill 1984). We cannot here deal with the considerable literature on the effects of different types of preschool equipment (e.g. Sylva, Roy and Painter 1980). A small-scale experimental study by Witt and Gramza (1970) indicates that positioning of preschool equipment can affect use. Witt and Gramza placed two trestles (climbing frames) in a small playroom used by four groups of 8–10 children, one by the wall and one in the centre of the room. They alternated which of the two frames was in each position and found that for three of the four groups whichever frame was in the centre of the room was played with more. Though Witt and Gramza suggest that 'purposeful positioning of play equipment' could 'permit unobtrusive modification of children's play behavior patterns' their study provides only limited evidence. It is uncertain how positioning interacts with the inherent popularity of play items, which varies considerably, with some types readily being ignored if others are available (Smith and Connolly 1980).

Nash (1981) reports that the complexity of children's educational activities was much increased when playrooms were partitioned into about four areas containing linked groups of equipment (for example, wood and tools for making models and paint for painting them). Children were more likely to make and decorate a construction when the related equipment was immediately available in this way (see also Kounin and Sherman 1979) than when they were scattered round the preschool in administratively convenient positions (for example, paint near a sink and wood outside where the noise of hammering would not disturb other activities). However, Nash was comparing preschools which had adopted a programme of his devising which stressed these spatial links between activities, with others which had not. The former would probably have had a more enterprising staff and the differences observed may well have been due to this factor rather than a direct effect of the manipulations themselves. Similarly Durlak, Beardsley and Murray (1972) found that open-plan elementary schools built by the Study of Educational Facilities differed from other open-plan and box classroom schools, probably because they attracted more committed staff.

This problem of non-random staff allocation may have been avoided to some extent in a study comparing practice in nursery schools and day nurseries of different designs (Neill 1982a, Neill et al. 1977), since the local authority controlled allocation of staff to units from the staff pool rather than staff choosing their own units; but the possibilities of selective allocation by the authority, and of staff, once allocated, staying in units they found congenial and moving out of uncongenial ones, cannot be eliminated. The results again probably confound building effects with staff and child population differences. A further problem was that the more visually open units were noisier, for the acoustic reasons mentioned above.

The study suggested that completely open units with large rectangular playrooms were less educationally successful than units with separate rooms to which children had free access or where an open space was subdivided into smaller areas by partitions or bays. In the more open units children spent less time in activities of the types considered by Sylva et al. (1980) to be educationally challenging, spent more time unoccupied or wandering around and suffered more aggression. Though the staff were not formally observed, the indications were that their behaviour reflected their conception of their role as facilitating children's free play rather than instructing them (see also Sylva et al. 1980, Griffin 1985). This meant that they tended to intervene mainly where children needed obvious assistance, in dealing with conflicts, supplying materials and assisting children in activities such as producing gifts for parents, where adult technical assistance was needed. In the more open rooms it was possible to see children from some distance, so staff tended to stay in a position where there was a good view, and at certain times the number of staff in the playroom was much reduced, with one remaining on surveillance duty while others took a break. As a result children tended to avoid calling on staff except where the assistance of an adult was essential (see also Wood, McMahon and Cranstoun 1980). By contrast, in the smaller spaces of the less open units, at least one member of staff normally had to be in each area to keep an eye on children, but with smaller numbers her duties were less onerous. She was therefore freer to become involved with the children in a range of educationally beneficial activities.

The 'less open' units in this study included two types which could be separated in Moore's (1987) study. From a rather larger pool of available units, six units were drawn, two each of the modern, modified open-plan type with free access through narrow doorways between spaces, and of the closed-plan type with separate rooms; there were also two conventional open-plan units. Moore matched units carefully for educational philosophy and child population. The modified open-plan centres seemed to be the most effective. Children in these sampled more activities, spent most time engaged in useful activities, initiated more activities themselves, explored more and were in smaller groups (though this last might not be desirable if it was a sign of stress – Smith and Connolly 1980). The open units showed more random, non-engaged activity by the children, and more caretaking and disciplinary control by the staff, while in the closed-plan centres children spent more time in transition between rooms, and more time withdrawn. Though great care was taken to match units and follow the requirements of valid quasi-experimental work by controlling for differences in the analysis (Cook and Campbell 1979), this study also draws on comparisons of existing units. Moore cites a third correlational study, by Field, which produced similar results to the two already discussed.

Legendre (1985) also suggests that preschool children prefer semi-enclosed bays and spend longer in them, in stable groups. However, at the ages of 2–3 which he studied, this relates to social competence; less competent children are dependent on the staff and restricted to their vicinity (Legendre 1989). As Legendre points out, little has been done to relate children's use of free space to development and personality. There is no corresponding evidence for older children, though we could expect, by analogy with the material on seat choice (chapter 7), that more independent children would choose positions further from the teacher.

If subdivision of playspace did lead to educationally valuable changes, it would be desirable to alter open spaces, such as the halls used by many playgroups. The effect of simple low-priced measures, which could be practical given the money and staffing available to many preschools, was investigated in a playgroup in an open hall (Neill 1982b). Screens were used to provide visual isolation and carpets to reduce noise levels. Their effect, separately and together, was assessed with the condition being changed on a daily basis, the arrangement of the playroom and daily regime being otherwise unchanged. The effects of the manipulations were slight, and a second study, using similar methods but with change on a weekly basis, produced equally slight but rather different results. The differences between conditions seemed therefore artifacts related to idiosyncrasies of the units studied. Observation of the staff showed that they did not change their behaviour in the different conditions, for example by dispersing into the screened-off areas. They continued to cluster together in particular areas, and to monitor what was happening elsewhere by ear or by going briefly to the screens and peering over. Children tended to cluster round the staff, so areas which had been under-used when the playroom was open continued to be under-used. As with the open-plan primary schools described above, the environmental changes were insufficient of themselves to produce alterations in behaviour, though they could potentially, like those described by Nash (1981), have been used with effect by a motivated staff.

Twardosz, Cataldo and Risley (1974) came to a rather different conclusion in their study of day nurseries. They partitioned off some or all areas by hanging a sheet from ceiling to floor and recorded that in the partitioned conditions children were more often out of sight of the staff, and staff more often out of sight of the supervisor. They therefore concluded that partitioning increased the difficulty of supervision, though their recording did not assess whether any behavioural changes occurred as a result of the manipulations. They also found that children participated just as well in adult-led preacademic activities in the open playroom as when the activities were conducted in a screened-off area or in a separate room. However, these activities only involved a single group of children for a ten-minute period. Their advocacy of the open playroom therefore seems inappropriate to older children or more complex activities.

Moore (1987) argues that conventional views, which see children manipulated by their environment, do not do justice to children's active agency in their own development, and their capacity to select the aspects of their situation which they will use. Many of the preschool studies have had the same ethos as the designers of open-plan schools mentioned earlier in the chapter. They have assumed that desirable outcomes can be planned by manipulating the educational setting. Children may be no less capable of subverting the educational plans of outside agencies than the teachers in Cooper's studies (1979 and 1981).

SUMMARY

Spatial arrangement of schools and rooms, like the seating arrangements discussed in the previous chapter, represents a formalisation of individual distance and mobility.

Open-plan school buildings, especially, were built with the intention of conveying a commitment to a child-centred education policy to teachers. They may also have been intended to impose it as the only practical method of teaching in an open space. They can create visual and noise distraction. However, the effects of distraction are not always as severe as might be expected; suitable organisation can be critical. Organisational problems can arise where staff continue to use traditional teaching methods in a building which is unsuited to them. Traditions of use may develop which persist despite being unsuited to changed circumstances. Reorganising the use of space can be effective, but it can be difficult to separate the effect of reorganisation itself from staff commitment, which can be the most influential factor. These conclusions apply to both preschools and primary schools.

Chapter 9
Differences between groups

Where appropriate in previous chapters we have mentioned differences in nonverbal signalling between different groups of children, especially in respect of age (chapter 2) but also in relation to sex, cultural or subcultural group and psychological condition. In this chapter I will consider the last three of these differentiations in more detail, after discussing the ways in which nonverbal signalling can break down. Most teachers in English-speaking Western countries are middle-class whites and this is the group on which most relevant nonverbal research has been done. The perspective adopted in other chapters has therefore inevitably been an ethnocentric one, though, as has been indicated, some nonverbal signals appear to be universal across all cultures and others can be observed across a wide range of cultures.

FACTORS LEADING TO BREAKDOWN IN NONVERBAL COMMUNICATION

In previous chapters we have assumed that nonverbal signals have been often adapted, either from a biological basis or from individual experience, to convey an 'honest' message to the recipient (e.g. chapter 3). In other circumstances nonverbal signals may leak information – for example that a teacher is more uncertain than she would wish to appear, or that she has low expectations for, or limited interest in, a child. This assumes that communicator and recipient are operating in essentially the same way. Where communicator and recipient belong to different groups communication may break down in different ways, as we have already seen in the case of young children. In assessing the types of breakdown that can occur between members of other groups it is useful to look at definitions of communication and the distinction between encoding and decoding.

Nonverbal communication need not be consciously intended (Bull 1987), or consciously received, but it does at least potentially have to convey information. Dawkins (1986) points out that there are many problems in constructing a watertight definition of communication, but for the purposes of this book the transmission of 'information', in its colloquial rather than its technical sense, is an appropriate definition. In many cases this information may be of mutual benefit, such as the communication between interested child and encouraging teacher (chapter 6). In other cases, such as the teacher who is an effective disciplinarian, the information is to the benefit of the communicator (chapter 3). In the case of the uncertain teacher who signals her uncertainty to the class (chapter 3), the information she conveys does not benefit her conscious intentions, but, as was argued there, this may be one case where a pattern of behaviour which is adaptive in other circumstances is maladaptive in the classroom.

In all these examples the information conveyed is *encoded* by the signaller and *decoded* by the recipient (Bull 1987). This process may break down for several reasons, apart from the trivial one that the recipient may simply fail to see the signal because he is looking elsewhere. Either encoding or decoding may be deficient, or the two participants may have incompatible expectations of the interaction. These three problems contribute differentially to communication problems between participants of different sexes, races and level of psychological deficit.

Firstly, we may consider encoding deficiencies. For example young children's lack of gestures (chapter 2) could hinder adults in understanding their explanations. Adults vary in their encoding effectiveness; for example marital difficulties are often related to poor encoding of nonverbal messages by the husband (Noller 1984). This is an example of the sex differences in sensitivity to nonverbal communication which are discussed below. The Japanese have cultural inhibitions against showing strong facial expressions of emotion in public (Ekman and Friesen 1975), though they will do so in private. This is an encoding deficiency from the Eurocentric point of view. However, where there are cultural or subcultural differences in the form or intensity of nonverbal signals, whether the problem is in encoding or decoding depends on one's viewpoint. This is well illustrated by emblematic gestures, which show strong local cultural differences even within Europe (Morris, Collett, Marsh and O'Shaughnessy 1979). Thus the English palm-back insult V-sign is encoded and decoded reliably in the United Kingdom but is liable to be decoded 'incorrectly' by a Greek as 'two' (Morris et al. op. cit.). Most of the problems in intercultural communication described below fall into this category of incompatible coding systems; most communicators are unaware that such incompatibilities exist, or of the form they take. They may completely fail to recognise a signal which is not in their own repertoire (for instance the *moutza*, a strong insult in Greece, resembles the non-emblematic fending hand (Figure 3.11)) or misinterpret the same physical signal which has different meanings in different cultures, such as the V-sign. The potential problems, especially in classes where English is being taught as a second language, are now beginning to be appreciated by educators (e.g. Soudek and Soudek 1985).

A further problem in communication between different cultures arises when the actual social relationships which underlie communication are different. For example in higher education problems sometimes arise with students from the Far East who have strong cultural expectations of a formal and inflexible lecturing style. Potentially training in nonverbal signals could assist such students in understanding the more informal, unpredictable, Western style, though an attempt to show this in practice was unsuccessful, apparently because the experimental group were so pleased with their new skill that they shared it with the control group (English 1985). Similar problems arise in communication between white teachers and American Indian schoolchildren, who tend to be silent and apparently uncooperative in class (Dumont 1972, Philips 1972). The Indian tradition is of leadership by consent, communal rather than individual effort, and learning by watching skilled performance, with the learners demonstrating their skill, or ability to participate in discussion, only when they feel ready to do so successfully. Indian children therefore find the conventional classroom situation, where the teacher has sole control, and learning is by individual, verbal trial and error in front of an audience, unfamiliar and unacceptable. Their silence and reluctance reflect this unacceptability.

Largely correct encoding and decoding of different social orientations underlies some of the communication differences between the sexes. Females tend to be less assertive than males, whether for biological or cultural reasons, and this underlies some of the differences in nonverbal signalling discussed below. In these cases it may be more appropriate to try to ensure realisation of the underlying differences in attitude than to dissociate the normal link between attitude and communication. In the case of children with special needs, or disruptive children, some differences may be due to accurate signalling of atypical social strategies. For example we discussed in chapter 4 the disruption of the normal level of advertance by which schizophrenic or depressed people signal their unwillingness to be members of social groups. However, as is indicated later, this is only part of the explanation for the differences between disruptive and normal children.

SEX DIFFERENCES IN NONVERBAL COMMUNICATION

Considerable attention has been devoted to sex differences in nonverbal communication between adults (e.g. review by Vrugt and Kerkstra 1984), and attention will only be given to this literature where it relates to aspects of behaviour which are relevant to classroom interaction. The main differences between the sexes which consistently reappear in the literature are greater female proficiency in encoding and decoding nonverbal signals and greater male nonverbal assertiveness. There are however many variations in this general picture. Thus Whitehurst and Derlega (1985) found that women's response to an apparently accidental touch in an experimental situation was related to their strength of preference for controlling social situations they found themselves in. As indicated in chapter 7, touch has controlling implications and men may use it as a controlling gesture to women (Henley and Harmon 1985; but see Vrugt and Kerkstra 1984). Women who preferred to be in control of social situations therefore reacted adversely to touch. This variation is likely to apply to other forms of nonverbal signal. Vrugt (n.d.) considers that behaviour may reflect differences in actual status, for example overriding the conventionally accepted cultural differences in status between men and women. Thus where a male layman is talking to a female expert, she will use dominant signals, reflecting her status. In Vrugt's view some of the differences proposed by Henley and others may have been accepted because they fit with subjective common-sense impressions, rather than having any objective basis.

Among these differences is women's suggested tendency to use a less dominant set of signals than men. Goffman (1979) illustrates a range of advertisements which draw on the culturally dominant position of men as depicted by their holding or directing women (compare Vrugt n.d. and Figure 7.1), showing them what to do, or occupying a higher position, for instance by standing over a sitting woman. He compares many of these behaviours to adults' behaviour towards children. All these signals commonly occur in teachers' behaviour towards children, in line with their dominant role. Women in advertisements also tend to adopt unstable postures, such as standing with one leg bent, leaning on someone else, while men adopt more stable (i.e. 'dependable') postures. Wex (1980) provides similar documentation from photographs, mostly in informal situations; a much higher proportion of men adopt the dominant postures discussed in chapter 3. Goffman also considers that women more frequently show self-touching or clinging to others; as discussed in chapter 3 these represent comfort movements. The effect of these types of signal may be the same whichever sex gives them but the controlling behaviour necessary for teachers may be a further departure from normal social behaviour for women than men, especially if we accept the view of Henley and Harmon (1985), that dominant signals given by women are taken less seriously than the same signals given by men.

A second characteristic difference related to dominance is the greater tendency of women to smile; as well as being an affiliative signal smiling has its origins as a submissive signal (chapter 3). The advice 'Don't smile till Christmas' may be particularly applicable to female teachers. Smiling pictures of teachers were seen as 'weaker' than frowning ones, though they were also seen as friendly (Neill 1989a; chapter 3); but this study did not include teacher sex as a variable.

Assertive behaviour provides an example of the difficulties in assessing the causes of the sex differences in signalling. Where there are physical differences between the sexes, the typical male patterns tend to be seen as dominant (often for either sex) which can be a disadvantage to women. The adolescent growth spurt makes more difference to men's faces than women's, so that men tend to have more 'mature' faces, with thicker eyebrows, more prominent jaws, narrower eyes and thinner lips. These features are seen by adults as conferring dominance on both male and female faces, though Keating noted that for female faces they were only effective in combination (Keating 1985). For male faces individual features conferred dominance. 'Dominant' features also made male, but not female, faces attractive. Beards are seen as dominant in comparison to clean-shaven male faces (Freedman 1971). Low voice pitch indicates calm dominance, while an increase in pitch signals stress; Atkinson (1984) notes that Mrs Thatcher took voice training which lowered her pitch by half the normal difference between men and women.

Height and size also favour men on average and are widely distributed indicators of dominance; many of the dominant signals described in chapter 3 such as erect posture and arms akimbo (Figures 3.2, 3.3) have the effect of increasing apparent height or size, whichever sex adopts them. Obviously a small person can adopt a dominant size-increasing signal, but it helps to be big to start with! Though there may be a cultural component in the recognition of these signals as dominant, they show such similarity to signals used by a wide range of species (e.g. Huntingford and Turner 1987, de Waal 1982) that there is probably a biological component as well. It therefore seems unlikely that any cultural change in expectations will completely eliminate the bias against which women who need to take a dominant position, including female teachers, have to work. However, the effectiveness of such fixed signals is limited; impressive appearance does not stand male teachers in good stead for long if they fail to show effective behavioural dominance and decisiveness (Hargreaves 1975) and small female teachers who possess the necessary skills have little difficulty in class control (Robertson 1989). These skills have been explored more fully in chapter 3.

Self-confidence and dominance are also necessary to pupils in competing for the teacher's attention. Whatever the classroom organisation, the simple mathematics of teacher–pupil ratios ensures competition for the teacher's attention. Unpredictable or attention-seeking children tend to get an undue share of the attention (Galton, Simon and Croll 1980) and these tend to be boys (Brophy and Good 1974). Boys' undue share may be due to two causes: their own more assertive behaviour and selectiveness by the teacher. Especially in informal situations they may be more willing to push girls aside in the queue to see the teacher, interrupt when girls are talking (as men interrupt women more than vice versa – Vrugt and Kerkstra 1984) and signal their stronger willingness to be called on in formal class discussions. This willingness may be signalled by general alertness and interest, parallel to the differences between high- and low-achieving children discussed in chapter 2. While there seems to be little research on sex differences in pupils' bids for attention under classroom conditions, girls who are effective at competing with other girls tend to avoid challenging boys, even those of lower ability, in situations both resembling physical education (catching a ball) and resembling oral classroom work (a spelling bee) (Cronin 1980). In the spelling bee experiment low-ability boys persisted in bidding to answer even when failure was penalised and it would have been more rational to allow the girls a first bid and benefit from any mistakes they made. As well as assertively out-competing girls, adolescent boys may undermine girls' status by harassment, including touching and other invasions of personal distance (Mahony 1985). These patterns are foreshadowed at the primary stage, when boys invade and disrupt girls' games, but not the reverse. Girls therefore tend to avoid boys, and only the most assertive manage to be accepted on equal terms (Thorne 1986). While assertiveness training may have value, separation into single-sex classes may be more effective in allowing girls to learn the skills associated with a full range of social roles, rather than some being customarily appropriated by boys (Mahony op. cit.).

Teachers may also preferentially call on boys, if not by intentional preference (many teachers of both sexes feel more warmly towards boys – Stanworth 1983), because of the greater assertiveness and unpredictability of boys mentioned above. Girls are well aware of and are upset by this. This problem may be made worse by the second major area of nonverbal difference between the sexes: the greater nonverbal 'politeness' of females (chapter 2). If correct, this would be consistent with the difficulties girls – and female teachers – can encounter in dominating classroom interaction. By disregarding the signals of uncertainty given by male opponents, they perceive them as more dominant and competent than they actually are, and effectively handicap themselves.

Females also show greater nonverbal expressiveness, but there is some evidence that even young children can discount this. Bugenthal, Love and Gianetto (1971) suggest that young children tended to disregard female smiles, because mothers tended to smile in relation to a wide range of messages and the information value of a smile was therefore low. They took more note of fathers' smiles because fathers smiled more contingently and their smiles therefore had greater information value. If preschool children can discriminate in this way it seems certain that school-age children could learn to discount the expressiveness of individual female teachers or that of female teachers in general. However, the only study related to this point is that of Woolfolk, Garlinsky and Nicolich (1977). Using a sample of only four teachers, they found no consistent overall differences related to teacher or pupil sex when they assessed the effect of teacher verbal and nonverbal communication on pupils' willingness to self-disclose. Though the validity of the study is limited by its short duration and the use of student teachers, it does suggest that children pay more attention to the teacher role in general than the sex of the teacher.

Secondary-school children seemed to behave in the same way in judging pictures of teachers' nonverbal signals (Neill 1986a; see also Brophy and

Good 1974). The sex of the teacher shown did not relate strongly to the responses that they gave, while other factors such as facial expression did. By contrast, children of the same age reacted to touch much more in terms of the sex of the person touching them than their role as teacher or non-teacher (Neill 1986c). The difference is probably related to the intimacy of the situation – where interaction is relatively distant the role predominates, while in closer interaction personal characteristics become more important.

CULTURAL AND SUBCULTURAL DIFFERENCES

The main possibilities for misunderstanding between cultural and subcultural groups arise when behavioural differences are relatively subtle. We are dealing here with misunderstanding rather than prejudice. Obvious differences, which can be consciously detected, will be seized on to support prejudiced views. Misunderstanding is likely where participants interpret the same cue in different ways, and are unaware that they are doing so.

Speech accent is relatively unmodifiable. Accented speech may be perfectly intelligible, but ridiculed by native speakers. This represents prejudice rather than misunderstanding. On the other hand there are cultural and subcultural differences in the wait time speakers allow during conversation. Thus New Yorkers have a very short wait time and readily interrupt other speakers (Tannen 1984). As a result they are seen as rude and pushy by residents of other parts of the United States who have a longer wait time (Tannen op. cit.). Finns, who have a long wait time, and listen silently without making 'back-channel' noises (approving noises such as ah'hm – see chapter 5, and below), are seen as disinterested or stupid by Swedish or other foreign speakers who have a short wait time (Lehtonen and Sajavarra 1985). The Finns therefore tend to be ignored; they may also contribute little to conversation because they cannot tolerate interruption when they are speaking, as this is not normal in Finnish conversation. Here cultural prejudice is based on genuine misunderstanding. No studies of this type of difference seem to have been carried out in the classroom context, but it is likely to be significant, given Rowe's (1974) work (chapter 6). It is probable that ethnic minority children have a longer wait time if English is their second language.

Further subtle differences which may cause misunderstanding are in signals of attention and respect, signals used to convey understanding, gestural style, and individual distance and touch. These differences should diminish as more ethnic minority children are born in this country, though they may be replaced by class-related differences; the London or Birmingham dialects of England-born minority children are a parallel. Gestural assimilation has certainly occurred with American immigrants of Jewish and Italian extraction, who originally had very different nonverbal styles (Ellis and Beattie 1986). Unfortunately there seems to be limited evidence on many aspects of cultural differences as they affect the classroom, at least in the

United Kingdom, let alone how the effects in the classroom vary with enculturation. This is not surprising as many of these effects have only recently been recognised at all, even in adults, and the same problem applies to areas such as counselling (Vogelaar and Silverman 1984).

The effect of these differences should not perhaps be overstated. Norton and Dobson (1976; see also Norton 1974) compared Caucasian, black and American Indian children's categorisations of pictures of teachers. They found that age (6 to 10) accounted for more differences between groups than ethnic background or sex, though ethnic and sex differences increased with age. Of the 15 pictures tested, 13 elicited significantly different responses from children of different ages, and for 9 of these the differences were highly significant. There were 7 significant differences between the three ethnic groups, 1 of which was highly significant, and only 1 significant difference related to sex. However, the three factors interacted; thus the Caucasian children's judgments changed more with age than those of the other two groups. Further, Caucasian boys tended to agree more closely with each other than boys of the other two races, but among girls it was the blacks who showed the most cohesive judgments. It is clear that cultures differ in the way children develop their relationships with teachers, and the way this interacts with sex differences, as indicated by nonverbal behaviour.

While most cultures tend to signal attention and respect in the same way, by the subordinate person gazing at the dominant, and lowering their gaze to indicate submission, for example when being criticised, cultures differ in the precise context in which these signals are used. These differences may also vary with age; Norton and Dobson (1976) found that Caucasian children considered eye contact as increasingly negative with age from 6 to 10, whereas black and American Indian children's opinions changed in the opposite direction. Many cultures consider a greater social distance between a child and a respected adult, such as a schoolteacher, appropriate than is the case in Western society. Thus, in the United States, white schoolteachers expect children to look them in the eye when being questioned, but for blacks (Feldman and Saletsky 1986) this is a sign of disrespect, and a downcast gaze would be correct, while the child nods or makes assenting 'um-hum' noises. The white teacher feels that the black child is being inattentive because he is not looking, but the black child is mystified to be criticised for insolence. On the other hand, American black children tend to use stylised 'sulks' in a way which can cause problems to white teachers who are unfamiliar with this cultural form (Gilmore 1985). According to Gilmore, 'sulking' girls tend to use the 'plus face' (Figure 2.1), cutting off eye contact by closing their eyes or looking away, while 'sulking' boys break the advertance rules (chapter 4) by slumping, with head down, legs splayed and desk pushed away. These displays of bad 'attitude' were recognised and dealt with severely by black parents and community figures. White teachers, especially if they were sensitive to the need to allow for cultural differences, tended to be more permissive, and this in turn led to classes displaying 'bad attitudes' more frequently. Black teachers and parents tended to be concerned about this permissive acceptance of 'low standards'. They felt teachers were not doing enough to pressure their children into accepting the education they needed to improve their status in society – indeed the teachers might almost be maintaining white superiority by default. However, teachers of either race could deal effectively with 'sulks' by humour, teasing or affectionate behaviour.

'Sulks' are an example of consciously controlled cultural variations in behaviour. There are similar consciously controlled cultural differences in other aspects of behaviour such as 'emblematic gestures' (such as the insult V-sign, which is little recognised outside Britain – Morris et al. 1979), but these are of little importance in the classroom.

Mediterranean peoples use more illustrative gestures (Graham and Argyle 1975a, Morris et al. op. cit.). Among adults a rich use of gesture makes for greater intelligibility. While this result has parallels with the importance of gesture to effective teaching (chapter 5) there is no definitive evidence in relation to Asian or Afro-Caribbean children, the most important groups in the English classroom context. There are also differences in the gestures shown to express agreement and disagreement – in Britain, nodding and head-shaking (Morris et al. op. cit., Eibl-Eibesfeldt 1972) – and in beckoning movements. Feldman and Saletsky (1986) point out that North American blacks use different 'back channel' or listening signals. Whites use attentive gaze (chapter 6) and nodding in combination, while blacks use one or other of these. Blacks also use a rather different, less emphatic form of nod, which may not be so salient to a white interactant, and they tend to nod almost continuously: the resultant continuous head-bobbing could appear impatient to a white speaker.

A further difference between cultures is the relationship of illustrative gestures to speech intonation and thought patterns. In general the maximum intensity of illustrative gestures in English coincides with the stressed syllable (Bull 1987). This applies in other languages where intonational stress is differently distributed, the pattern being different in languages such as French where intonational stress is little used (Creider 1986). Secondly, the type of gesture used varies across cultures (Creider op. cit.), for example the use of *conduit gestures* (chapter 5). Both these types of difference could potentially make it much more difficult for children familiar with different language systems to grasp what was being said to them in English, since the differences in gestural systems would be working against rather than assisting their understanding of the spoken language (see also English 1985).

Cultural differences in patterns of proximity and, especially, touch are likely to have practical implications because of the salience of touch and close approach (chapter 7). Again our evidence for patterns occurring in the United Kingdom is incomplete. In the United States black children tend to approach each other more closely than white children and to touch each other more (chapter 7). English infant teachers tend to touch black children more than white children, especially directing more controlling touch to black boys (Evans 1979b) and more affectionate touch to black girls. Evans was somewhat suspicious of the teachers' rationalisations of this extra touch, in terms of showing concern for the black children which society rejected; she felt the touch might have a controlling intention. However, if the English black children, like their American counterparts, were more willing to accept touch than their white peers, the teachers' greater use of touch might be acceptable in line with their expressed intentions. Differences occur with age in the acceptability of touch across cultures and the acceptability of touch may differ depending on whether the toucher is of the same or a different culture (chapter 7).

There are also well-documented differences between the personal space customary in different cultural groups (Jones and Aiello 1973, Willis, Carlson and Reeves 1979) though these differences are likely to be overridden by age differences and the teacher's ability to invade children's personal space. However, the most salient intercultural aspect of space, which relies on both sides' ability to interpret its meaning, is the greater space maintained between rather than within racial groups (Jones and Aiello op. cit., Willis et al. op. cit., Willis and Hoffman 1975, Willis and Reeves 1976, Willis, Reeves and Buchanan 1976, Willis, Rinck and Dean 1978). This is reflected in the use of seating positions to indicate the differences between cultural groups. Campbell, Kruskal and Wallace (1966) compared classroom seating positions in American high schools in the 1950s and 1960s. They felt that there had been some improvement over this period in interracial attitudes as indicated by seating positions, but there was still considerable segregation by race and sex. Feldman and Saletsky (1986) also report research indicating that white interviewers sit closer to white than black interviewees.

Feldman and Saletsky report research done in their own group, using the widely adopted methodology of one student tutoring another (chapter 6). They found that both black and white tutors were judged from videotapes to be more pleased with students of their own race than of the other race, but this judgment could only be made accurately by judges of the same race as the tutor. Feldman and Saletsky do not describe what the interracial differences in nonverbal cues might be which would account for this. The potential implications of this are serious, as the teacher might be expressing prejudice against minority group pupils which was apparent to pupils who were fellow members of the majority group, but to which the minority group pupils were unable to react because they were not aware of it. Using a similar method, they found that nonverbal signals were consistent with level of prejudice, judged on a standard questionnaire; white tutors who were highly racially prejudiced were more negative to their black tutees than those who were less prejudiced; though both groups were more positive to white tutees, the differential was more marked among the more prejudiced tutors. In both these experiments the tutee made few errors; in a third experiment white tutors dealt with either a tutee who made few errors or one who made many. Tutors' more positive behaviour to white tutees appeared again, as did more positive behaviour to more successful tutees, as might be expected. Interestingly, however, the differential related to success was greater for white than black tutees; in other words blacks were being given less adequate feedback about their performance, as well as being rewarded less. Though these experiments illustrate the potential of nonverbal signals for transmitting prejudice in a way which the recipients would find difficult to challenge, evidence is needed as to whether they apply in the normal classroom situation with younger children as well as in the one-to-one undergraduate tutoring situation which Feldman and Saletsky studied.

PSYCHOLOGICAL DIFFERENCES

The effects of psychological abnormalities on children's behaviour fall, from the point of view of classroom management, broadly into three groups, because of the pressure of time on teacher–child relationships and the resulting competition between children for the teacher's attention (chapter 6). These groups are children who fail to compete adequately and are therefore 'invisible' to the teacher; children who fail to respond adequately to the teacher's educational initiatives and are therefore unrewarding to teach; and children who are disruptive.

Into the first group fall children who are withdrawn or depressed. These children, especially if young, continue to show the patterns of behaviour which would be appropriate for a child who was a stranger to the group, when a normal child would have settled in and would be showing established prosocial behaviour (Putallaz and Gottman 1981). Uncertain preschool children tend to hover, watching a group; together with other tactics, this makes them more likely to be ignored (Putallaz and Gottman op. cit.). Depressed children tend to avert their gaze; this also encourages other members of the classroom group to ignore them. Such children give the teacher little trouble, and because their behaviour lies within the range adopted by normal children at some times, there is a tendency for the teacher to treat them like normal children undergoing stress; in other words to leave them until they show signs of improvement. The teacher's task may be made more difficult by the child's behaviour showing abnormalities only in certain situations. Thus Rutter and O'Brien (1980) found (under laboratory conditions) that withdrawn adolescent girls met an adult's gaze less than aggressive girls from the same schools for maladjusted children. However, this difference only appeared during discussions of personal topics, not when discussing television. Thus differences might not show up if a teacher's contacts with a child were mainly impersonal and work-oriented.

Similar but more extreme patterns of behaviour are shown by children suffering from more serious disabilities such as autism or Down's syndrome. Down's patients tend to communicate differences in social relationships with strange and familiar adults by posture (Leudar 1981). They tend to face away from strangers, or to use barrier signals (Figures 3.7, 3.8, 3.9). The adults, on the other hand, differentiate in the way they talk to them. Autistic children show very severe gaze avoidance, and will only respond to adults at all if they can ensure little or no meeting of gaze (e.g. Hutt and Hutt 1970). At this level the differences are sufficiently clear to make adults consciously modify their behaviour to allow for the child. However, these modifications may work against allowing the child to interact normally. If he can never take the initiative, as a normal individual would, he may become passive and unresponsive. For example, in some cases Down's syndrome children may talk when they are alone with peers but not when staff are present (Leudar 1981). Other children may also talk to children with learning difficulties in different ways from those which they would use with normal peers, which may not be productive for the child with learning difficulties. Infant-school children tend to treat peers with learning difficulties as if they are very young normal children (Lewis 1987; this relates to one of the explanations the normal children consistently use to explain the behaviour of the children with learning difficulties – Lewis and Lewis 1988). Some young normal children are relatively skilled at modifying and simplifying their speech, explaining and questioning, approaching the level of skill of the staff. Others are more prone to take a controlling role by repeating and requesting until the child with learning difficulties responds, or using motherese. However, the normal children's feelings about the children with learning difficulties are considerably more tolerant than about low-achieving normal classmates.

The abnormal behaviour of such children may cause problems to the teacher but is not overtly disruptive. Disruptive children lack responsiveness to the controlling tactics of their teachers. The disruptive child may be less prone to stress than normal children (Davies and Maliphant 1971a, 1971b). As was discussed in chapter 3, stress and signals of stress are an adaptive response to risk which ensure that in most cases normal individuals avoid undue exposure to risk. If disruptive children do not find punishments as stressful as normal children they will lack the same incentive to learn the early warning signals of risk as do normal children. Whereas normal children move from overt conflict with peers and adults in the preschool years to more sophisticated avoidance of conflict (Sluckin 1979), disruptive children continue to decode signals inaccurately. McCuller (1983) found that disruptive children interpreted pictures of classroom situations, including confrontations, differently from normal children. They were less sensitive to signals the teacher used to indicate annoyance or control, and they were prone to explanations blaming the teacher more than the child in the picture. These responses would have been more likely to get them into trouble in the corresponding real situations.

As indicated in chapter 2 older children are well aware of the implicit meanings carried in nonverbal signals, and irony or sarcasm are frequently used by both children and teachers to show up the other (chapter 4). Younger children are insensitive to these nonverbal messages, as are both older children and adults suffering from mental disability (Reilly and Muzekari 1986). Reilly and Muzekari tested male normals and schizophrenics at the ages of 7–9, 10–12, 13–15 and 17–54 with consistent friendly and hostile messages, in which words and nonverbal signals agreed, and inconsistent messages, with friendly words and hostile facial expression and vocal tone, or vice versa. Both groups performed similarly on the consistent messages. The patients attended purely to the verbal content of the inconsistent messages, gaining the opposite message to normal adults, who were mainly influenced by the nonverbal component. Normal children moved progressively from attending primarily to the words to attending to the nonverbal component, making this transition between the ages of 10–12 and 13–15. Given that the patients were hospitalised, in the case of the adults, or in special schools, their inability to pick up the nonverbal content of messages probably exceeds that of children still in normal schools, but this study reinforces that of McCuller (1983) in showing the lack of ability to pick up the more subtle cues commonly used by normal interactants. While these problems of communication will be familiar to experienced teachers of children with special educational needs, with the current move for such children to be taught in normal schools, they may encounter teachers who are unfamiliar with these aspects of their communicative abilities.

It is less clear whether there are any differences related to academic ability. Grogan (1988) investigated whether poor readers showed behaviour related to poor social skill, which might have led to their getting less help from teachers. She looked for signs of anxiety and defensiveness in conversation with an educational tester, especially when the children were talking about school-related topics. She found no differences in two prosocial behaviours, smiling and gaze, related to reading ability (or to age or sex), and both good and poor readers showed the same differences when discussing school as opposed to out-of-school topics. Poor readers did show more filled pauses ('er's and 'um's), especially when discussing out-of-school topics. Grogan thought the most likely explanation of this was that the poor readers found the discussion more difficult, especially when they were unexpectedly confronted with discussing out-of-school topics in a very school-oriented situation.

SUMMARY

Nonverbal communication involves both encoding rules controlling the signals used to convey a message and decoding rules by which the receiver interprets the message received. As these rules are rarely explicit, problems arise when sender and receiver belong to different groups. A message will be encoded using one set of rules and decoded using another. Neither party may be aware of the resulting misunderstanding. Further difficulties may arise when sender and receiver interpret the same relationship differently, for example if the teacher sees a teaching relationship as more egalitarian than a student from a different culture, who is used to showing more respect. Neither party may be aware of their difference in viewpoint if the message is conveyed nonverbally.

Females tend to be less assertive than males, and to be seen as less assertive when they use similar behaviour. This can cause problems to female teachers, and to girls in gaining an equal share of the teacher's attention. However, under classroom conditions, children appear to attend more to the teacher role than to the sex of the person occupying it.

Cultural differences may lead to prejudice even where there is no misunderstanding. More often, interactants may be unaware of cultural differences in nonverbal behaviour, leading to misinterpretation. These differences tend to increase in a complex fashion with age. For example, differences in the signals used to show attention may lead to teachers misinterpreting 'attention' signals from one culture as inattention, while displays of inattention or insolence from another culture are not recognised and dealt with. Cultural differences occur in most aspects of nonverbal communication. Most of the evidence relates to American children, and there is little evidence for British children, especially on whether differences in nonverbal behaviour decrease with integration.

In most cases children with psychological abnormalities display normal nonverbal signals, but their selection of behaviours is abnormal for the context. They may also fail to develop normal sensitivity to nonverbal signals with age. This causes problems under the social pressures of the classroom. Thus depressed or withdrawn children fail to behave assertively enough to be noticed. Disruptive children fail to respond to low-intensity control signals from teachers, and therefore fail to avoid confrontations. However, there do not seem to be nonverbal skill deficits related to poor academic ability.

Chapter 10

Implications for teacher training

Are nonverbally skilled teachers 'born' or are their skills 'made'? We have seen in chapter 2 that nonverbal skills develop over childhood, and that Zivin's (1982) model of development as a result of individual experience is the most probable account even for those behaviours where there is clear evidence of an innate component, in a strict sense. However, if we take entry into teacher training as metaphorical 'birth', the question, as rephrased, remains a useful one.

The problems in answering it are evident from the general literature on the influences on new teachers. As Zeichner (1986) points out, in his review, there are some studies suggesting that teacher-training courses 'wash over' students, leaving the views they have formed in their own schooling intact; but these may discount the more subtle 'hidden curriculum' of the courses. Further, student teachers are likely to be selective in their acceptance of the various experiences they are exposed to. This active selection is likely to be rather less powerful, however, in the case of nonverbal skills, in so far as student teachers are not consciously aware of them. Here we look at the evidence on the stage at which nonverbal teaching skills are learnt, and consider whether they can be explicitly trained.

ALTERNATIVE MODELS OF THE DEVELOPMENT OF TEACHING SKILLS

There are three possible situations so far as the development of nonverbal skills by trainee teachers is concerned. Firstly, (the 'born teacher' model) they may already have all the skills they need on entry, perhaps as a result of course selectors accepting only those candidates who have the relevant skills. In this case skill at the end of the course should be perfectly correlated with skill at entry.

An alternative possibility is that the skills students possess when they leave the course are 'learnt'; they relate to course experience rather than the skills at entry. If this was the case there would be no relationship between level of skill at entry onto the course and skill at leaving it. Skill at leaving would depend entirely on the quality of the experience provided by the course.

The third possibility is that there is an interaction. Entrants to training, while not possessing all the necessary specific teaching skills, have to varying degrees either the nonverbal awareness to detect and copy the skills of teachers whom they watch or sufficient self-awareness to detect and build on their own successes and errors. Differences between more and less skilled students at intake would increase, as the initially more skilled were more receptive to new experiences and built more rapidly on their existing superior foundations. This might occur through their own experience, as mentioned above, or due to their better responsiveness to teaching.

This third model is difficult to distinguish in practice from the first unless detailed information is available both on behaviour at different stages and on the situations in which it is elicited. If superior students, while maintaining their superior skills in general, change in the skills they display over the course, the interactive model would be favoured. If they continue to display the same skills, this would favour the 'born teacher' model.

Both the 'born teacher' and interactive models would be supported by evidence suggesting consistency over the duration of the course. Consistency would be indicated by a close correlation between the behaviour of candidates before acceptance, for instance as reported by their referees or at interview, and their performance as they progressed through the course. However, behaviour is influenced by context. Recordings from different situations (for example interview and classroom) would elicit different sets of behaviour, even if there is no underlying change. Correlation would depend on similarity between the stresses exerted by the interview, where the candidate is performing in front of one or two people of superior status, and the classroom, where the performance is to a larger number of inferior status. In theory measures at intake could predict teaching performance at outcome perfectly, but in practice, even if this model was correct, differences in situations would reduce the value of the correlation. Both for teaching (reviewed by Crocker 1974) and for other occupations (reviewed by McHenry 1981) the predictive value of interviews across a range of situations is limited, as discussed below.

We therefore need to know whether nonverbal behaviour changes in the teaching situation itself over the duration of the course. Detailed observation of classroom behaviour at, for instance, entry and on leaving would be needed. Such information is not available at present, but we may look at the available literature to see what information it throws on the ways in which student teachers develop their skills.

INTERVIEWS AND THE IMPACT OF NONVERBAL SKILLS

Selectors for teacher-training courses are more likely to interview candidates than selectors for other university courses. The aim is to assess candidates' personal qualities (Coleman 1985). The Elton Report (Department of

Education and Science and Welsh Office 1989) felt that the personal qualities of intending teachers were so important that no candidate for teacher training or for a post as a licensed teacher should be selected without an interview addressed to these qualities. The emphasis which has been put on interpersonal skills in this book supports the need for assessing them in some way; the question is whether the interview is an effective method. Direct observational evidence from interviews for teacher training is not available, and we therefore have to collate data from other sources. In general, research on interviews has criticised their effectiveness as a selection method (e.g. McHenry 1981, Hoskin and Steele 1988). Coleman (1985) found that interviewers' assessments of teacher-training candidates varied markedly even when assessing the same candidates. Morgan, Hall and MacKay (1983) trenchantly criticised the interview as normally used in selecting senior-school staff, and suggested a range of selection methods which they felt more accurately represented the conditions under which senior staff worked. However, they found great difficulty in persuading education authorities to try using these methods, or, having tried them, to continue with them. The main objection was the time and expense involved relative to the conventional interview, despite the major implic- ations of making an unsatisfactory appointment in a senior position. It seems highly unlikely, given the current constraints on expenditure and the much larger number of candidates to be considered at selection for training, that the conventional interview will be replaced, despite its inadequacy.

NONVERBAL BEHAVIOUR IN SELECTION INTERVIEWS

There is some evidence on the nonverbal qualities which lead to selection at interview. Raffler-Engel (1983) found that interviewers for management posts in industry preferred confident candidates. Willingness to make eye contact was seen as a mark of forcefulness and appropriate use of gestures was taken to indicate an interest in the job. Eye contact as a dominant behaviour was rated significantly higher by the referees for the successful teacher-training applicants in Neill (1989c), and gesture as an enthusiastic behaviour slightly higher, than for the unsuccessful applicants. Forbes and Jackson (1980) found a similar, but less assertive, constellation of behaviours in 17–19-year-old interviewees for places on an engineering training scheme. Eye contact was again characteristic of the more successful interviewees, but they also smiled more, and nodded or shook their heads more; there were no differences in gesture. In general these candidates were rather tense, sitting still with upright bodies and hands clasped in their laps. Less assertiveness would clearly be expected in trainees than potential managers. Hollandsworth, Kazelkis, Stevens and Dressel (1979) compared the effects of verbal and non-verbal behaviour on interviewers' ratings of the employability of college students in preliminary interviews for commercial posts. They found that appropriate verbal content, with concise and relevant answers, had the greatest influence, followed by two indicators of self-confidence, fluency of speech and composure. Less important, in decreasing order, were eye contact, posture, gesture and facial expression, a firm voice, and appropriate dress and grooming. The jobs involved were not specified. It would be interesting to do a similar comparison for teacher-training candidates, for whom it is possible that nonverbal factors would assume more importance, and to assess whether nonverbal skills differ according to their intended area of specialisation, as would be implied by Lawes's (1987a) work discussed below. In other words one might expect selectors for secondary courses to prefer a more assertive style than selectors for primary courses.

Another point raised by Raffler-Engel (1983) is the similarity between successful candidates and their interviewers. Interviewers for management posts prefer candidates who resemble themselves. Forbes and Jackson (1980) suggest that one possible reason for the more confident behaviour shown by successful candidates is that the interviewers may be giving them more encouraging feedback. They point out that contingent behavioural echo occurs between participants in conversations (chapter 5; Figure 4.4). Since the literature indicates that interviewers tend to come to a decision very early in the interview, the more confident behaviour of successful candidates could be a result of their foreshadowed success rather than the cause of it. However, Forbes and Jackson feel that the interviewer's decision itself may result from the candidate's behaviour in the first section of the interview. An alternative explanation would be provided by the correlation between referees' and interviewers' ratings found by Neill (1989c). Though these ratings were made independently, the interviewers had the standard references, and would therefore have formed impressions of the candidates before meeting them. It is therefore likely that a candidate with a good reference would have been met more positively by interviewers from the start of the interview. This lends added weight to Forbes and Jackson's suggestion that the style of the interviewers and the sequential patterning of behaviour through the interview should be investigated.

The importance and stressful nature of the interview may lead to candidates behaving differently from the way they would in similar but less critical situations (Hocking and Leathers 1980). Candidates who believed they were in a critical selection test showed differences in nonverbal behaviour related to deception, compared to the classic Ekman and Friesen (1969b) pattern (chapter 1). Unlike Ekman and Friesen, Hocking and Leathers found that deceivers showed fewer bodily signs of nervousness such as foot movements, but more vocal signs of stress. Deceivers' eye contact was briefer. Hocking and Leathers suggest that self-monitoring capability was critical; their subjects, who were intending to train in criminal justice, were better at this than Ekman and Friesen's mental patients. There are obvious parallels here to the importance of self-monitoring in transmitting expectations (chapter 6).

It is doubtful whether many applicants get specific training in interviewing for teacher-training places, though it is more commonly included as part of training courses to prepare students in applying for jobs. Both student interviewees and interviewers (school governers etc.) on an interview training course felt they benefited from practising skills in a simulation of selection for first teaching posts (Seddon and Thorp 1989). It is not clear whether there were any alterations in actual behaviour and the interviewees' subsequent success in actually getting jobs was not assessed.

CHILDREN'S PERCEPTIONS OF STUDENT TEACHERS

A number of authors have suggested that pupils, both primary and secondary, are accurate judges of teachers' skills (Cortis and Grayson 1978, Meighan 1977), whose opinions are consistent with those of other judges such as course supervisors and supervising class teachers, and that they could therefore play a useful part in teacher education (e.g. Hull 1985).

As discussed in chapters 4, 5 and 6, calm control, enthusiasm and friendliness distinguish effective from ineffective experienced teachers. Children have strong views on what is appropriate behaviour for teachers (Nash 1974), and we may regard the children as acting as selective agents against teachers who do not show these behaviours, and are therefore rejected as ineffective (see also Gannaway 1976). This selective action will operate in the same way against student teachers as against their experienced colleagues, if not more strongly, since children may rate students as less firmly controlling and poised (Veldman 1970). Student teachers therefore face the same task of immediately showing appropriate behaviour on first contact with the children if they are not to lose them (chapter 4). On the other hand, students' greater friendliness, cheerfulness, liveliness and interest may make children prefer them, at least slightly, to experienced teachers.

DOES 'PERSONALITY' PREDICT?

Children's awareness of teaching skill could potentially be put into practice immediately; pupils moving into initial training courses have more 'recent and relevant experience' of teaching – at least from the receiving end – than those who are training them. For example, the views of sixth-formers, who are potential candidates for teaching, on what is effective and ineffective teacher behaviour (James and Choppin 1977) are similar to those expressed by student teachers who were assessed as effective and ineffective by their college tutors (Davis and Satterley 1969). In both cases insecurity, tenseness and lack of conscientiousness mark the poor teacher. Davis and Satterley found that these personality characteristics were stable between the application of their questionnaire when students entered the course and 26 months later, just before final teaching practice. (This supports the 'born teacher' model.)

Though attempts to relate teaching success to personality characteristics have had mixed results, Davis and Satterley felt that there were clear relationships between personality and poor teaching performance at least.

Preece's (1979) study attempted to assess the causal relationship between personality and teaching effectiveness. Does a confident personality predict success or does success boost confidence? It is quite possible that student teachers lose confidence in themselves after their first devastating foray into the classroom jungle and that some personalities should never have ventured into it in the first place. Preece asked students to rate themselves on a four-point scale, while their tutors rated class control on a ten-point scale. These ratings were performed at the beginning and end of teaching practice. Cross-lagged panel correlations were used to assess whether anxiety was causing control problems or whether control problems were leading to increased anxiety. He found that general levels of anxiety decreased as the students gained experience. Anxiety predicted future problems of class control across the group as a whole, but not at a significant level. Though the raw correlation was significant, the differential – which indicates the direction in which causation acts – between the correlation for early anxiety and later control, and the correlation for early control and later anxiety, was not. The differential effect was considerably stronger for science teachers, though still not significant. However, it did not apply for other teachers. Preece considered that these differences were probably real, since they appeared when male and female students were considered separately. He thought it might be related to the pressures on science teachers related to controlling practical lessons, with their possible hazards. For other subjects the less dangerous implications of discipline problems may have meant that anxiety was less important.

However, studies of the predictive value of personality tests for teaching success (reviewed by Crocker 1974) have generally produced inconclusive or contradictory results. This may be due to the general lack of a relationship between tested personality and nonverbal behaviour (reviewed by Bull 1983). However, Bull's review suggests that individual differences in physiological arousability may be better correlated with nonverbal expressiveness than ratings from conventional personality tests. In other words the lack of relation between personality test results and teaching success may be due to the tests not relating accurately to the only cues which are directly available to the children: the actual nonverbal and verbal signals emitted by the teachers.

STUDENTS' NONVERBAL AWARENESS AND TEACHING SKILL

Although Lawes (1987a, 1987b) was not able to follow the development of students' skills through their course, he provides some of the best information on the relationship between students' nonverbal skill and teaching ability. Student teachers' rating of their own nonverbal behaviour (on an inventory which used general descriptions of the different functional types of behaviour and their intensity and clarity) was correlated with, firstly, supervisors' ratings using the same scale, and secondly, the normal assessments of teaching competence made by the supervisor and the supervising teacher (Lawes 1987a). So far as competence was concerned, different relationships occurred for secondary and junior students. Competent secondary students used more enthusiastic nonverbal behaviour (see also chapter 5). They saw themselves as using a high level of nonverbal activity, with large and rapid movements. They felt they could convey their intended meaning with clarity, and one contributory factor seemed to be a greater use of illustrative gestures. These patterns are consistent with the rather theatrical role of the secondary teacher, and the better students may be more aware of this need for an effective performance.

By contrast, no overall trend appeared for the junior teachers, but more detailed analyses suggested curvilinear relationships, with self-reported nonverbal activity having different correlates for above-average and below-average student teachers. For above-average students, greater competence was related to less use of illustrative and controlling or attention-getting signals, less 'housekeeping' manipulation of objects (not intended to communicate to the children) and slower movements. For below-average students these relationships were reversed (except for 'housekeeping' where there was no relationship); more competent students used more controlling and illustrative behaviours and faster movements.

Lawes explains the difference between these and the secondary students by the more intimate teaching to small groups or individuals which occurs in the junior classroom. The more confident and competent students, he feels, can handle this situation well with their normal, unconscious interpersonal skills. For less confident students, by contrast, conscious monitoring of what they are doing may make the difference between a poor teaching performance and a moderate one, in Lawes's view. Lawes's view contrasts somewhat with that of Calderhead (1986) who found that the better primary students were more prone to look at their lessons in a detached way, as a performance, separate from their true identity. This suggests that the successful students both had a greater awareness of their own behaviour and were less prone to anxiety when problems did occur. However, Calderhead did not specifically investigate nonverbal behaviour. It may be that in fact superior primary students are monitoring themselves closely, but that they are aware that their teaching situation, working largely with individuals or small groups of children, requires only low-key nonverbal communication, and they are reporting this fact accurately.

This is consistent with Lawes's (1987a) second finding. The relationship between students' self-reports of their nonverbal signals and their supervisors' reports was taken as an index of nonverbal self-awareness. Nonverbal self-awareness was correlated with teaching competence, and Lawes concluded that an interactive model, similar to that discussed at the start of the chapter, is the most likely explanation for this. He found that, in general, students were aware of their own facial expression, gaze, eye contact, and head moves, but less aware of movements of their hands, arms, feet and body. This pattern parallels closely that found by Ekman and Friesen (1969b) for nonverbal leakage, which, in their view, reflected decreasing awareness as one moves from face to feet. Again we see a parallel between the nonverbal behaviour of teachers and non-teachers. However, the student teachers did differ in their awareness of their own orientation and proximity to pupils. This factor was not relevant in Ekman and Friesen's work, which was based on (presumably seated) psychiatric interviews.

Lawes also (1987b) investigated students' comprehension of children's nonverbal signals. He asked students to judge comprehension, attention, interest and ability from a silent videotape of 10-year-olds in a lesson with a familiar teacher (the cues used are described in chapter 6). Accuracy of nonverbal decoding was greater in student teachers who scored at the stable end of the neuroticism/stability scale on the Eysenck personality inventory. The more neurotic students might be less receptive to signals from others, and it might be possible and appropriate to select applicants for teacher training on this basis. The advantage shown by stable personalities is consistent with the greater success of student teachers who had high scores for calmness and dominance at entry in Neill (1989c), discussed below, and Calderhead's work, mentioned above. Crocker (1974) also considered that tested flexibility was a useful predictor of teaching success, more valid than G.C.E. results, I.Q. and the interview, and should be included in the battery of selection tests for student teachers.

It is perhaps not surprising, given the evidence in chapter 2 of children's ability to signal their level of interest deliberately at the age (10–11 years) the student teachers were watching, that faced with video material, the students can make judgments of comprehension and interest. While these findings suggest that 'innate' factors, present before entering the course, are important, another finding of Lawes's study suggests a role for experience. For junior specialists, whose experience would usually have included the age-group used in these tests, students who had been rated as having high or medium competence on teaching practice scored better on decoding than those of low teaching competence. This is consistent with a model where a threshold of nonverbal competence is necessary for satisfactory teaching performance. (It could be suggested that the difference between high and medium competence relates to the students' own communicative skills, including nonverbal skills.) For secondary specialists, however, both high teaching practice competence students and low competence students scored worse than medium competence students. While the difference between medium and low competence students is consistent with the junior specialists, the high competence students represent a problem. Lawes suggests various solutions, including that verbal processes may be of more importance at the secondary level, or that nonverbal cues related to disruption or originating from the whole class are of more importance. An alternative possibility is that the most effective secondary teachers are sensitised to the more subtle nonverbal cues produced by secondary children (chapters 2 and 4), and may over-interpret the cues produced by junior children. One might expect students to learn from their own experience the meaning of nonverbal signals emitted by their own specialist age-range, but this information would be more or less misleading for other age-ranges. Without evidence on exactly what students were taught on the course, a third explanation, that they were taught differentially in relation to their age specialisation, cannot be ruled out. As Lawes suggests, more work on this area is necessary, but in any case the result may suggest that teaching skill depends on experience, the effect of which is to some extent specific to the age-groups taught. The ability of teachers to cope with a range of age-groups is an area which needs further investigation.

Evidence from Neill, Fitzgerald and Jones (1983) on the development of student teachers' perceptions of nonverbal behaviour appears at first sight contradictory to that of Lawes (1987b). Neill et al. scored third-year students' and probationers' responses for mentions of nonverbal communication, either their own signals or signals from the class, in three classroom situations – how they could tell if a lesson had gone well, what immediate action they would take if they felt a lesson was not going well, and how they got the attention of the class at the start of a lesson. The students made very few mentions of nonverbal communication and there was no correlation between the number of times they mentioned it and their rated classroom performance. As Lawes (1987b) points out, the difference relates to the test situation; in his work the students' attention was drawn to nonverbal factors by the videotapes used. Without such prompting, nonverbal factors were not salient enough in most students' minds for them to mention them. The probationers in the Neill et al. study, by contrast, mentioned nonverbal signals more often and in their case number of mentions and rated performance were related. This suggests that with increasing experience the more able probationers were becoming more reflectively aware of their own and the children's signals. Informal contact (by Fitzgerald) with the probationers as their careers developed suggested that ratings as probationers had good predictive value for the subsequent development of their careers (see also Cortis (1972, 1973) and Crocker (1974) for college assessments).

This suggests that conscious awareness and use of nonverbal signals develops relatively slowly, but that Lawes's more competent students would probably become the more proficient teachers as their careers progressed. Calderhead (1987) suggests that student teachers go through a stage where they use tactics such as patrolling the classroom because they have seen the classroom teacher use them and because their tutors expect them to. By contrast, Calderhead found experienced class teachers often used these same tactics in a sophisticated way based on their previous knowledge of the class and individual children. They might, for instance, move into the area of particular children who they knew needed settling, as a way of settling them without exerting overt pressure (chapters 3 and 7). Calderhead felt that student teachers simply felt they needed to look busy while the children worked. However, they often received high marks from their tutors for doing so – Calderhead seems to feel this was cheating! Nevertheless, tutors and children have no way of knowing whether the student teacher's planning is less sophisticated than that of the experienced teacher unless their behaviour shows it. If the students give a performance consistent with that of an experienced teacher, the children should react in the same way. Where their performance differs from that of an experienced teacher, through inexperience or for other reasons, the children are likely to detect this. Calderhead gives an example – students' controlling behaviours may be less effective because the liberal ethos of their university course makes them feel unhappy as figures of authority.

COULD NONVERBAL SKILLS BE TRAINED?

The previous section suggested that if students can accurately replicate the full range of the experienced teacher's behaviour they should get the same reactions. Once they have behaved successfully without understanding, they might then begin to analyse what they are doing. This development of skills might happen without explicit training. What evidence is there that they could be, and currently are being, trained? In theory we can separate the issue of how the skills are acquired – by observation and imitation of teachers they encounter on the course, by self-observation, or by specific training or instruction – from where they are acquired. Jecker, Maccoby and Beitrose's study (1965) on teachers' perceptions of children's nonverbal signals of understanding is relevant. Experienced teachers made little use of these cues, and were no more perceptive of cues from children in their own class than those in other classes. This implied that there had been little learning from experience, without the benefit of prompting to focus teachers' attention on suitable cues. Hall, Rosenthal, Archer, DiMatteo and Rogers (1977) found that experienced teachers were actually less perceptive than students (a result they also found for a group of clinicians – psychiatrists and clinical psychologists who seemed to 'suffer' from experience in the same way). The teachers as a group were no more perceptive than high-school students or businessmen, and less perceptive than college students, clinicians, students on visual arts and nonverbal communication courses and actors (listed in order of increasing skill).

RESEARCH ON TRAINING TEACHERS IN NONVERBAL SKILLS

Although, as we shall see, specific training in nonverbal skills is relatively infrequent in teacher-training courses, attempts to train teachers in nonverbal skills go back some time. Jecker et al.'s (1965) early work showed that 6–8 hours of training produced a 7 per cent improvement in perceptiveness to students' cues, both training and testing using film clips of specially set up lessons. Though this was statistically significant, and they were satisfied with it, the absolute improvement was rather small.

Recent work on nonverbal training is reviewed by Klinzing and Tisher (1986). The majority of the studies used student teachers, but studies with experienced teachers have equally positive outcomes. An overview is provided by Klinzing and Jackson (1987), who contrast *direct* training approaches, which focus on specific behaviours, with *indirect* training, which aims to change more general personality attributes, such as assertiveness. Indirect training on its own is generally ineffective, unlike a combination of direct and indirect methods, or direct methods alone. Though few experiments have been done, they suggest combined courses would improve communication over a wider range of skills and contexts than pure direct training.

Effective direct training courses contain at least two of the following four elements: presentation of theory, training in discriminating nonverbal signals, modelling of the skills involved, and practice of the new skills with feedback – preferably in this order. Courses which are too short, especially if participants get two or fewer practice sessions, are less effective. However, courses are also less effective if participants do not know what they are supposed to be practising, or if feedback is so extensive that it leads to self-consciousness and anxiety. The effects were slightly stronger when follow-up assessments were done in actual classrooms than for follow-ups in microteaching or other scaled-down situations. As might be expected, effects are greatest in skills directly related to those trained; such skills can be transferred to normal classrooms and persist when course participants are reassessed up to three months later. In most studies, however, the follow-up period was shorter. In some cases desirable changes in behaviour occurred beyond those directly related to the training.

Smaller effects were registered for more global outcomes, such as clarity, persuasiveness, assertiveness and interest; and also for improving children's application to work and the correctness of their answers. However, effects on children's attitudes and achievement are less consistent; non-significant, or even negative, effects have been found. Klinzing and associates suggest that, apart from some cases where the amount of training was inadequate (e.g. Hodge 1974), teachers may have used their new skills over-enthusiastically, so that the medium interfered with the message. Where pupils are interested in their work in any case, because the material is interesting, or discovery or discussion methods are used, the effects of the teacher's nonverbal techniques are likely to be much slighter. This is likely to apply especially in primary education, where children's willingness to learn tends to be higher, especially child-centred progressive primary classes (see also chapter 1). All three factors applied, for example, to Bettencourt, Gall and Hull's (1980) study of training in enthusiasm.

Raymond (1973) was concerned to encourage student science teachers in positive nonverbal skills, including listening, as she felt current teacher behaviour worked against modern enquiry learning methods in science. She found that the group who had received nonverbal training showed more positive nonverbal behaviour. Students saw nonverbally positive teachers as more effective. However, the significance of the results was limited by the small numbers involved, and when the progress of individuals was followed, it was not possible to predict from good performance in the earlier part of the training that a teacher would do well in the later stages.

More evidence is needed on whether training is equally effective for different groups of student teachers. Though a four-session course on nonverbal behaviour and perceptiveness led to student teachers being assessed significantly more positively by their pupils, when Garratt (1979) looked at the sexes separately this applied only to female student teachers. There were no significant differences for males. She did not discuss possible reasons for this, but it may be related to females' greater nonverbal perceptiveness (chapter 2). If, as Lawes's work discussed above suggests, perceptiveness is related to performance, the rather short course used (four 50-minute sessions) may have been sufficient to sensitise the more perceptive females, but not male student teachers. The experimental group were judged better than the control group by their children for sociability, expertise, interest, control and democratic attention to children's views.

CURRENT TRAINING OF STUDENT TEACHERS IN NONVERBAL SKILLS

It is difficult to be sure how far nonverbal skills are taught to teachers in training in this country, especially on a systematic basis. Relatively few books intended for trainee teachers mention them explicitly, Robertson (1989) being an exception. A sample of 92 third-year students in one institution considered, with few exceptions, that their courses had been of virtually no value in giving them skills to deal with specific classroom situations such as starting lessons and assessing whether a lesson was progressing satisfactorily (Neill et al. 1983). Similar views were expressed by about half a group of 40 probationer primary teachers, all of whom had attended different colleges, so the problem does not appear confined to one institution (see also Cortis and Dean 1970). Certainly there does not seem to have been the effort devoted to the specifics of classroom communication in this country which has been devoted to presentations in industry (e.g. Turk 1985) or to police work

(Ainsworth and Pease 1987). However, the more effective probationers in the Neill et al. study did mention advice on their college courses on classroom technique including use of gaze, and voice projection and volume. This suggests that the advice given on these areas may be valuable in assisting students to develop effective technique, though we cannot rule out the alternative possibility that the more perceptive students are likely to attend to and recall advice. Unfortunately it is not possible to discriminate between these possibilities on the second-hand evidence which interviews with the teachers provides. Cortis (1972; Cortis and Dean 1972) found, similarly, that poorer probationer teachers reported they had had less help on classroom management on their training courses.

NONVERBAL SKILL AT ENTRY AS A PREDICTOR OF TEACHING SUCCESS ON COURSE

Ideally we would like not only to observe students' progress in nonverbal skill when they are on the course but also their level of skill at entry. Neill (1989c) attempted to follow the progress of entrants to a P.G.C.E. course. Unfortunately it was not possible to get permission to observe the interviews directly, and the study therefore had to be based on questionnaires to candidates' referees, and reports from interviewers, supervisors, supervising teachers and course tutors, sources of information considerably less reliable than direct observation. The questionnaire to referees asked them to rate four aspects of behaviour which are important in classroom interaction, and were deduced from the literature to be important in non-educational contexts. These were erectness and directness of gaze, which have been related to dominance (Weisfield 1980, Weisfield and Linkey 1985); their use of gestures, related to enthusiasm (Neill 1986b, McNeill 1985a), and their tendency to fidget, which gives an impression of lack of calmness and confidence (Exline 1985). Dominance, calmness and enthusiasm were rated from interviewers, and from supervisors' and supervising teachers' reports, and information was also collected about academic qualifications, reasons for withdrawal from the course and success in getting a job at the end of the course.

One striking result was the difference between interviewers' and referees' judgments of accepted and rejected candidates. Interviewers rated accepted candidates as significantly more dominant, calm and enthusiastic than rejected candidates. While referees rated accepted candidates as more erect and direct in their gaze, these differences were relatively small. Without evidence from direct observation it is not possible to be sure whether these differences reflect real differences in behaviour, or a 'halo effect' whereby interviewers emphasise differences to account for their decision. It is possible that some of the candidates who are rejected on their reaction to the stresses at interview would have performed satisfactorily as teachers, in line with their referees' assessments. Behaviour clearly had an important influence on selection; candidates were usually rejected for personality rather than academic reasons. There was no significant relationship between academic qualifications and selection, or progress once on the course.

This is consistent with the view of the classroom as a social system, and teaching effectiveness as being dependent on social skills, which has been mentioned throughout this book. However, Parkes (1989) found a strong relationship between academic success (primarily degree class, as this subsumed A-level results) and teaching practice success, which was strongly related to success in getting a teaching post. She was somewhat surprised at this effect of academic factors, and suggested that they may operate through increased self-confidence. In other words students who really know their subject reflect this in their confident behaviour and the children respond to this. Professional commitment and motivation to take up teaching as a career were also related; it is likely that these would be related to motivation and enthusiasm in the classroom. However, the study contained no direct evidence on behaviour.

Interpretation of the results of the Neill study once the candidates were on the course was complicated by the low amount of variation between students, with very few leaving the course and the great majority being rated as performing at least satisfactorily. In addition, the five reports and ratings from supervisors of teaching practice, supervising teachers, and tutors were highly correlated with each other, partly as a result of the amount of contact between staff. Correlations with the interviewers' ratings were much weaker, suggesting that what is described as enthusiasm, for instance, in interviews is different from enthusiasm under classroom conditions. The latter was more closely related to calm dominant behaviour as rated by referees and at interview. This suggests that, as was the case for experienced teachers (chapter 3), calm control was a prerequisite; student teachers who could not control their classes were not in a position to show enthusiasm.

As mentioned above, one of the problems in analysis was the small proportion of students who left the course, though greater numbers of candidates who had been accepted withdrew before starting the course. The majority of the small number of students who dropped out of the course before completing it did so because of poor teaching performance on either the first or the second teaching practice and had been accepted with reservations by the interviewers. Though the numbers are too low to make a definite judgment, it does seem that here the selection system is working effectively.

Potentially of more concern are those candidates who do not start the course, and may have accepted a place only as insurance in case they could not get a better prospect. This is significant because of current concern about the difficulty of recruiting adequate numbers of teachers for the sciences and mathematics, especially. The problems are likely to increase as the number of 18-year-olds decreases in the next few years. However, candidates who dropped out did not show any systematic difference from those who actually started the course in the ratings they had received from interviewers or reports from referees. Many candidates who withdrew gave an explanation of their reasons. Again there was no significant difference between those who had withdrawn as a result of getting another job (who might have been expected to be more competent, including more socially skilled) and the others, though the number involved was fairly small. Though this question needs to be addressed in a more specific study, there is therefore no evidence that the course was being systematically deprived of its highest quality recruits. There is of course no evidence as to how those who apply for teacher training compare in their behavioural skills with those who reject teaching as a career and apply for other jobs.

STUDENT TEACHERS' NONVERBAL BEHAVIOUR IN THE CLASSROOM

Although there is a considerable literature on student teachers' behaviour, often either it tends to omit aspects of nonverbal behaviour (for example Dreyfus and Eggleston 1979, where it is apparent that classroom control is disintegrating, but only subject-oriented behaviours are recorded) or student teachers are used only for convenience, and the research does not refer to them as students (for example the research by the Woolfolks mentioned in chapter 6). The work of the Teacher Education Project (Partington and Hinchcliffe 1979, Wragg and Dooley 1984) is an exception.

Partington and Hinchcliffe's pilot case studies covered particularly effective or ineffective incidents of class control. They felt that successful teachers always maintained the initiative and control of the class. Critical incidents occurred especially at transitions (chapter 4). Specific skills subserved global factors such as the establishment of good relationships with their classes, effective preparation before lessons and organisation during them. However, they also considered that more information was necessary on these specific teaching skills, which were independent of the subject taught.

Wragg and Dooley (1984) studied P.G.C.E. students in comprehensive schools. They paid particular attention to discipline, which was generally good: 83 per cent of incidents recorded were considered to be mild, and only 2 per cent serious. However, some deviant action was recorded in 76 per cent of the 3-minute recording units used; in half of these five or more children were involved. (It would be interesting to have comparable figures for experienced teachers.) Older secondary classes were more troublesome than younger ones. This success was probably due to the accuracy of the teacher's response; 73 per cent of responses occurred before the deviant incident escalated; less than 1 per cent were to inappropriate target children. This can be related to the point made in chapter 3, that nonverbal signals are only 'promises' of action, and will lose their force if they are not related to appropriate action. In 79 per cent of incidents, the students remained calm; they became agitated in only 16 per cent of incidents. In the remaining 5 per cent they were angry, though it was impossible to tell if the anger was genuine or put on. The results do not indicate whether the outcome was related to the teacher's calmness or otherwise in dealing with the incident.

A large proportion of the misbehaviour which occurred in the student teachers' lessons was nonverbal, in the broad sense. The 76 per cent of lesson units where deviant behaviour occurred, mentioned above, included 24 per cent where nonverbal behaviour was inappropriate to the task, 20 per cent where materials or equipment were used inappropriately, 12 per cent where children ate or drank illicitly, 11 per cent where they moved about inappropriately, and 9 per cent where they fidgeted. The 6 per cent of units where they provoked derision probably involved some interesting play-acting too! By contrast, noisy talk occurred in 38 per cent of segments, irrelevant talk in 23 per cent and interruptions in 5 per cent. There were also a range of misdemeanours, both verbal and nonverbal, which occurred in 2 per cent of units or less. This fits with the pattern described in chapter 4 that nonverbal misbehaviour is used because of its unattributability. It is also consistent with the pattern of misdemeanours teachers reported in the survey produced for the Elton Report (Department of Education and Science and Welsh Office 1989) – wearing and niggling, rather than serious.

The student teachers' responses, by contrast, tended to be mainly verbal. The most common nonverbal response was moving closer to the deviant pupil, which occurred in 20 per cent of the lesson units where the teacher made a response; facial expressions were used in 8 per cent, a dramatic pause in 7 per cent and a gesture in 5 per cent. Direct comparison between these figures and those for experienced teachers in Neill (1986b) is difficult because of differences in the recording systems. The only comparison which can be made with any confidence is that the effective experienced teachers used considerably more gestures, while the ineffective teachers' use of gesture was more comparable to the students'. Wragg and Dooley's (1984) student teachers moved the pupil in only 3 per cent of units and touched him in 1 per cent. By contrast, pupils were told to stop in 61 per cent of units, reprimanded in 25 per cent and threatened in 10 per cent. Rules were restated in 24 per cent of incidents and pupils encouraged to become more fully involved in their work in 16 per cent. The teachers' explicit and verbal efforts to regain control contrast with the pupils' implicit and nonverbal challenges. However, the use of gaze was not reported, and this may have been a common nonverbal control measure (though more difficult to observe reliably than those which were reported). In addition, the success of the verbal control measures may have been dependent on the nonverbal signals accompanying them, as discussed for experienced teachers in chapter 3.

IMPLICATIONS FOR FUTURE DEVELOPMENT OF TRAINING

Future development in nonverbal training would be valuable in two areas: in training teachers in classroom skills, and as a component of personal and social education, to prepare children for adult life, especially in workplace relationships.

As discussed earlier in this chapter, there is research evidence both that nonverbal skills can be trained and that student teachers currently receive little training in classroom interaction. The Elton Report (D.E.S. and Welsh Office 1989) assigns a central role in maintaining discipline in schools to group management skills, though it does not neglect the effects of school organisation and the leadership and support offered by senior staff, together with factors such as teacher morale, the attitude of parents and the image of teachers conveyed by the media. Group management included aspects such as scanning the class, appropriate posture and intonation, liberal encouragement to pupils who are working well and firm but restrained control, as well as lesson and curriculum planning matched to the needs of the pupils. Though the Report does not go into the appropriate behaviours in detail, it recommends guides such as Robertson (1989) which do so.

Both initial and in-service training in group management is recommended, the in-service training to include discussion and mutual support among teachers. Initial training should contain compulsory and specific training on group management, linked to teaching practice. These recommendations are in line with the research reviewed above.

However, a further recommendation of the Report, now adopted by the Council for the Accreditation of Teacher Education, is more dubious. This is that all course tutors involved in training classroom management should have recent experience of teaching, or should return to the classroom for teaching experience at regular intervals. This assumes that the ability to act skilfully in the classroom correlates with the ability to present the skills analytically. Tomlinson and Smith (1985) suggest that, if anything, the reverse is the case: high facility in using classroom skills automatically and without reflection militates being able to analyse and explain them explicitly. Indeed the Elton Report's own concern at the widespread belief among teachers that classroom management skills are a natural gift which cannot be trained or learned underlines the problem. If classroom skills are seen as low-level craft knowledge this devalues them relative to the more academic elements of the course. If, as the Report suggests, they are central to the classroom teacher's role, this could be taken as implying that the role is one of artisan rather than professional. Although the theoretical elements in teacher-training courses have attracted much criticism over the years, there is a strong case for a research-based element in classroom skills courses. One of the aims of this book is to show the range of relevant research.

Much of the research cited has been based on situations outside the classroom, and this brings us to the second area, the training of children in skills relevant to outside life. Duck's (1983) complaint that children are not educated in the social skills of friendship, with serious implications for their domestic and social life as adults, applies also to work-related social skills. However, the increased emphasis on the world of work is reflected in emphasis on the skills needed to relate to and work cooperatively with others (D.E.S. 1988). These career-related skills tend to be more apparent in cooperative project work at primary level than in many secondary-school situations, but explicit personal and social education has to date been more developed in secondary schools. Primary schools have not seen it as a specific part of their role. This implies a need to develop communication skills across the curriculum, via a coordinated personal and social education policy extending across all subjects (National Curriculum Council 1989b). Material specifically addressed to communication skills has to date been developed largely for post-16 careers courses (e.g. Berry 1985) though some material addressed to younger age-groups is available (e.g. Blatchford and Pellicer 1984). A general approach, addressed to skills which will be valuable in both work and leisure contexts, is likely to be more useful than the very specific training given, for example, to salespeople (Pease 1984). Especially in a multicultural society, it is essential to get pupils to analyse the message more carefully, rather than to misunderstand and reject the messenger.

SUMMARY

The available evidence suggests that teaching skills are acquired interactively, both pre-existing skill and perceptiveness and course experience contributing, rather than the popular view that effective teachers are 'born' with the gift of being able to relate to and control children.

The predictive value of interviews for teacher training, as for other situations, is limited. This may be due to the subordinate role of the interviewee, as compared to the dominant role of the class teacher. However, confident, enthusiastic behaviour leads to selection in interviews for teaching as for other positions. Nonverbal behaviour makes a considerable contribution to selection, though less than what the candidate actually says.

Children have clear ideas of what characterises competent teachers, and student teachers' previous experience as pupils appears to have a lasting effect. Student teachers' success is related to their nonverbal skills assessed before and during the course, and to their ability to make deductions from pupils' nonverbal signals. However, increased skill may be confined to the age-group with which the student has experience. Teachers' perceptiveness increases with experience, at least initially, though this increase may not be sustained. The classroom behaviour and control of student teachers is generally satisfactory. Many of their problems relate to their lower ability to analyse and predict classroom situations, by comparison with experienced teachers.

Direct training in specific skills is more effective than general training. Courses need to be of sufficient length and to include discrimination and role-play practice. Currently most courses include very little training in classroom group management skills, including nonverbal skills, and this needs to be increased. Children also need more practice with nonverbal and other interactive skills to prepare them for adult life.

References

Abramovitch, R. (1977) 'Children's recognition of situational aspects of facial expression'. *Child Development* 48: 459–63.
Abramovitch, R. and Daly, E.M. (1979) 'Inferring attributes of a situation from the expressions of peers'. *Child Development* 50: 586–9.
Adams, R.S. and Biddle, B.J. (1970) *Realities of Teaching: Explorations with Videotape.* New York: Holt, Rinehart & Winston.
Ainsworth, P.B. and Pease, K. (1987) *Police Work.* London: B.P.S./Methuen.
Aitchison, J. (1983) *The Articulate Mammal.* (2nd edn) London: Hutchinson.
Allen, V.L. and Atkinson, M.L. (1978) 'Encoding of nonverbal behavior by high-achieving and low-achieving children'. *Journal of Educational Psychology* 70: 298–305.
Allen, V.L. and Feldman, R.S. (1976) 'Studies on the role of tutor'. In Allen, V.L. (ed.) *Children as Teachers.* New York: Academic Press.
Anderson, L.M., Evertson, C.M. and Emmer, E.T. (1980) 'Dimensions in classroom management derived from recent research'. *Journal of Curriculum Studies* 12: 343–56.
Angus, M.J., Evans, K.W. and Parkin, B. (1975) *An Observational Study of Selected Pupil and Teacher Behaviour in Open Plan and Conventional Design Classrooms.* Australian Open Area Schools Project Technical Report No. 4.
Ardrey, R. (1967) *The Territorial Imperative.* New York: Atheneum.
Argyle, M. and Dean, J. (1965) 'Eye contact, distance and affiliation'. *Sociometry* 28: 289–304.
Argyle, M., Lalljee, M. and Cook, M. (1968) 'The effects of visibility on interaction in a dyad'. *Human Relations* 21: 3–17.
Atkinson, M. (1984) *Our Masters' Voices.* London: Methuen.
Baldwin, D. and Lister, C. (1987) *Safety When Alone.* Hove: Wayland.
Ball, S.J. (1980) 'Initial encounters in the classroom and the process of establishment'. In Woods, P. (ed.) *Pupil Strategies: Explorations in the Sociology of the School.* London: Croom Helm.
Barkow, J.H. (1980) 'Prestige and self-esteem: a biosocial interpretation'. In Omark, D., Strayer, F.F. and Freeman, D. (eds) *Dominance Relations.* New York: Garland.
Bates, J.E. (1976) 'Effects of children's nonverbal behavior upon adults'. *Child Development* 47: 1079–88.
Baxter, J.C. (1970) 'Interpersonal spacing in natural settings'. *Sociometry* 33: 444–56.
Beattie, G. (1983) *Talk: An Analysis of Speech and Non-verbal Behaviour in Conversation.* Open University Press: Milton Keynes.
Bellaby, P. (1979) 'Towards a political economy of decision-making in the classroom'. In Eggleston, J. (ed.) *Teacher Decision-making in the Classroom.* London: Routledge & Kegan Paul.

Bennett, N., Andrae, J., Hegarty, P. and Wade, B. (1980) *Open Plan Schools*. Slough: N.F.E.R.
Bennett, N. and Blundell, D. (1983) 'Quantity and quality of work in rows and classroom groups'. *Educational Psychology* 2: 94–105.
Bennett, N., Desforges, C., Cockburn, A. and Wilkinson, B. (1984) *The Quality of Pupil Learning Experiences*. London: Lawrence Erlbaum.
Berry, M. (ed.) (1985) *Communication: Themes and Skills*. Sheffield: Careers and Occupational Information Centre, Manpower Services Commission.
Bettencourt, E.M., Gall, M.D. and Hull, R.E. (1980) 'Effects of training teachers in enthusiasm on student achievement and attitudes'. Paper presented at the Annual Meeting of the American Educational Research Association, Boston, April 1980.
Bevan, K. and Wheldall, K. (1985) 'A touching way to teach: teacher touch behaviour in nursery and infant school classrooms'. Paper presented at the Annual Conference of the Education Section of the British Psychological Society, York, September 1985.
Beynon, J. (1985) *Initial Encounters in the Secondary School*. London: Falmer.
Blanck, P.D. and Rosenthal, R. (1982) 'Developing strategies for decoding "leaky" messages: on learning how and when to decode discrepant and consistent social communications'. In Feldman, R.S. (ed.) *Development of Nonverbal Behavior in Children*. New York: Springer-Verlag.
Blatchford, R. and Pellicer, C. (1984) *W.A.L.R.U.S.* Harlow: Longman.
Boileau, D.M. (1981) 'Nonverbal communication: classroom influence and topic'. *Communication Education* 30: 305–10.
Bower, R.L. (1980) 'A study in nonverbal behaviour: the influence of an instructor's posture on student task performance'. *International Journal of Instructional Media* 7: 257–67.
Bowers, T. (1986) 'Interpersonal skills and conflict management'. In Tattum, D.P. (ed.) *Management of Disruptive Pupil Behaviour in Schools*. London: Wiley.
Boydell, D. (1978) *The Primary Teacher in Action*. London: Open Books.
Brazil, D., Coulthard, M. and Johns, C. (1980) *Discourse Intonation and Language Teaching*. London: Longman.
Brophy, J.E. (1981) 'Teacher praise: a functional analysis'. *Review of Educational Research* 51: 5–32.
Brophy, J.E. and Good, T.L. (1970) 'Teachers' communication of differential expectations for children's classroom performance: some behavioral data'. *Journal of Educational Psychology* 61: 365–74.
Brophy, J.E. and Good, T.L. (1974) *Teacher–Student Relationships*. New York: Holt, Rinehart & Winston.
Brown, G.A. and Armstrong, S. (1984) 'Explaining and explanations'. In Wragg, E.C. (ed.) *Classroom Teaching Skills*. London: Croom Helm.
Brown, R. (1973) *A First Language*. London: Allen & Unwin.
Bugenthal, D.E., Love, L.R. and Gianetto, R.M. (1971) 'Perfidious feminine faces'. *Journal of Personality and Social Psychology* 17: 314–18.
Bull, P. (1983) *Body Movement and Interpersonal Communication*. Chichester: Wiley.
Bull, P. (1987) *Posture and Gesture*. Oxford: Pergamon.
Bull, P. and Brown, R. (1977) 'The role of postural change in dyadic conversations'. *British Journal of Social and Clinical Psychology* 16: 29–33.
Byrne, R. and Whiten, A. (1988) *Machiavellian Intelligence*. Oxford: Clarendon.
Calderhead, J. (1986) 'The contribution of field experience to student primary teachers' professional learning'. Paper presented at the Annual Conference of the British Educational Research Association, Bristol, September 1986.
Calderhead, J. (1987) 'Developing a framework for the elicitation and analysis of teachers' verbal reports'. *Oxford Review of Education* 13: 183–9.

Campbell, D.T., Kruskal, W.H. and Wallace, W.P. (1966) 'Seating aggregation as an index of attitude'. *Sociometry* 29: 1–15.

Caproni, V., Levine, D., O'Neal, E., McDonald, P. and Garwood, G. (1977) 'Seating position, instructor's eye contact availability and student participation in a small seminar'. *Journal of Social Psychology* 103: 315–16.

Caswell, C.R. (1982) 'Pupil strategies affecting classroom control'. Unpublished M.Ed. thesis, University of Warwick.

Chafe, W. (1980) 'Some reasons for hesitating'. In Dechert, H.W. and Raupach, M. (eds) *Temporal Variables in Speech*. The Hague: Mouton.

Chaikin, A.L., Sigler, E. and Derlega, V.J. (1974) 'Nonverbal mediators of teacher expectancy effects'. *Journal of Personality and Social Psychology* 30: 144–9.

Chance, M.R.A. (1967) 'Attention structure as the basis of primate rank orders'. *Man* (N.S.) 2: 503–18.

Chance, M.R.A., Callan, H.M.W. and Pitcairn, T.K. (1973) 'Attention and advertance in human groups'. *Social Science Information* 12: 27–41.

Clarke, D.D., Parry-Jones, W.Ll., Gay, B.M. and Smith, C.M.B. (1981) 'Disruptive incidents in secondary school classrooms: a sequence analysis approach'. *Oxford Review of Education* 7: 111–17.

Clements, J.E. and Tracy, D.B. (1977) 'Effects of touch and verbal reinforcement on the classroom behavior of emotionally disturbed boys'. *Exceptional Children* 43: 453–4.

Clift, S., Hutchings, R. and Povey, R. (1984) 'School-related attitudes of 11-year-old pupils in spacious and space-restricted classrooms'. *Educational Research* 26: 208–13.

Cohen, A.A. and Harrison, R.P. (1973) 'Intentionality in the use of hand illustrators in face-to-face communication situations'. *Journal of Personality and Social Psychology* 28: 276–9.

Coleman, B.J. (1985) 'Inter-interviewer agreement in the selection of P.G.C.E. students'. *Educational Research* 27: 127–32.

Cook, T.D. and Campbell, D.T. (1979) *Quasi-experimentation: Design and Analysis Issues for Field Settings*. Chicago: Rand McNally.

Cook-Gumperz, J. and Gumperz, J.J. (1982) 'Communicative competence in educational perspective'. In Wilkinson, L.C. (ed.) *Communicating in the Classroom*. New York: Academic Press.

Cooper, I. (1979) 'Design and use of primary school buildings; an examination of government-endorsed advice'. Paper presented at the International Conference of Environmental Psychology, Guildford.

Cooper, I. (1981) 'The politics of education and architectural design; the instructive example of British primary education'. *British Educational Research Journal* 7: 125–35.

Cooper, I. (1985) 'Teachers' assessments of primary school buildings: the role of the physical environment in education'. *British Educational Research Journal* 11: 253–69.

Cortis, G.A. (1972) 'A longitudinal study of college assessments'. *Education for Teaching* 89: 35–41.

Cortis, G.A. (1973) 'The assessment of a group of teachers in relation to earlier career experience'. *Educational Review* 25: 112–23.

Cortis, G.A. and Dean, A.J. (1970) 'Teaching skills of probationary primary teachers – a follow-up study'. *Educational Research* 14: 200–3.

Cortis, G.A. and Dean, A.J. (1972) 'Teaching skills of probationary primary teachers'. *Educational Research* 12: 230–4.

Cortis, G.A. and Grayson, A. (1978) 'Primary school pupils' perceptions of student teachers' performance'. *Educational Review* 30: 93–101.

Creider, C.A. (1986) 'Interlanguage comparisons in the study of the interactional use of gesture: progress and prospects'. *Semiotica* 62: 147–63.

Crocker, A.C. (1974) *Predicting Teaching Success*. Slough: N.F.E.R..
Cronin, C.L. (1980) 'Dominance relations and females'. In Omark, D., Strayer, F.F. and Freeman, D. (eds) *Dominance Relations*. New York: Garland.
Davies, J.G.V. and Maliphant, R. (1971a) 'Refractory behaviour at school in normal adolescent males in relation to psychopathy and early experience'. *Journal of Child Psychology and Psychiatry* 12: 35–41.
Davies, J.G.V. and Maliphant, R. (1971b) 'Autonomic responses of male adolescents exhibiting refractory behaviour in school'. *Journal of Child Psychology and Psychiatry* 12: 115–27.
Davis, T.N. and Satterley, D.J. (1969) 'Personality profiles of student teachers'. *British Journal of Educational Psychology* 39: 183–7.
Dawkins, M.S. (1986) *Unravelling Animal Behaviour*. Longman: Harlow.
Dean, L.M., Willis, F.N. and Hewitt, J. (1975) 'Initial interaction distance among individuals equal and unequal in military rank'. *Journal of Personality and Social Psychology* 32: 294–9.
Delamont, S. (1976) *Interaction in the Classroom*. London: Methuen.
Delamont, S. (1983) 'The ethnography of transfer'. In Galton, M. and Willcocks, J. (eds) *Moving from the Primary Classroom*. London: Routledge & Kegan Paul.
Delamont, S. and Galton, M. (1986) *Inside the Secondary Classroom*. London: Routledge & Kegan Paul.
Denscombe, M. (1980) 'Pupil strategies and the open classroom'. In Woods, P. (ed.) *Pupil Strategies*. London: Croom Helm.
Department of Education and Science (1975) *Acoustics in Educational Buildings*. Building Bulletin 51. London: H.M.S.O.
Department of Education and Science (1976) *Guillemont Junior School, Farnborough, Hampshire*. Building Bulletin 53. London: H.M.S.O.
Department of Education and Science (1978) *Nursery Education in Converted Space*. Building Bulletin 56. London: H.M.S.O.
Department of Education and Science (1987) *Building for Success: Schools and Colleges in the 1980s*. London: H.M.S.O.
Department of Education and Science (1988) *Careers Education and Guidance from 5 to 16*. Curriculum Matters 10. London: H.M.S.O.
Department of Education and Science and Welsh Office (1989) *Discipline in Schools: Report of the Committee of Enquiry chaired by Lord Elton*. London: H.M.S.O.
DePaulo, B.M. and Rosenthal, R. (1979a) 'Age changes in nonverbal decoding skills: evidence for increasing differentiation'. *Merrill-Palmer Quarterly* 25: 145–50.
DePaulo, B.M. and Rosenthal, R. (1979b) 'The structure of nonverbal decoding skills'. *Journal of Personality* 47: 506–17.
Docking, J.W. (1980) *Control and Discipline in Schools*. London: Harper & Row.
Dovidio, J.F. and Ellyson, S.L. (1985) 'Patterns of visual dominance behaviour in humans'. In Ellyson, S.L. and Dovidio, J.F. (eds) *Power, Dominance and Nonverbal Behavior*. New York: Springer.
Doyle, W. (1983) 'Academic work'. *Review of Educational Research* 53: 159–99.
Drake, K. (1979) 'Decision-making in the classroom; a microeconomic analysis'. In Eggleston, J. (ed.) *Teacher Decision-making in the Classroom*. London: Routledge & Kegan Paul.
Dreyfus, A. and Eggleston, J.F. (1979) 'Classroom transactions of student-teachers of science'. *European Journal of Science Education* 1: 75–86.
Duck, S. (1983) *Friends, for Life*. Brighton: Harvester.
Dumont, R.V. (1972) 'Learning English and how to be silent: studies in Sioux and Cherokee classrooms'. In Cazden, C.B., John, V.P. and Hymes, D. (eds) *Functions of Language in the Classroom*. New York: Teachers College Press.

Durlak, J.T., Beardsley, B.E. and Murray, J.S. (1972) 'Observation of user activity patterns in open and traditional environments'. In Mitchell, W.J. (ed.) *Environmental Design: Research and Performance*. Proceedings of the E.D.R.A.3 Conference, University of California.

Durlak, J.T. and Lehman, J. (1972) 'User awareness and sensitivity to open space: a study of traditional and open plan schools'. In Canter, D. and Lee, T. (eds) *Psychology and the Built Environment*. London: Architectural Press.

Durlak, J.T. and Lehman, J. (1974) 'User awareness abd sensitivity to open space: a study of traditional and open plan schools'. In Canter, D. and Lee, T. (eds) *Psychology and the Built Environment*. London: Architectural Press.

Edwards, A.D. and Furlong, V.J. (1978) *The Language of Teaching*. London: Heinemann.

Eibl-Eibesfeldt, I. (1972) 'Similarities and differences between cultures in expressive movements'. In Hinde, R.A. (ed.) *Non-verbal Communication*. London: Cambridge University Press.

Ekman, P. and Friesen, W.V. (1969a) 'The repertoire of nonverbal behavior: categories, origins, usage and coding'. *Semiotica* 1: 49–98.

Ekman, P. and Friesen, W.V. (1969b) 'Nonverbal leakage and clues to deception'. *Psychiatry* 32: 88–105.

Ekman, P. and Friesen, W.V. (1975) *Unmasking the Face*. Englewood Cliffs, N.J.: Prentice-Hall.

Ekman, P., Friesen, W.V. and Ancoli, S. (1980) 'Facial signs of emotional experience'. *Journal of Personality and Social Psychology* 39: 1125–34.

Ekman, P., Roper, G. and Hager, J.C. (1980) 'Deliberate facial movement'. *Child Development* 51: 886–91.

Ellis, A. and Beattie, G. (1986) *The Psychology of Language and Communication*. London: Weidenfeld & Nicolson.

English, S.L. (1985) 'Kinesics in academic lectures'. *E.S.P. Journal* 4: 161–70.

Enquist, M., Plane, M. and Roed, J. (1985) 'Aggressive communication in fulmars (*Fulmarus glacialis*) competing for food'. *Animal Behaviour* 33: 1007–20.

Erickson, F. (1982) 'Classroom discourse as improvisation: relationships between academic task structure and social participation structure in lessons'. In Wilkinson, L.C. (ed.) *Communicating in the Classroom*. New York: Academic Press.

Evans, K. (1974) 'The spatial organisation of infants' schools'. *Journal of Architectural Research* 3: 26–33.

Evans, K. (1979a) 'The physical form of the school'. *British Journal of Educational Studies* 27: 29–41.

Evans, K. (1979b) 'A touch of control in the classroom'. *New Society* 47: 187–9.

Exline, R.V. (1985) 'Multichannel transmission of nonverbal behavior and the perception of powerful men: the presidential debates of 1976'. In Ellyson, S.L. and Dovidio, J.F. (eds) *Power, Dominance and Nonverbal Behavior*. New York: Springer.

Feldman, R.S. (1976) 'Nonverbal disclosure of teacher deception and interpersonal affect'. *Journal of Educational Psychology* 68: 807–16.

Feldman, R.S., Devin-Sheehan, L. and Allen, V.L. (1978) 'Nonverbal cues as indicators of verbal dissembling'. *American Educational Research Journal* 15: 217–31.

Feldman, R.S., Jenkins, L. and Popoola, O. (1979) 'Detection of deception in adults and children via facial expressions'. *Child Development* 50: 350–5.

Feldman, R.S. and Prohaska, T. (1979) 'The student as Pygmalion; effect of student expectation on the teacher'. *Journal of Educational Psychology* 71: 485–93.

Feldman, R.S. and Saletsky, R.D. (1986) 'Nonverbal communication in interracial teacher–student interaction'. In Feldman, R.S. (ed.) *The Social Psychology of Education*. New York: Cambridge University Press.

Foot, H.C., Chapman, A.J. and Smith, J.R. (1980) *Friendship and Social Relations in Children*. Chichester: Wiley.
Forbes, R.J. and Jackson, P.R. (1980) 'Non-verbal behaviour and the outcome of selection interviews'. *Journal of Occupational Psychology* 53: 65–72.
Freedman, D.G. (1971) 'An evolutionary approach to research on the life cycle'. *Human Development* 14: 87–99.
Freedman, D.G. (1980) 'Sexual diomorphism and the status hierarchy'. In Omark, D.R., Strayer, F.F. and Freedman, D.G. (eds) *Dominance Relations*. New York: Garland.
Freedman, R., van Meel, J.M., Barroso, F. and Bucci, W. (1986) 'On the development of communicative competence'. *Semiotica* 62: 77–105.
Friedman, H.S. (1979) 'The interactive effects of facial expressions of emotion and verbal messages on perceptions of affective meaning'. *Journal of Experimental and Social Psychology* 15: 453–69.
Furlong, V.J. (1976) 'Interaction sets in the classroom; towards a study of pupil knowledge'. In Stubbs, M. and Delamont, S. (eds) *Explorations in Classroom Observation*. London: Wiley.
Galloway, C.M. (1974) 'Nonverbal teacher behaviors: a critique'. *American Experimental Research Journal* 11: 305–6.
Galton, M. (1989) *Teaching in the Primary School*. London: David Fulton.
Galton, M. and Simon, B. (eds) (1980) *Progress and Performance in the Primary Classroom*. London: Routledge & Kegan Paul.
Galton, M., Simon, B. and Croll, P. (1980) *Inside the Primary Classroom*. London: Routledge & Kegan Paul.
Galton, M. and Willcocks, J. (1983) *Moving from the Primary Classroom*. London: Routledge & Kegan Paul.
Gannaway, H. (1976) 'Making sense of school'. In Stubbs, M. and Delamont, S. (eds) *Explorations in Classroom Observation*. London: Wiley.
Garner, J. and Bing, M. (1973) 'Inequalities of teacher–pupil contacts'. *British Journal of Educational Psychology* 43: 234–43.
Garratt, B.A. (1979) 'Pupil perceptions of selected Mississippi State University student teacher participants in a nonverbal communication training program as measured by the pupil observation survey'. D.Ed. dissertation, Mississippi: Mississippi State University.
Garvey, C. (1977) *Play*. Glasgow: Fontana.
Getzels, J.W. (1974) 'Images of the classroom and visions of the learner'. *School Review* 82: 527–40.
Gillis, J.R. (1975) *Youth and History*. London: Academic Press.
Gilmore, P. (1985) 'Silence and sulking: emotional displays in the classroom'. In Tannen, D. and Saville-Troike, M. (eds) *Perspectives on Silence*. Norwood, N.J.: Ablex.
Ginsburg, H.J., Pollman, V.A. and Wauson, M.S. (1977) 'An ethological analysis of nonverbal inhibitors of aggressive behavior in male elementary school children'. *Developmental Psychology* 13: 417–18.
Gladwin, T. (1970) *East is a Big Bird*. Cambridge, Mass: Harvard University Press.
Goffman, E. (1972) *Relations in Public*. Harmondsworth: Penguin.
Goffman, E. (1979) *Gender Advertisements*. London: Macmillan.
Goodwin, C. (1986) 'Gestures as a resource for the organisation of mutual orientation'. *Semiotica* 62: 29–49.
Goodwin, M.H. and Goodwin, C. (1986) 'Gesture and coparticipation in the activity of searching for a word'. *Semiotica* 62: 51–75.
Graham, J.A. and Argyle, M. (1975a) 'A cross-cultural study of the communication of extra-verbal meaning by gestures'. *Journal of Human Movement Studies* 1: 33–9.
Graham, J.A. and Argyle, M. (1975b) 'The effects of different patterns of gaze combined

with different facial expressions, on impression formation'. *Journal of Human Movement Studies* 1: 178–82.
Graham, J.A., Ricci Bitti, P. and Argyle, M. (1975) 'A cross-cultural study of the communication of emotion by facial and gestural cues'. *Journal of Human Movement Studies* 1: 68–77.
Grammer, K., Schiefenhovel, W., Schleidt, M., Lorenz, B. and Eibl-Eibesfeldt, I. (1988) 'Patterns on the face: the eyebrow flash in crosscultural comparison'. *Ethology* 77: 279–99.
Grant, B.M. and Hennings, D.G. (1971) *The Teacher Moves*. New York: Teachers College Press.
Grant, E.C. (1969) 'Human facial expression'. *Man* (N.S.) 4: 525–36.
Gray, J.A. (1984a) 'The science of teaching the art of dance: a description of a computer-aided system for recording and analyzing dance instructional behaviors'. *Journal of Education for Teaching* 9: 264–78.
Gray, J.A. (1984b) 'A computerised technique for recording and analysing teacher mobility'. *Educational Studies* 10: 23–9.
Green, J.L. and Harker, J.O. (1982) 'Gaining access to learning: conversational, social and cognitive demands of group participation'. In Wilkinson, L.C. (ed.) *Communicating in the Classroom*. New York: Academic Press.
Greenfield, P. and Lave, J. (1982) 'Cognitive aspects of informal education'. In Wagner, D.A. and Stevenson, H.W. (eds) *Cultural Perspectives on Child Development*. San Francisco: Freeman.
Griffin, S. (1985) 'What else happens in playgroups?' *Education 3–13* 13 (1): 3–4.
Griffith, C.R. (1921) 'A comment on the psychology of the audience'. *Psychological Monographs* 30: 36–47.
Grogan, S.C. (1988) 'Nonverbal communication in children with reading problems'. *Journal of Learning Disabilities* 21: 364–8.
Gump, P.V. (1975) 'Operating environments in schools of open and traditional design'. In David, T.G. and Wright, B.D. (eds) *Learning Environments*. Chicago: University of Chicago Press.
Haber, G.M. (1980) 'Territorial invasion in the classroom'. *Environment and Behavior* 12: 17–31.
Hadar, U., Steiner, T.J. and Clifford Rose, F. (1985) 'Head movement during listening turns in conversation'. *Journal of Nonverbal Behavior* 9: 214–28.
Hall, E.T. (1966) *The Hidden Dimension*. New York: Doubleday.
Hall, J.A., Rosenthal, R., Archer, D., DiMatteo, M.R. and Rogers, P.L. (1977) 'Nonverbal skills in the classroom'. *Theory into Practice* 16: 162–6.
Hammersley, M. (1976) 'The mobilisation of pupil attention'. In Hammersley, M. and Woods, P. (eds) *The Process of Schooling*. Milton Keynes: Open University Press.
Hammersley, M. (1984) 'Staffroom news'. In Hargreaves, A. and Woods, P. (eds) *Classrooms and Staffrooms*. Milton Keynes: Open University Press.
Hammersley, M. and Turner, G. (1980) 'Conformist pupils?' In Woods, P. (ed.) *Pupil Strategies*. London: Croom Helm.
Hargreaves, D.H. (1967) *Social Relations in a Secondary School*. London: Routledge & Kegan Paul.
Hargreaves, D.H. (1975) *Interpersonal Relations and Education*. London: Routledge & Kegan Paul.
Hargreaves, D.H. (1982) *The Challenge for the Comprehensive School*. London: Routledge & Kegan Paul.
Heath, A. (1981) *Social Mobility*. Glasgow: Fontana.
Heinig, R.B. (1975) 'A descriptive study of teacher–pupil tactile communication in grades four through six'. Unpublished Ph.D. thesis, University of Pittsburgh.
Henley, N.M. and Harmon, S. (1985) 'The nonverbal semantics of power and gender: a

perceptual study'. In Ellyson, S.L. and Dovidio, J.F. (eds) *Power, Dominance and Nonverbal Behavior*. New York: Springer.
Heslin, R. and Alper, T. (1983) 'Touch: a bonding gesture'. In Wiemann, J.M. and Harrison, R.P. (eds) *Nonverbal Interaction*. Beverley Hills: Sage.
Hiers, J.M. and Heckel, R.V. (1977) 'Seating choice, leadership, and locus of control'. *Journal of Social Psychology* 103: 313–14.
Hinde, R.A. (1974) *Biological Bases of Human Social Behaviour*. New York: McGraw-Hill.
Hinde, R.A. (1987) *Individuals, Relationships and Culture*. Cambridge: Cambridge University Press.
Hocking, J.E. and Leathers, D.G. (1980) 'Nonverbal indicators of deception: a new theoretical perspective'. *Communication Monographs* 47: 119–31.
Hodge, R.L. (1974) 'An empirical study of the acquisition of nonverbal teaching behaviors by secondary teaching candidates in a teaching laboratory'. Paper presented at the Annual Meeting of the American Educational Research Association, Chicago, Illinois, April 1974.
Hold-Cavell, B.C.L., Stohr, C. and Schneider, J. (1985) 'The significance of attention-structure: when do children attend to each other?' Paper presented at the 19th International Ethological Conference, Toulouse, August 1985.
Hollandsworth, J.G., Kazelkis, R., Stevens, J. and Dressel, M.E. (1979) 'Relative contributions of verbal, articulative, and nonverbal communication to employment decisions in the job interview setting'. *Personnel Psychology* 32: 359–67.
Hook, C.M. and Rosenshine, B.V. (1979) 'Accuracy of teacher reports of their classroom behavior'. *Review of Educational Research* 49: 1–12.
Hoskin, K.W. and Steele, A. (1988) 'Assessing the Business Professional'. Report to the Institute of Chartered Accountants of England and Wales.
Hull, C. (1985) 'Pupils as teacher educators'. *Cambridge Journal of Education* 15: 1–8.
Humphrey, N.K. (1976) 'The social function of intellect'. In Bateson, P.P.G. and Hinde, R.A. (eds) *Growing Points in Ethology*. Cambridge: Cambridge University Press.
Humphreys, A.P. and Smith, P.K. (1984) 'Rough-and-tumble in preschool and playground'. In Smith, P.K. (ed.) *Play in Animals and Humans*. Oxford: Blackwell.
Humphries, S. (1981) *Hooligans or Rebels?* Oxford: Blackwell.
Huntingford, F. (1984) *The Study of Animal Behaviour*. London: Chapman and Hall.
Huntingford, F. and Turner, A. (1987) *Animal Conflict*. London: Chapman and Hall.
Hutt, C. (1972) *Males and Females*. Harmondsworth: Penguin.
Hutt, S.J. and Hutt, C. (1970) *Direct Observation and Measurement of Behavior*. Springfield, Ill.: Thomas.
Jackson, P.W. and Lahaderne, H.M. (1967) 'Inequalities of teacher–pupil contacts'. *Psychology in the Schools* 4: 204–11.
Jaffe, J., Stern, D.N. and Peery, J.C. (1973) '"Conversational" coupling of gaze behavior in prelinguistic human development'. *Journal of Psycholinguistic Research* 2: 321–9.
James, G. and Choppin, B. (1977) 'Teachers for tomorrow'. *Educational Research* 19: 184–91.
Jecker, J.D., Maccoby, H. and Beitrose, H.S. (1965) 'Improving accuracy in interpreting non-verbal cues of comprehension'. *Psychology in the Schools* 2: 239–44.
Jenkins, J.R. and Deno, S.L. (1969) 'Influence of student behavior on teacher's self-evaluation'. *Journal of Educational Psychology* 60: 439–42.
Jones, S.E. and Aiello, J.R. (1973) 'Proxemic behavior of black and white first-, third- and fifth-grade children'. *Journal of Personality and Social Psychology* 25: 21–7.
Jourard, S.M. (1966) 'An exploratory study of body-accessibility'. *British Journal of Social and Clinical Psychology* 5: 221–31.
Kazdin, A.E. and Klock, J. (1973) 'The effect of nonverbal teacher approval on student attentive behavior'. *Journal of Applied Behavior Analysis* 6: 643–54.

Keating, C.F. (1985) 'Human dominance signals: the primate in us'. In Ellyson, S.L. and Dovidio, J.F. (eds) *Power, Dominance and Nonverbal Behavior*. New York: Springer.
Keith, L.T., Tornatzky, L.G. and Pettigrew, L.E. (1974) 'An analysis of verbal and non-verbal classroom teaching behaviors'. *Journal of Experimental Education* 42: 30–8.
Kendon, A. (1967) 'Some functions of gaze direction in social interaction'. *Acta Psychologica* 26: 22–63.
Kendon, A. (1970) 'Movement coordination in social interaction: some examples described'. *Acta Psychologica* 32: 100–25.
Kenner, A.N. (1984) 'The effect of task differences, attention and personality on the frequency of body-focussed movement'. *Journal of Non-Verbal Behavior* 8: 159–71.
Klein, S.S. (1971) 'Student influence on teacher behavior'. *American Educational Research Journal* 8: 403–21.
Klinzing, H.G. and Jackson, I. (1987) 'Training teachers in nonverbal sensitivity and nonverbal behaviour'. *International Journal of Educational Research* 11: 589–600.
Klinzing, H.G. and Tisher, R.I. (1986) 'Expressive nonverbal behaviours; a review of research on training with consequent recommendations for teacher education'. In Raths, J.D. and Katz, L.G. (eds) *Advances in Teacher Education*. (Vol 2.) Norwood, N.J.: Ablex.
Koneya, M. (1976) 'Location and interaction in row-and-column seating arrangements'. *Environment and Behaviour* 8: 265–82.
Kounin, J.S. (1970) *Discipline and Group Management in Classrooms*. Huntington, N.Y.: Robert E. Krieger.
Kounin, J.S. and Sherman, L.W. (1979) 'School environments as behavior settings'. *Theory into Practice* 18: 145–51.
Lasley, T.J. (1981) 'Classroom misbehavior: some field observations'. *High School Journal* 64: 142–9.
Lawes, J.S. (1987a) 'The relationship between nonverbal awareness of self and teaching competence in student teachers'. *Journal of Education for Teaching* 13: 145–54.
Lawes, J.S. (1987b) 'Student teachers' awareness of pupils' nonverbal responses'. *Journal of Education for Teaching* 13: 257–66.
Leathers, D.G. (1979) 'The impact of multichannel message inconsistency on verbal and nonverbal decoding behaviors'. *Communication Monographs* 46: 88–100.
Legendre, A. (1985) 'L'expérimentation écologique dans l'approche des comportements sociaux des jeunes enfants en groupes'. In Baudonnière, P.-M. (ed.) *Étudier l'enfant de la naissance a 3 ans*. Paris: Collection Comportements CRNS.
Legendre, A. (1989) 'Young children's social competence and their use of space in day-care centres'. In Schneider, B.H. (ed.) *Social Competence in Developmental Perspective*. Dordrecht: Kluwer Academic Publishers.
Lehtonen, J. and Sajavarra, K. (1985) 'The silent Finn'. In Tannen, D. and Saville-Troike, M. (eds) *Perspectives on Silence*. Norwood, N.J.: Ablex.
Leudar, I. (1981) 'Strategic communication in mental retardation'. In Fraser, W.I. and Grieve, R. (eds) *Communicating with Normal and Retarded Children*. Bristol: John Wright.
Lewis, A. (1987) 'Modification of discourse strategies by mainstream 6–7 year olds towards peers with special learning difficulties'. In Griffiths, P., Local, J. and Mills, A. (eds) *Proceedings of the Child Language Seminar*. York: University of York.
Lewis, A. and Lewis, V. (1988) 'Young children's attitudes, after a period of integration, towards peers with severe learning difficulties'. *European Journal of Special Needs Education* 3: 161–71.
Lewis, R. and Lovegrove, R. (1984) 'Teachers' classroom control procedures: are students' preferences being met?' *Journal of Education for Teaching* 10: 97–105.

Licata, J.W. (1978) 'Student brinkmanship and school structure'. *Educational Forum* 42: 345–50.

Lovegrove, M.N. and Lewis, R. (1982) 'Classroom-control procedures used by relationship-centred teachers'. *Journal of Education for Teaching* 8: 55–66.

McCuller, C.C. (1983) 'Perceptions of videotaped classroom simulations by disruptive and nondisruptive students'. Paper presented at the Annual Meeting of the American Educational Research Association, Montreal, April 1983.

McHenry, R. (1981) 'The selection interview'. In Argyle M. (ed.) *Social Skills and Work*. Methuen: London.

Maclure, S. (1984) *Educational Development and School Building: Aspects of Public Policy 1945–1973*. Harlow: Longman.

McMillan, M. (1983) *An Open Question: a Study of the Use of Open-Plan Areas in Secondary Schools*. Edinburgh: Scottish Council for Research in Education.

McNeill, D. (1985a) 'So you think gestures are nonverbal?' *Psychological Review* 92: 350–71.

McNeill, D. (1985b) 'Temanotics, or the wisdom of the hands'. Paper given at the Eastern States Conference on Linguistics, SUNY, Buffalo, October 1985.

McNeill, D. (1986) 'Iconic gestures of children and adults'. *Semiotica* 62: 107–28.

McNeill, D. (1987) 'So you *do* think gestures are nonverbal. Reply to Feyereisen'. *Psychological Review* 94: 499–504.

Macpherson, J. (1983) *The Feral Classroom*. London: Routledge & Kegan Paul.

Mahony, P. (1985) *Schools for the Boys?* London: Hutchinson.

Maxwell, G.M. and Cook, M.W. (1985) 'Postural congruence and judgements of liking and perceived similarity'. *New Zealand Journal of Psychology* 14: 20–6.

Maynard Smith, J. (1982) *Evolution and the Theory of Games*. Cambridge: Cambridge University Press.

Meighan, R. (1977) 'Pupils' perceptions of the classroom techniques of postgraduate student teachers'. *British Journal of Teacher Education* 3: 139–48.

Merritt, M. (1982) 'Distributing and directing attention in primary classrooms'. In Wilkinson, L.C. (ed.) *Communicating in the Classroom*. New York: Academic Press.

Meyenn, R.J. (1980) 'School girls' peer groups'. In Woods, P. (ed.) *Pupil Strategies: Explorations in the Sociology of the School*. London: Croom Helm.

Miller, J.F. (1979) 'Proxemics; a hidden dimension in the classroom'. *International Journal of Instructional Media* 7: 55–8.

Moore, D.W. and Glynn, T. (1984) 'Variation in question rate as a function of position in the classroom'. *Educational Psychology* 4: 233–48.

Moore, G.T. (1987) 'The physical environment and cognitive development in child-care centres'. In Weinstein, C.S. and David, T.G. (eds) *Spaces for Children: The Built Environment and Child Development*. New York: Plenum.

Morgan, C., Hall, V. and MacKay, H. (1983) *The Selection of Secondary School Headteachers*. Milton Keynes: Open University Press.

Morris, D. (1977) *Man-watching*. London: Triad Panther.

Morris, D., Collett, P., Marsh, P. and O'Shaughnessy, M. (1979) *Gestures: Their Origin and Distribution*. London: Jonathan Cape.

Mortimore, P., Sammons, P., Stoll, L., Lewis, D. and Ecob, R. (1988) *School Matters*. Wells: Open Books.

Moskowitz, G. and Hayman, J.L. (1974) 'Interaction patterns of first-year, typical and 'best' teachers in inner-city schools'. *Journal of Educational Research* 67: 224–30.

Moskowitz, G. and Hayman, J.L. (1976) 'Success strategies of inner-city teachers: a year-long study'. *Journal of Educational Research* 69: 283–9.

Nash, B.C. (1981) 'The effects of classroom spatial organisation on four and five year old children's learning'. *British Journal of Educational Psychology* 51: 144–55.

Nash, R. (1974) 'Pupils' expectations for their teachers'. *Research in Education* 12: 47–61.
National Curriculum Council (1989a) *An Introduction to the National Curriculum*. Milton Keynes: Open University.
National Curriculum Council (1989b) *The National Curriculum and Whole Curriculum Planning: Preliminary Guidance*. Circular Number 6. York: National Curriculum Council.
Neill, S.R. St J. (1976) 'Aggressive and non-aggressive fighting in twelve-to-thirteen year old pre-adolescent boys'. *Journal of Child Psychology and Psychiatry* 17: 213–20.
Neill, S.R. St J. (1982a) 'Preschool design and child behaviour'. *Journal of Child Psychology and Psychiatry* 23: 309–18.
Neill, S.R. St J. (1982b) 'Experimental alterations in playroom layout and their effect on staff and child behaviour'. *Educational Psychology* 2: 103–19.
Neill, S.R. St J. (1983a) 'Choosing an appropriate observation method for science lessons'. *European Journal of Science Education* 5: 327–31.
Neill, S.R. St J. (1983b) 'Children's social relationships and education – an evolutionary effect?' *Social Biology and Human Affairs* 47: 48–55.
Neill, S.R. St J. (1984) 'The effects of preschool playgroup equipment'. *Education 3–13* 12 (1): 4–6.
Neill, S.R. St J. (1985) 'Rough-and-tumble and aggression in schoolchildren: serious play?' *Animal Behaviour* 33: 1380–2.
Neill, S.R. St J. (1986a) 'Children's reported response to teachers' nonverbal signals: a pilot study'. *Journal of Education for Teaching* 12: 53–63.
Neill, S.R. St J. (1986b) 'An ethological approach to teachers' nonverbal communication'. In Le Camus, J. and Cosnier, J. (eds) *Ethology and Psychology*. Readings from the 19th International Ethological Conference. Toulouse: Privat/Université Paul Sabatier.
Neill, S.R. St J. (1986c) 'Children's responses to touch'. Paper presented at the Fifth International Conference on Human Ethology, Tutzing, West Germany, 27–31 July.
Neill, S.R. St J. (1987) 'Nonverbal communication – implications for teachers'. In Martinsson, B.-G. (ed.) *On Communication 4*. Linkoping: University of Linkoping.
Neill, S.R. St J. (1989a) 'The effects of facial expression and posture on children's reported responses to teacher nonverbal communication'. *British Educational Research Journal* 15: 195–204.
Neill, S.R. St J. (1989b) 'Children's reported responses to teachers' and non-teachers' nonverbal communication'. *Educational Research* 31: 71–4.
Neill, S.R. St J. (1989c) 'The predictive value of assessments of the non-verbal skills of applicants to postgraduate teacher training'. *Journal of Education for Teaching* 15: 149–59.
Neill, S.R. St J., Denham, E.J.M., Schaffer, H.R. and Markus, T.A. (1977) *Psychological Influence of Spatial Design Factors in Nurseries*. Glasgow: University of Strathclyde.
Neill, S.R. St J., Fitzgerald, J.M. and Jones, B. (1983) 'The relation between reported awareness of non-verbal communication and rated effectiveness in probationer and student teachers'. *Journal of Education for Teaching* 9: 16–29.
Noller, P. (1984) *Nonverbal Communication and Marital Interaction*. Oxford: Pergamon.
Norton, L. (1974) 'Elementary School Age Children's Perceptions of Teachers' Nonverbal Behavior'. Unpublished D.Ed. thesis, Oklahoma State University, Stillwater, Oklahoma.
Norton, L. and Dobson, R. (1976) 'Perceptions of teachers' nonverbal behaviors by children of different race, age and sex'. *Humanist Educator* 14: 94–102.

O.E.C.D. (1976) *Providing for Future Change: Adaptability and Flexibility in School Building*. Paris: Organisation for Economic Cooperation and Development.

Olson, D.R. (1976) 'Culture, technology and intellect'. In Resnick, L.B. (ed.) *The Nature of Intelligence*. Hillsdale, N.J.: Lawrence Erlbaum.

Parkes, K.R. (1989) 'The performance and subsequent employment status of PGCE students: academic and attitudinal predictors'. *British Educational Research Journal* 15: 231–48.

Parry-Jones, W.L. and Gay, B.M. (1980) 'The anatomy of disruption: a preliminary consideration of interaction sequences within disruptive incidents'. *Oxford Review of Education* 6: 213–20.

Partington, J. (1984) *Law and the New Teacher*. London: Holt, Rinehart & Winston.

Partington, J.A. and Hinchcliffe, G. (1979) 'Some aspects of classroom management'. *British Journal of Teacher Education* 5: 231–41.

Pease, A. (1984) *Body Language*. London: Sheldon.

Perdue, V.P. and Connor, J.M. (1978) 'Patterns of touching between preschool children and male and female teachers'. *Child Development* 49: 1258–62.

Perry, A. (1908) *The Management of a City School*. New York: Macmillan.

Peterson, P.L. and Swing, S.R. (1982) 'Beyond time on task: students' reports of their thought processes during classroom instruction'. *Elementary School Journal* 82: 481–91.

Philips, S.U. (1972) 'Participant structures and communicative competence: Warm Springs children in community and classroom'. In Cazden, C.B., John, V.P. and Hymes, D. (eds) *Functions of Language in the Classroom*. New York: Teachers College Press.

Pitcairn, T. (1985) 'Young infants' knowledge of faces'. Paper presented at International Conference on the Meaning of Faces, Cardiff, June 1985.

Preece, P.F.W. (1979) 'Student teacher anxiety and class-control problems on teaching practice: a cross-lagged panel analysis'. *British Educational Research Journal* 5: 13–19.

Proshansky, E. and Wolfe, M. (1975) 'The physical setting and open education'. In David, T.G. and Wright, B.D. (eds) *Learning Environments*. Chicago: University of Chicago Press.

Putallaz, M. and Gottman, J.M. (1981) 'Social skills and group acceptance'. In Asher, S.R. and Gottman, J.M. (eds) *The Development of Children's Friendships*. Cambridge: Cambridge University Press.

Raffler-Engel, W. von (1983) 'The perception of nonverbal behavior in the career interview'. *Pragmatics and Beyond* IV: 4. Amsterdam: John Benjamin.

Raymond, A. (1973) 'The acquisition of nonverbal behaviors by preservice science teachers and their application during student teaching'. *Journal of Research in Science Teaching* 10: 13–24.

Reid, D.J. (1980) 'Spatial involvement and teacher–pupil interaction patterns in school biology laboratories'. *Educational Studies* 6: 31–40.

Reilly, S.S. and Muzekari, L.H. (1986) 'Effects of emotional illness and age upon the resolution of discrepant messages'. *Perceptual and Motor Skills* 62: 823–9.

Rivlin, L.G. and Rothenberg, M. (1976) 'The use of space in open classrooms'. In Proshansky, H.M., Ittelson, W.H. and Rivlin, L.G. (eds) *Environmental Psychology*. New York: Holt, Rinehart & Winston.

Rivlin, L.G. and Wolfe, M. (1972) 'The early history of a psychiatric hospital for children; expectations and reality'. *Environment and Behavior* 4: 31–71.

Robbins, E.S. and Haase, R.F. (1985) 'Power of nonverbal cues in counseling interactions: availability, vividness, or salience?' *Journal of Counseling Psychology* 32: 502–13.

Robertson, J. (1989) *Effective Classroom Control*. London: Hodder & Stoughton.

Roehler, L.R. and Duffy, G.G. (1986) 'What makes one teacher a better explainer than another'. *Journal of Education for Teaching* 12: 273–84.

Roskraft, E., Jarvi, T., Bakken, M., Beeh, C. and Reinertsen, R.E. (1986) 'The relationship between social status and resting metabolic rate in great tits (*Parus major*) and pied flycatchers (*Ficedula hypoleuca*)'. *Animal Behaviour* 34: 838–42.

Rowe, M.B. (1974) 'Wait time and reward as instructional variables; their influence on language, logic and fate control'. *Journal of Research in Science Teaching* 11: 81–94.

Rutter, D.R and O'Brien, P. (1980) 'Social interaction in withdrawn and aggressive maladjusted girls: a study of gaze'. *Journal of Child Psychology and Psychiatry* 21: 59–66.

Rutter, D.R., Stephenson, G.M., Ayling, K. and White, P.A. (1978) 'The timing of Looks in dyadic conversation'. *British Journal of Social and Clinical Psychology* 17: 17–21.

Scheman, J.D. and Lockard, J.S. (1979) 'Development of gaze aversion in children'. *Child Development* 50: 594–6.

Schwebel, A.I. and Cherlin, D.L. (1972) 'Physical and social distancing in teacher–pupil relationships'. *Journal of Educational Psychology* 63: 543–50.

Seabrook, J. (1982) *Working-class Childhood*. London: Gollancz.

Seddon, G.M. and Thorp, J. (1989) 'A method of training selection panels and applicants for teaching appointments'. *Journal of Education for Teaching* 15: 239–46.

Shorter, E. (1976) *The Making of the Modern Family*. London: Fontana.

Silberman, M.L. (1969) 'Behavioral expression of teachers' attitudes toward elementary school students'. *Journal of Educational Psychology* 60: 402–7.

Sinclair, J.McH. and Coulthard, R.M. (1975) *Towards an Analysis of Discourse*. London: Oxford University Press.

Sluckin, A.M. (1979) 'Avoiding violence in the playground'. *Educational Research* 21: 83–8.

Sluckin, A.M. (1980) 'Dominance relationships in preschool children'. In Omark, D.R., Strayer, F.F. and Freedman, D.G. (eds) *Dominance Relations: An Ethological View of Human Conflict and Social Interaction*. New York: Garland.

Sluckin, A.M. (1981) *Growing Up in the Playground*. London: Routledge & Kegan Paul.

Smith, H.A. (1979) 'Nonverbal communication in teaching'. *Review of Educational Research* 49: 631–72.

Smith, P.K. and Ahmad, Y. (1989) 'The playground jungle: bullies, victims and intervention strategies'. Unpublished paper, Department of Psychology, University of Sheffield.

Smith, P.K., Boulton, M. and Cowie, H. (1989) 'ERSC-funded project on ethnic relations in middle school'. Unpublished report, Department of Psychology, University of Sheffield.

Smith, P.K. and Connolly, K.J. (1980) *The Ecology of Preschool Behaviour*. Cambridge: Cambridge University Press.

Snodgrass, S.E. and Rosenthal, R. (1985) 'Interpersonal sensitivity and skills in decoding nonverbal channels: the value of face value'. *Basic and Applied Social Psychology* 6: 243–55.

Solomon, J. (1983) 'Messy, contradictory and obstinately persistent: a study of children's out-of-school ideas about energy'. *School Science Review* December: 225–9.

Sommer, R. (1969) *Personal Space*. Englewood Cliffs, N.J.: Prentice-Hall.

Soudek, M. and Soudek, L.I. (1985) 'Non-verbal channels in language learning'. *E.L.T. Journal* 39: 109–13.

Spiegel, J. and Machotka, P. (1974) *Messages of the Body*. New York: Free Press.

Stanners, R.F., Byrd, D.M. and Gabriel, R. (1985) 'The time it takes to identify facial expressions: effects of age, gender of subject, sex of sender, and type of expression'. *Journal of Nonverbal Behavior* 9: 201–13.

Stanworth, M. (1983) *Gender and Schooling*. London: Hutchinson.
Stebbins, R.A. (1970) 'The meaning of disorderly behavior: teacher definitions of a classroom situation'. *Sociology of Education* 44: 217–36.
Stebbins, R.A. (1973) 'Physical context influences on behavior: the case of classroom disorderliness'. *Environment and Behavior* 5: 291–314.
Stein, S.A. (1976) 'Selected teacher verbal and nonverbal behaviors as related to grade level and student classroom behaviors'. Unpublished Ph.D. dissertation, Northwestern University, Evanston, Illinois.
Streeck, J. (1983) 'Social order in child communication: a study in microethnography'. *Pragmatics and Beyond* IV: 8. Amsterdam: John Benjamin.
Sullins, E.S., Friedman, H.S. and Harris, M.J. (1985) 'Individual differences in expressive style as a mediator of expectancy communication'. *Journal of Nonverbal Behavior* 9: 229–38.
Sundstrom, E. and Altman, I. (1976) 'Interpersonal relationships and personal space: research review and theoretical model'. *Human Ecology* 4: 47–67.
Sylva, K., Roy, C. and Painter, M. (1980) *Childwatching at Playgroup and Nursery School*. London: Grant McIntyre.
Tann, S (1981) 'Grouping and group work'. In Simon, B. and Willcocks, J. (eds) *Research and Practice in the Primary Classroom*. London: Routledge & Kegan Paul.
Tannen, D. (1984) *Conversational Style*. Norwood, N.J.: Ablex.
Taylor, R.B. (1988) *Human Territorial Functioning*. Cambridge: Cambridge University Press.
Thorne, B. (1986) 'Girls and boys together ... but mostly apart: gender arrangements in elementary schools'. In Hartup, W.W. and Rubin, Z. (eds) *Relationships and Development*. Hillsdale, N.J.: Lawrence Erlbaum.
Tizard, B. and Hughes, M. (1984) *Young Children Learning*. London: Fontana.
Tomlinson, P. and Smith, R.(1985) 'Training intelligently skilled teachers'. In Francis, H. (ed.) *Learning to Teach: Psychology in Teacher Training*. London: Falmer.
Torode, B. (1976) 'Teachers' talk and classroom discipline'. In Stubbs, M. and Delamont, S. (eds) *Explorations in Classroom Observation*. London: Wiley.
Touhey, J.C. (1974) 'Effects of dominance and competence on heterosexual attraction'. *British Journal of Social and Clinical Psychology* 13: 22–6.
Trevarthen, C. (1977) 'Descriptive analyses of infant communicative behaviour'. In Schaffer, H.R. (ed.) *Studies in Mother–Infant Interaction*. London: Academic Press.
Trivers, R. (1985) *Social Evolution*. Menlo Park: Benjamin/Cummings.
Trower, P., Bryant, B. and Argyle, M. (1978) *Social Skills and Mental Health*. London: Methuen.
Turk, C. (1985) *Effective Speaking*. London: Spon.
Turner, G. (1982) 'The distribution of classroom interactions'. *Research in Education* 27: 41–8.
Turner, G. (1983) *The Social World of the Comprehensive School*. London: Croom Helm.
Twardosz, S., Cataldo, M.F. and Risley, T.R. (1974) 'Open environment design for infant and toddler day care'. *Journal of Applied Behavior Analysis* 7: 529–46.
Van Hooff, J.A.R.A.M. (1972) 'A comparative approach to the phylogeny of laughter and smiling'. In Hinde, R.A. (ed.) *Non-verbal Communication*. London: Cambridge University Press.
Van Houten, R., Nau, P.A., MacKenzie-Keating, S.E., Sameoto, D. and Colavecchia, B. (1982) 'An analysis of some variables influencing the effectiveness of reprimands'. *Journal of Applied Behavior Analysis* 15: 65–83.
Veldman, D.J. (1970) 'Pupil evaluation of student teachers and their supervisors'. *Journal of Teacher Education* 21: 165–7.
Vogelaar, L.M.E. and Silverman, M.S. (1984) 'Nonverbal communication in

crosscultural counselling: a literature review'. *International Journal of Advances in Counselling* 7: 41–57.

Volkmar, F.R. and Siegel, A.E. (1982) 'Responses to consistent and discrepant social communications'. In Feldman, R.S. (ed.) *Development of Nonverbal Behavior in Children*. New York: Springer-Verlag.

Vrugt, A. (n.d.) 'The meaning of nonverbal sex differences'. Unpublished manuscript.

Vrugt, A. and Kerkstra, A. (1984) 'Sex differences in nonverbal communication'. *Semiotica* 50: 1–41.

Waal, F. de (1982) *Chimpanzee Politics*. London: Jonathan Cape.

Wachter, O. (1986) *No More Secrets for Me*. Harmondsworth: Penguin.

Wade, B. and Moore, M. (1986) 'Making meaningful choices: an investigation into young children's use of intonation patterns in storytelling'. *Educational Psychology* 6: 45–56.

Waldron, J. (1975) 'Judgment of like–dislike from facial expression and body posture'. *Perceptual and Motor Skills* 41: 799–804.

Walker, A.G. (1985) 'The two faces of silence: the effect of witness hesitancy on lawyers' impressions'. In Tannen, D. and Saville-Troike, M. (eds) *Perspectives on Silence*. Norwood, N.J.: Ablex.

Walker, R. and Adelman, C. (1975) *A Guide to Classroom Observation*. London: Methuen.

Walker, R. and Adelman, C. (1976) 'Strawberries'. In Stubbs, M. and Delamont, S. (eds) *Explorations in Classroom Observation*. London: Wiley.

Waller, W. (1932) *The Sociology of Teaching*. (Paperback edition, 1967.) New York: Wiley.

Wardhaugh, R. (1985) *How Conversation Works*. Oxford: Blackwell.

Watts, M. and Bentley, D. (1987) 'Constructivism in the classroom: enabling conceptual change by words and deeds'. *British Educational Research Journal* 13: 145–54.

Wawra, M. (1986) 'Vigilance in *Homo sapiens*'. Paper presented at 5th. International Conference on Human Ethology, Tutzing, West Germany, July 1986.

Weinstein, C.S. (1977) 'Modifying student behavior in an open classroom through changes in the physical design'. *American Educational Research Journal* 14: 249–62.

Weinstein, C.S. (1979) 'The physical environment of the school; a review of the research'. *Review of Educational Research* 49: 577–610.

Weinstein, C.S. (1982) 'Privacy-seeking behavior in an elementary classroom'. *Journal of Environmental Psychology* 2: 23–35.

Weinstein, C.S. (1987) 'Designing preschool classrooms to support development'. In Weinstein, C.S. and David, T.G. (eds) *Spaces for Children: The Built Environment and Child Development*. New York: Plenum.

Weinstein, C.S. and Weinstein, N.D.(1979) 'Noise and reading performance in an open space school'. *Journal of Educational Research* 72: 210–13.

Weinstein, C.S. and Woolfolk, A.E. (1981) 'The classroom setting as a source of expectations about teachers and pupils'. *Journal of Environmental Psychology* 1: 117–29.

Weisfeld, G.E. (1980) 'Social dominance and human motivation'. In Omark, D., Strayer, F.F. and Freeman, D. (eds) *Dominance Relations*. New York: Garland.

Weisfeld, G.E. and Laehn, T.L. (1986) 'Eye gaze and posture related to arrogation of a resource and dominant personality'. Paper presented at 5th International Conference on Human Ethology, Tutzing, West Germany, July 1986.

Weisfeld, G.E. and Linkey, H.E. (1985) 'Dominance displays as indicators of a social success motive'. In Ellyson, S.L. and Dovidio, J.F. (eds) *Power, Dominance and Nonverbal Behavior*. New York: Springer.

Wex, M (1980) *'Weibliche' und 'Mannliche' Korpersprache als Folge patriarchalischer*

Machtverhaltnisse. Frankfurt: Frauenliteraturvertrieb Hermine Fees.
Wheldall, K., Bevan, K. and Shortall, K. (1986) 'A touch of reinforcement: the effects of contingent teacher touch on the classroom behaviour of young children'. *Educational Review* 38: 207–16.
Wheldall, K. and Glynn, T. (1989) *Effective Classroom Learning*. Oxford: Blackwell.
Wheldall, K. and Lam, Y.Y. (1987) 'Rows vs. tables. II. The effects of two classroom seating arrangements on classroom disruption rate, on-task behaviour and teacher behaviour in three special school classes'. *Educational Psychology* 7: 303–12.
Wheldall, K., Morris, M., Vaughan, P. and Ng, Y.Y. (1981) 'Rows vs. tables: an example of the use of behavioural ecology in two classes of eleven year old children'. *Educational Psychology* 1: 171–84.
Wheldall, K. and Olds, D. (1987) 'Of sex and seating: the effects of mixed and same-sex seating arrangements in junior classrooms'. *New Zealand Journal of Educational Studies* 22: 71–85.
Whitehurst, T.C. and Derlega, V.J. (1985) 'Influence of touch and preferences for control on visual behavior'. In Ellyson, S.L. and Dovidio, J.F. (eds) *Power, Dominance and Nonverbal Behavior*. New York: Springer.
Whiten, A. and Byrne, R.W. (1988) 'Tactical deception in primates'. *Behavioral and Brain Sciences* 11: 233–73.
Willes, M.J. (1983) *Children into Pupils*. London: Routledge & Kegan Paul.
Willett, T.H. (1976) 'A descriptive analysis of nonverbal behaviors of college teachers'. Unpublished Ph.D. thesis, University of Missouri – Columbia. (University Microfilms 77–15, 564.)
Willis, F.N., Carlson, R. and Reeves, D. (1979) 'The development of personal space in primary school children'. *Environmental Psychology and Nonverbal Behavior* 3: 195–204.
Willis, F.N. and Hoffman, G.E. (1975) 'The development of tactile patterns in relation to age, sex and race'. *Developmental Psychology* 11: 866.
Willis, F.N. and Reeves, D.L. (1976) 'Touch interactions in junior high school students in relation to sex and race'. *Developmental Psychology* 12: 91–2.
Willis, F.N., Reeves, D.L. and Buchanan, D.R. (1976) 'Interpersonal touch in high school relative to sex and race'. *Perceptual and Motor Skills* 43: 843–47.
Willis, F.N., Rinck, C.M. and Dean, L.M. (1978) 'Interpersonal touch among adults in cafeteria lines'. *Perceptual and Motor Skills* 47: 1147–52.
Witt, P.A. and Gramza, A.F. (1970) 'Position effects in play equipment preferences of nursery school children'. *Perceptual and Motor Skills* 31: 431–34.
Wolfe, M. and Rivlin, L. (1972) 'Evolution of space utilization patterns in a children's psychiatric hospital'. In Mitchell, W.J. (ed.) *Environmental Design: Research and Practice*. Proceedings of the EDRA 3/AR8 Conference, University of California.
Wood, D. (1986) 'Aspects of teaching and learning'. In Richards, M.P.M. and Light, P. (eds) *Children of Social Worlds*. Cambridge: Polity.
Wood, D., McMahon, L. and Cranstoun, Y. (1980) *Working with Under-Fives*. London: Grant McIntyre.
Woods, P. (1975) '"Showing them up" in secondary school'. In Chanan, G. and Delamont, S. (eds) *Frontiers of Classroom Research*. Slough: N.F.E.R.
Woolfolk, A.E. (1978) 'Student learning and performance under varying conditions of teacher verbal and nonverbal evaluative communication'. *Journal of Educational Psychology* 70: 87–94.
Woolfolk, A.E., Garlinsky, K.S. and Nicolich, M.J. (1977) 'The impact of teacher behavior, teacher sex and student sex upon student self-disclosure'. *Contemporary Educational Psychology* 2: 124–32.
Woolfolk, A.E. and Woolfolk, R.L. (1975) 'Student self-disclosure in response to

teacher verbal and nonverbal behaviors'. *Journal of Experimental Education* 44: 36–40.

Woolfolk, R.L. and Woolfolk, A.E. (1974) 'Effects of teacher verbal and nonverbal behaviors on student perceptions and attitudes'. *American Educational Research Journal* 11: 297–303.

Woolfolk, R.L., Woolfolk, A.E. and Garlinsky, K.S. (1977) 'Nonverbal behavior of teachers: some empirical findings'. *Environmental Psychology and Nonverbal Behavior* 2: 45–61.

Wragg, E.C. and Dooley, P.A. (1984) 'Class management during teaching practice'. In Wragg, E.C. (ed.) *Classroom Teaching Skills*. London: Croom Helm.

Wragg, E.C. and Wood, E.K. (1984) 'Teachers' first encounters with their classes'. In Wragg, E.C. (ed.) *Classroom Teaching Skills*. London: Croom Helm.

Yerrell, P., Lovell, R., Stote, W. and Rosenthal, R. (1986) 'Pupils' sensitivity to teachers' nonverbal behaviour: a study of the mediation of interpersonal expectancies (SMILE)'. Paper presented at the Annual Conference of the British Educational Research Association, Bristol, September 1986.

Young, M. and Willmott, P. (1957) *Family and Kinship in East London*. London: Routledge & Kegan Paul.

Zeichner, K.M. (1986) 'Individual and institutional influences on the development of teacher perspectives'. In Raths, J.D. and Katz, L.G. (eds) *Advances in Teacher Education*. (Vol 2.) Norwood, N.J.: Ablex.

Ziv, A., Gorenstein, E. and Moris, A. (1986) 'Adolescents' evaluation of teachers using disparaging humour'. *Educational Psychology* 6: 37–44.

Zivin, G. (1982) 'Watching the sands shift: conceptualizing the development of nonverbal mastery'. In Feldman, R.S. (ed.) *Development of Nonverbal Behaviour in Children*. New York: Springer.

Zuckerman, M., Blanck, P.D., DePaulo, B.M. and Rosenthal, R. (1980) 'Developmental changes in decoding discrepant and nondiscrepant nonverbal cues'. *Developmental Psychology* 16: 220–8.

Name index

Abramovitch, R. 22
Adams, R.S. 112
Adelman, C. 9, 29, 49, 54, 68
Ahmad, Y. 117
Aiello, J.R. 94, 142
Ainsworth, P.B. 159
Aitchison, J. 16, 70
Allen, V.L. 19, 81
Alper, T. 95
Altman, I. 94
Ancoli, S. 14
Anderson, L.M. 30
Andrae, J. 121, 124, 125, 127
Angus, M.J. 125
Archer, D. 156
Ardrey, R. 120
Argyle, M. 39, 69, 72, 88, 141
Armstrong, S. 5
Atkinson, M. 18, 68, 70, 72, 137
Atkinson, M.L. 19
Ayling, K. 71

Bakken, M. 34
Baldwin, D. 99
Ball, S.J. 29
Barkow, J.H. 59
Barroso, F. 18
Bates, J.E. 84
Baxter, J.C. 94
Beardsley, B.E. 122, 129
Beattie, G. 16, 69, 71, 74, 139
Beeh, C. 34
Beitrose, H.S. 156–7
Bellaby, P. 10
Bennett, S.N. 4, 20, 64, 115, 121, 124, 125, 127
Bentley, D. 58, 64–5, 87
Berry, M. 10, 164

Bettencourt, E.M. 156
Bevan, K. 95, 98
Beynon, J. 29, 35, 56, 59, 108
Biddle, B.J. 112
Bing, M. 24, 91, 111
Blanck, P.D. 23, 24
Blatchford, R. 164
Blundell, D. 115
Boileau, D.M. 16
Boulton, M. 117
Bower, R.L. 67
Bowers, T. 27, 32
Boydell, D. 111
Brazil, D. 73
Brophy, J.E. 21, 24, 80, 90–1, 98, 137, 138
Brown, G.A. 5
Brown, R. 16, 70
Bryant, B. 39
Bucci, W. 18
Buchanan, D.R. 94, 99, 142
Bugenthal, D.E. 138
Bull, P. 5, 7, 18, 39, 68, 70, 71, 74–5, 84–7, 93, 133, 134, 141, 152, 22
Byrd, D.M. 22
Byrne, R.W. 10

Calderhead, J. 153, 155–6
Callan, H.M.W. 50–1
Campbell, D.T. 125, 130, 142
Caproni, V. 114
Carlson, R. 93, 142
Caswell, C.R. 54
Cataldo, M.F. 131
Chafe, W. 68
Chaikin, A.L. 81
Chance, M.R.A. 48, 50–1
Chapman, A.J. 10, 67

Cherlin, D.L. 114
Choppin, B. 151
Clarke, D.D. 26
Clements, J.E. 97
Clifford Rose, F. 71
Clift, S. 127
Cockburn, A. 4, 20, 64, 115
Cohen, A.A. 69
Colavecchia, B. 98
Coleman, B.J. 148, 149
Collett, P. 69, 134, 141
Connolly, K.J. 128, 129, 130
Connor, J.M. 98
Cook, M. 72
Cook, M.W. 68
Cook, T.D. 125, 130
Cook-Gumperz, J. 49
Cooper, I. 48, 119, 120 123, 125–6, 126
Cortis, G.A. 151, 155, 158–9
Coulthard, R.M. 49, 72, 89
Cowie, H. 117
Cranstoun, Y. 130
Creider, C.A. 141
Crocker, A.C. 148, 152, 154, 155
Croll, P. 4, 9, 115, 124, 125, 137
Cronin, C.L. 35, 138

Daly, E.M. 22
Davies, J.G.V. 144
Davis, T.N. 151
Dawkins, M.S. 33, 133
Dean, A.J. 158–9
Dean, J. 88
Dean, L.M. 93, 99, 142
Delamont, S. 8, 58, 119
Denham, E.J.M. 121
Deno, S.L. 84
Denscombe, M. 53, 108, 120
Department of Education and Science
    26, 58, 119, 120, 122–3, 148, 162, 163,
    164
DePaulo, B.M. 22, 23, 24
Derlega, V.J. 81, 135
Desforges, C. 4, 20, 64, 115
Devin-Sheehan, L. 82
DiMatteo, M.R. 156
Dobson, R. 140
Docking, J.W. 45
Dooley, P.A. 161–2
Dovidio, J.F. 71
Doyle, W. 87
Drake, K. 29

Dressel, M.E. 149–50
Dreyfus, A. 161
Duck, S. 164
Duffy, G.G. 77
Dumont, R.V. 135
Durlak, J.T. 122, 125, 129

Ecob, R. 124
Edwards, A.D. 8, 52, 87
Eggleston, J.F. 161
Eibl-Eibesfeldt, I. 13, 141
Ekman, P. 8, 14, 22, 23, 33, 62, 69–70,
    74, 82, 85, 134, 150, 154
Ellis, A. 16, 69, 71, 74, 139
Ellyson, S.L. 71
Emmer, E.T. 30
English, S.L. 135, 141
Enquist, M. 33
Erickson, F. 49
Evans, K.W. 95–6, 119, 125, 142
Evertson, C.M. 30
Exline, R.V. 33, 39, 72, 159

Feldman, R.S. 24, 81–2, 140–1, 142–3
Fitzgerald, J.M. 155, 158
Foot, H.C. 10, 67
Forbes, R.J. 149, 150
Freedman, D.G. 8, 137
Freedman, R. 18
Friedman, H.S. 83, 92
Friesen, W.V. 8, 14, 22, 23, 33, 62,
    69–70, 74, 82, 85, 134, 150, 154,
Furlong, V.J. 8, 28–9, 52, 87

Gabriel, R. 22
Gall, M.D. 156
Galloway, C.M. 91
Galton, M. 4, 9, 53, 58, 115, 124, 125, 137
Gannaway, H. 151
Garlinsky, K.S. 92, 138
Garner, J. 24, 91, 111
Garratt, B.A. 158
Garvey, C. 16
Garwood, G. 114
Gay, B.M. 26
Getzels, J.W. 119
Gianetto, R.M. 138
Gillis, J.R. 11
Gilmore, P. 49, 87, 140
Ginsburg, H.J. 40
Gladwin, T. 10, 76
Glynn, T. 114, 115

Name index

Goffman, E. 95, 119, 136
Good, T.L. 24, 80, 137, 139
Goodwin, C. 69, 70
Goodwin, M.H. 69
Gorenstein, E. 90
Gottman, J.M. 15, 67–8, 143
Graham, J.A. 39, 69, 88, 141
Grammer, K. 13
Gramza, A.F. 129
Grant, B.M. 3, 9
Grant, E.C. 33, 45
Gray, J.A. 110
Grayson, A. 151
Green, J.L. 49
Greenfield, P. 79
Griffin, S. 130
Griffith, C.R. 113
Grogan, S.C. 145
Gump, P.V. 36, 111, 127
Gumperz, J.J. 49

Haase, R.F. 80
Haber, G.M. 113
Hadar, U. 71
Hager, J.C. 14
Hall, E.T. 93
Hall, J.A. 156
Hall, V. 149
Hammersley, M. 11, 49, 119
Hargreaves, D.H. 10, 11, 35, 137
Harker, J.O. 49
Harmon, S. 35, 68, 108, 136
Harris, M.J. 83
Harrison, R.P. 69
Hayman, J.L. 29, 45, 90
Heath, A. 11
Heckel, R.V. 114
Hegarty, P. 121, 124, 125, 127
Heinig, R.B. 94, 95
Henley, N.M. 35, 68, 108, 136
Hennings, D.G. 3, 9
Heslin, R. 95
Hewitt, J. 93
Hiers, J.M. 114
Hinchcliffe, G. 161
Hinde, R.A. 6, 10, 13, 48
Hocking, J.E. 23, 150
Hodge, R.L. 157
Hoffman, G.E. 94, 99, 142
Hold-Cavell, B.C.L. 48
Hollandsworth, J.G. 149–50
Hook, C.M. 9, 47–8, 83

Hoskin, K.W. 149
Hughes, M. 9
Hull, C. 151
Hull, R.E. 158
Humphrey, N.K. 1, 27
Humphreys, A.P. 36
Huntingford, F. 35, 37, 111, 137
Hutchings, R. 127
Hutt, C. 35, 144
Hutt, S.J. 144

Jackson, I. 157–8
Jackson, P.R. 149, 150
Jackson, P.W. 111
Jaffe, J. 70
James, G. 151
Jarvi, T. 34
Jecker, J.D. 156–7
Jenkins, J.R. 84
Jenkins, L. 24
Johns, C. 73
Jones, B. 155, 158
Jones, S.E. 94, 142
Jourard, S.M. 94, 95

Kazdin, A.E. 97
Kazelkis, R. 149–50
Keating, C.F. 108, 137
Keith, L.T. 90
Kendon, A. 67, 70, 71
Kenner, A.N. 84
Kerkstra, A. 135, 136, 137
Klein, S.S. 83–4
Klinzing, H.G. 157–8
Klock, J. 97
Koneya, M. 112–13
Kounin, J.S. 36, 59, 129
Kruskal, W.H. 142

Laehn, T.L. 39, 40, 60
Lahaderne, H.M. 111
Lalljee, M. 72
Lam, Y.Y. 115
Lasley, T.J. 59
Lave, J. 79
Lawes, J.S. 19–20, 62–3, 85, 150, 152–5
Leathers, D.G. 23, 150
Legendre, A. 130
Lehman, J. 125
Lehtonen, J. 139
Leudar, I. 144
Levine, D. 114

Lewis, A. 144
Lewis, D. 124
Lewis, R. 31
Lewis, V. 144
Licata, J.W. 51, 57
Linkey, H.E. 60, 159
Lister, C. 99
Lockard, J.S. 14
Lorenz, B. 13
Love, L.R. 138
Lovegrove, M.N. 31
Lovegrove, R. 31
Lovell, R. 21

Maccoby, H. 156–7
Machotka, P. 43, 48
McCuller, C.C. 144–5
McDonald, P. 114
McHenry, R. 148, 149
MacKay, H. 149
Mackenzie-Keating, S.E. 98
Maclure, S. 120
McMahon, L. 130
McMillan, M. 120
McNeill, D. 17–18, 69, 74–6, 159
Macpherson, J. 10, 27, 36, 39, 54, 113–14
Mahony, P. 99, 138
Maliphant, R. 144
Markus, T.A. 121
Marsh, P. 69, 134, 141
Maxwell, G.M. 68
Maynard Smith, 27, 29
Meighan, R. 151
Merritt, M. 49
Meyenn, R.J. 27
Miller, J.F. 108
Moore, D.W. 114
Moore, G.T. 121, 124, 130, 131
Moore, M. 16
Morgan, C. 149
Moris, A. 90
Morris, D. 33, 39, 54, 69, 77, 112, 134, 141
Morris, M. 115
Mortimore, P. 124
Moskowitz, G. 29, 45, 90
Murray, J.S. 122, 129
Muzekari, L.H. 23, 145

Nash, B.C. 129, 131
Nash, R. 28, 68, 151
National Curriculum Council 10, 164

Nau, P.A. 98
Neill, S.R. St J. 9, 11, 23, 24, 29, 33, 35, 36, 39–40, 45, 59, 60, 64, 66, 72, 74, 76–7, 88, 90, 95–6, 99, 109, 121, 128, 129–31, 136, 138–9, 149, 150, 154, 155, 158, 159–61, 162
Ng, Y.Y. 115
Nicolich, M.J. 138
Noller, P. 67, 134
Norton, L. 21, 96, 140

O'Brien, P. 143
O'Neal, E. 114
O'Shaughnessy, M. 69, 134, 141
O.E.C.D. 120
Olds, D. 115–16
Olson, D.R. 10, 76

Painter, M. 128, 129, 130
Parkes, K.R. 160
Parkin, B. 125
Parry-Jones, W.Ll 26
Partington, J.A. 30, 161
Pease, A. 164
Pease, K. 159
Peery, J.C. 70
Pellicer, C. 164
Perdue, V.P. 98
Perry, A. 1
Peterson, P.L. 60–1
Pettigrew, L.E. 90
Philips, S.U. 135
Pitcairn, T.K. 50–1, 75
Plane, M. 33
Pollman, V.A. 40
Popoola, O. 24
Povey, R. 127
Preece, P.F.W. 152
Prohaska, T. 82
Proshansky, E. 119, 126
Putallaz, M. 15, 67–8, 143

Raffler-Engel, W.von 149, 150
Raymond, A. 158
Reeves, D.L. 93–4, 99, 142
Reid, D.J. 110–11
Reilly, S.S. 23, 145
Reinertsen, R.E. 34
Ricci Bitti, P. 88
Rinck, C.M. 94, 99, 142
Risley, T.R. 131
Rivlin, L.G. 124, 125

Name index

Robbins, E.S. 80
Robertson, J. 70, 74, 87, 137, 158, 163
Roed, J. 33
Roehler, L.R. 77
Rogers, P.L. 156
Roper, G. 14
Rosenshine, B.V. 9, 47–8, 83
Rosenthal, R. 21, 22, 23, 24, 156
Roskraft, E. 34
Rothenberg, M. 125
Rowe, M.B. 89–90, 139
Roy, C. 128, 129, 130
Rutter, D.R. 71, 143

Sajavarra, K. 139
Saletsky, R.D. 140–1, 142–3
Sameoto, D. 98
Sammons, P. 124
Satterly, D.J. 151
Schaffer, H.R. 121
Scheman, J.D. 14
Schiefenhovel, W. 13
Scheidt, M. 13
Schneider, J. 48
Schwebel, A.I. 114
Seabrook, J. 11
Seddon, G.M. 151
Sherman, L.W. 129
Shortall, K. 98
Shorter, E. 11
Siegel, A.E. 23
Sigler, E. 81
Silberman, M.L. 83
Silverman, M.S. 140
Simon, B. 4, 9, 115, 124, 125, 137
Sinclair, J. McH. 49, 72, 89
Sluckin, A.M. 8, 10, 28, 36, 144
Smith, C.M.B. 26
Smith, H.A. 2, 3
Smith, J.R. 10, 67
Smith, P.K. 36, 117, 128, 129, 130
Smith, R. 163
Snodgrass, S.E. 24
Solomon, J. 87
Sommer, R. 112, 114–115
Soudek, L.I. 134
Soudek, M. 134
Spiegel, J. 43, 48
Stanners, R.F. 22
Stanworth, M. 24, 138
Stebbins, R.A. 32, 122
Steele, A. 149

Stein, S.A. 80
Steiner, T.J. 71
Stephenson, G.M. 71
Stern, D.N. 70
Stevens, J. 149–50
Stohr, C. 48
Stoll, L. 124
Stote, W. 21
Streeck, J. 116–17
Sullins, E.S. 83
Sundstrom, E. 94
Swing, S.R. 60–1
Sylva, K. 128, 129, 130

Tann, S. 117
Tannen, D. 139
Taylor, R.B. 120–1
Thorne, B. 138
Thorp, J. 151
Tisher, R.I. 157–8
Tizard, B. 9
Tomlinson, P. 163
Tornatzky, L.G. 90
Torode, B. 54
Touhey, J.C. 108
Tracy, D.B. 97
Trevarthen, C. 17, 70
Trivers, R. 8
Trower, P. 39
Turk, C. 68, 112, 158
Turner, A. 35, 37, 137
Turner, G. 10, 11, 51, 112
Twardosz, S. 131

Van Hooff, J.A.R.A.M. 45
Van Houten, R. 98
van Meel, J.M. 18
Vaughan, P. 115
Veldman, D.J. 151
Vogelaar, L.M.E. 140
Volkmar, F.R. 23
Vrugt, A. 135, 136, 137

Waal, F. de 137
Wachter, O. 99
Wade, B. 16
Wade, B. 121, 124, 125, 127
Waldron, J. 88
Walker, A.G. 73
Walker, R. 9, 29, 49, 54, 68
Wallace, W.P. 142
Waller, W. 1

Wardhaugh, R. 4, 5, 9
Watts, M. 58, 64–5, 87
Wauson, M.S. 40
Wawra, M. 54
Weinstein, C.S. 3, 109, 112, 119–20, 123, 126
Weinstein, N.D. 123
Weisfield, G.E. 39, 40, 59–60, 159
Welsh Office 26, 58, 119, 122, 148, 162, 163
Wex, M. 35, 136
Wheldall, K. 95, 98, 115–16
White, P.A. 71
Whitehurst, T.C. 135
Whiten, A. 10
Wilkinson, B. 4, 20, 64, 115
Willcocks, J. 53
Willes, M.J. 8
Willett, T.H. 66–7

Willis, F.N. 93–4, 99, 142
Willmott, P. 11
Witt, P.A. 129
Wolfe, M. 119, 124, 126
Wood, D. 79, 130
Wood, E.K. 29, 90
Woods, P. 57–9
Woolfolk, A.E. 23, 91–2, 119–20, 138
Woolfolk, R.L. 23, 91–2
Wragg, E.C. 29, 90, 161–2

Yerrell, P. 21
Young, M. 11

Zeichner, K.M. 147
Ziv, A. 90
Zivin, G. 15, 45, 49, 108, 147
Zuckerman, M. 24

Subject index

ability, differences related to 80-3, 89-90, 117, 145, 154
abnormal behaviour 36-9, 135, 143-5
acoustics 121-3
action zone 112
advertance 50-3, 87
age difference 13-25, 93-9, 115, 116, 130, 140, 145, 154-5
akimbo posture 40, 138
ambiguity of nonverbal communication 1, 5-8, 59
animal behaviour 27, 110, 111-12
arms-fold 14, 15, 20, 38, 39-43
assault 26, 39, 43, 94, 97, 117
attention 47-63, 96, 97, 111-12, 111-12, 140-1; distribution of 48-9, 137-8

backward lean 32, 50, 58
barrier signals 14, 15, 20, 34, 37, 38, 39, 40, 56, 57, 86, 96, 144
baton signals 39, 74
beats 18, 74
blinking 39, 70
brow raise 7, 18, 38, 46, 81, 92
building design 133-46

challenges: closed 54-7; open 54-7
classroom social system 8-11, 27-9, 67-8, 71-2, 90
classroom subculture 7
clothing signals 150, 151, 156; by teachers 19-20, 62-3, 119-20, 140-1, 152-7

definition of nonverbal communication 2-4
development of nonverbal skill 5, 13-25, 45, 47, 67, 145, 147-8, 152-6, 159, 163-4

discrepant messages 23-4, 145
disruptive behaviour 28, 51-2, 54-7, 68, 113-14, 121-2, 141-2, 144, 161-2
distraction 121-3, 127
distribution of time 4, 8, 49, 127, 151, 156; by teachers 19-20, 62-3, 119-20, 140-1, 152-7
dominant signals 14, 15, 26-46, 51, 59, 60, 61, 66, 71, 86, 94, 95-8, 99, 108, 110, 136-8, 142, 149-50, 157

echo, behavioural 53, 68, 150
effective teachers 14, 15, 27, 29-31, 37, 39, 41, 42, 66-7, 75, 81, 89, 90, 91, 94-7, 109, 124, 162
elementary school student (age-group) *see* primary school children
emblematic gestures 69, 134, 141
encoding 134-5
encouragement 7, 87-9, 91, 95, 97-8, 109, 142-3, 144, 150, 163
enthusiasm 7, 18, 64-79, 81, 89, 91, 95, 153, 157, 160
equipment effects, preschool 128-9
ethnic differences 54, 90, 93-4, 117, 133-5, 139-43, 164
expectations, transmission of 19-20, 80-3
explanations 77-9
eye contact *see* gaze
eyebrow flash 13
eyes side 37

face structure 136-7
failure of communication 4-5, 36-9, 133-5
feedback to speakers 20, 50, 60, 65-6, 70, 83-4, 86
fidgeting 39, 43, 50, 63, 82, 84, 85, 150, 159, 162

flick check 54, 55
forward lean 1, 5, 6, 7, 14, 23, 32, 44, 55, 65, 75, 77, 80–2, 88, 89, 97, 109
frown 7, 20, 23, 30, 32, 42–3, 50, 58, 62, 72, 75, 76–7, 88, 91–2
furniture arrangement 48, 115–16, 126, 129

gaze 7, 14–15 20, 23, 28, 30, 31, 32, 37, 38, 41, 42, 45, 48, 49, 50, 51, 52, 53, 55, 60–3, 65, 66, 70, 71, 80–2, 86, 88, 89, 95–7, 109–10, 112, 114, 140, 143, 144, 149–50, 154, 159, 162, 163; aversion 6, 15, 44, 50–1, 61, 84, 93
gestures 2, 17–19, 21, 28, 37, 41, 42, 55, 58, 65–6, 69–70, 74–6, 77, 78, 81, 89, 134, 141, 149–50, 153, 159; beats 18, 74; conduit 18, 66, 76, 77, 78, 89, 141; iconix 17–18, 37, 75–6; metaphorix 17–18, 66, 74, 76, 77, 78, 89
grooming 28, 33, 34, 39, 43, 45, 84, 136
group work 115, 116–17

hands on hips 30, 39–40, 43, 44, 46, 51, 58, 97, 138; in pockets 30, 42, 43, 52, 61
head cant 88, 95
head prop 50, 56, 84, 86
hesitancy 34, 38, 40, 41, 44, 51, 61, 68–9, 73, 88–90, 143, 149–50, 151–2
high school student (age-group) *see* secondary school children
honest communication 27, 32–6, 133
humour 90, 97

iconic gesture 17–18, 75–6
ideographic gestures 74
illustrative gestures 18, 37, 66, 69, 74–6, 77, 78, 89, 141, 153
inconsistent messages 23–4, 145
individual distance 35, 88, 93–118, 141–2, 154
informal classrooms 53, 119–21, 124–7
initial encounters 29–32, 90
intention movements 6–7, 109
interaction set 28–9
interest 20, 50, 60–3, 80–92, 154, 158
interpersonal distance 35, 88, 93–118
interviews 148–51, 154, 159–60
intonation 16, 69, 91, 141, 150, 159, 163; animated 39, 74; emphatic 16, 150; proclaiming 16, 73–4; referring 16, 73–4; shouting 39

leaning 7, 23, 31, 44, 50, 51, 110
lecturing 66–7, 68
listening signals 57, 68–73, 87–8, 141, 158

marker signals 13, 49, 73
metacommunications 50–3
metaphoric gestures 17–18, 66, 74, 76, 77–8, 89
minus face 15, 44, 45, 96
models, animal-based 27, 29, 33–4, 110, 111–12, 120
motherese 16–17, 18, 144
mouth hiding 57
moving children's position 114

nod 80–1, 141, 149
noise 121–3, 162
nonverbal leakage 8, 23–4, 32, 34, 37, 38, 40, 41, 82–3, 90–1, 150, 154
nonverbal style 8, 15–16, 19

openness, measures of 121
open-plan preschools 129–31
open-plan primary schools 119–27
open-plan secondary schools 120

pantomiming 69, 76
partitions 122, 125, 131
pauses in speech 68–9, 73, 82, 88–90, 139, 145
personal and social education 164
personal space 35, 88, 93–118, 142
personality 152, 154
pictographic gestures 69
plus face 14, 15, 43
pointing 2, 28, 37, 58, 81
position in classroom, teacher's 108–112, 114
position in classroom, children's 111–16
postural echo 53, 68
posture 7–8, 14–15, 20, 21, 23, 28, 30, 31, 32, 35, 41, 44, 46, 49, 50, 51, 52, 53, 55, 56, 57, 58, 61, 62, 65, 67, 71, 75, 80–2, 84–7, 89, 96, 97, 109, 110, 136, 144, 149–50, 159, 163
praise 90–2, 97–8
preschool children 8, 16–17, 22, 33, 48, 79, 88, 98–9, 127–32, 138, 143, 144
preschool design 127–32
primary school children (age-group) 4–5, 8, 14–15, 17–24, 28, 29–30, 39–45, 47 49–50, 60–3, 64, 67–8, 80–2, 84, 85,

87, 89–90, 91–2, 93–9, 111, 112, 114, 115–17, 119–20, 122, 123–7, 135, 137–8, 140, 142, 144–5, 151, 154–6, 164
public speaking 72–3
puzzle frown 20, 76, 88

racial differences 54, 90, 93–4, 117, 133–5, 139–43, 164
regulator gestures 69, 74
relative height 42, 43, 72, 97, 108, 109, 110, 136, 137
relative importance of nonverbal signals 23–4, 91–2, 145, 149–50
room appearance 119–20
room arrangement 48, 115–16, 125–6, 128–31
row seating 115–16
rules 53–4

sad brow 32, 38, 41, 96
sarcasm 23
seating position 111–17
secondary school children (age-group) 1, 9, 11, 14, 23–4, 26, 27–31, 35–6, 39–45, 49, 51–3, 54–60, 64–6, 76–9, 82–3, 85–7, 90, 93–9, 108, 110–11, 112, 113–14, 116, 117, 122, 138–9, 140–2, 143, 144–5, 151, 154–5, 161–2
self-awareness 153–4
self-esteem 59–60
self-holding 15, 20, 34, 37, 38, 39–43, 136, 149
settings, classrooms as 119–20
sex differences 24, 34–6, 72, 84, 92, 94–9, 115–16, 117, 134, 135–9, 158
sexual abuse 99, 138
silence 49, 68–9, 135
showing up 35, 57–9
smile 6, 7, 13, 14, 23, 28, 42, 45, 46, 51, 52, 53, 56, 58, 59, 76, 78, 80–2, 85, 88, 89, 90, 91–2, 95, 97, 110, 136, 138, 149

social behaviour, informal 28, 67–71, 116–17, 153, 164
space 127–8
special needs children 97, 115, 135, 143–5
status signals 6, 14, 15, 20, 30, 31, 32, 34, 37, 38, 40, 41, 42, 44, 50, 52, 53, 58, 61, 65, 66, 81, 85, 86, 93, 94, 95, 96, 97, 109, 110
stress 37, 148, 150, 152
structuring of speech 65
students (college/university) 3, 19, 22, 24, 66–7, 81–4, 84–5, 92, 112–13, 114, 135, 142–3, 149–50, 164
student teachers 19–20, 62–3, 84, 90, 91–2, 111, 119–20, 147–65
subordinate signals 15, 34, 38, 39–45, 61, 72, 96, 109
synchronisation of nonverbal signals and speech 70–1, 72, 74–5

table seating 115–17
territoriality 120–1
threat 30–2, 36, 162
tidy classrooms 119–20
time, organisation of 4, 8, 49, 127
touch 6, 34, 35, 38, 43, 91, 94, 95–108, 135–6, 139, 141–2
traditions of building use 124–6
traditional societies 10–11, 60, 76, 79
training 147–65
transitions between activities 49, 161
turn–taking signals 71

uncertainty, signals of 20, 21, 38, 40, 41, 70, 73, 87–90, 152
understanding, signal of 19–20, 60–3

wait time 89–90
wielding 2, 3
withitness 59

yawning 50